We'll Always Be United

The History of Spennymoor United F.C.

Ray Simpson

First published in Great Britain in 2007 by
Ray Simpson
166 Byerley Road
Shildon
Co. Durham
DL4 1HW

© Ray Simpson 2007

This book is sold subject to the condition that it shall not, by way of trade or otherwise, be lent, resold, hired out or otherwise circulated without the publisher's prior written consent in any form of binding or cover other than that in which it is published and without a similar condition including this condition being imposed upon the subsequent purchaser.

ISBN xxx-x-xxxxxxx-x-x

A CIP record for this book is available from the British Library

Printed by Lintons Printers, County Durham

Foreword

I felt honoured when I was approached by Spennymoor Town chairman Alan Murray to write the foreword of this book.

As a young schoolboy, I didn't appreciate that when I made my one appearance for the club over thirty years ago what a long and glorious history it had. For a club to exist for over a century and win so many honours says plenty about the passion and commitment of the people who have been a part of it over the years, and hopefully for many years to come.

Grassroots clubs like Spennymoor Town are vitally important to the survival of football, as they give many a young footballer a nurturing hand in their football careers, a fact which seems to be forgotten sometimes in the multi million pound world of the upper echelons of professional football.

I was very sad when I learned that Spennymoor United had folded in 2005, but I was just as happy when I learned that a new club had been formed with Alan as chairman. Its progress in just two years has been very encouraging and heartwarming, but I'm sure that everyone is aware that there is still plenty of hard work in the years ahead. It just goes to show what can be achieved when everybody pulls together, and the local community supports its club.

This book is not only a history of the club's honours, but also an enthralling insight of the thoughts and memories of some of the players who have worn the black and white shirt. Even if you're not a Spennymoor fan, it will be of interest to anybody who loves their local football club and football in general.

Eric Gates, Ipswich, Sunderland and England.

Hartlepool Beer & Wine

Company Limited

Security House • Usworth Road • Hartlepool • TS25 1PD
Tel: 01429 265087 • Fax: 01429 867931
Email: philgallagher1969@yahoo.co.uk • www.hartlepoolbeer.com

Notes by the author

This isn't meant to be a definitive history of Spennymoor United Football Club and some of the other names it has had, but the club achieved so much during its long history that I felt that every cup final it played in - and there have been plenty of those as you'll see by the list of honours - should be recorded. The Durham Challenge Cup seemed to be the club's personal property at times.
Maybe there are one or two pivotal moments that have been inadvertently omitted, but I'd like to think that many of the club's ups and downs have been recalled, in some cases, with the memories of people who were involved.
I also learned some little known facts. One of the most successful managers in modern times - Spurs' Bill Nicholson - played for the Moors. Also, the man who lifted the 1957 FA Cup for Aston Villa - Johnny Dixon - was a star and helped to bring in the crowds just after the Second World War. Players, such as John Mordue and Eric Gates, who won England caps have also worn the black and white colours.
I have contacted many former players and officials, and if I have missed any favourites out, then apologies, but I either ran out of time, some couldn't be traced, and others, like Butch Simpson and Bill Gates, are abroad. The budget didn't stretch that far! (Unless this book is turned into a film, in which case I'm sure the chairman would fly me to Australia to write a sequel).
Several emotions were prominent when I spoke to players, fans and officials. Their deep passion for the club is undeniable, whatever the era; the camaraderie was unsurpassed, especially in the seventies and early nineties; but the most noticeable emotion was the deep heartache of missing out on a place in the FA Trophy final in 1978. It was very clear that even thirty years on, the second half against Leatherhead on that fateful day at the Brewery Field weighs heavily on the minds of those who were part of it, either on the field or on the terraces. The Northern Echo report of one of the most disappointing playing days in the club's history suggested that centre forward Geoff Hart cried at the final whistle. I asked Geoff to confirm the story, and choking back a tear, he said: "Yes, I bloody cried all right."
Despite extensive research, in some instances it has been impossible to establish the Christian names of some players, especially before the Second World War. In those situations I have just recorded the surname. Where attendance figures have been noted, these have been obtained from

newspapers and club records.

It has also been difficult to establish team line ups in some cases - for example the 1913 Spennymoor FA Cup team at Gillingham - so apologies for any omissions. There weren't many Spennymoor fans at the game that day.

My research jogged the memories of so many people, and that prompted a real surge of anecdotes and stories, both serious and amusing. I hope you enjoy reading them.

Front cover: Albert Hickman lifts the Durham Challenge Cup after Moors beat Willington in the 1976 Durham Challenge Cup final.

Back cover: Six people (of many) who have played a major part in the club over the years.

Club History

As Spennymoor United
Mid Durham League 1904-05
Northern League 1905-08
North Eastern League 1908-1937
Wearside League 1937-38
North Eastern League 1938-1958
Midland League 1958-1960
Northern League 1960-1990
Northern Counties East League 1990-1993
Northern Premier League 1993-2005

Honours
North Eastern League winners 1910, 1945, 1946, 1957
North Eastern League non reserve winners 1937
Northern Premier League Cup winners 1994
Northern League championship winners 1968, 1972, 1974, 1977, 1978, 1979
Northern Counties East League winners 1993
Northern Counties East league Cup winners 1993
Durham Challenge Cup winners 1930, 1946, 1954, 1963, 1968, 1973, 1974, 1975, 1976, 1979, 1983, 1994, 1995, 1996, 1998
Durham Wartime Cup winners 1945
Northern League cup winners 1966, 1968, 1980, 1981, 1987
FA Trophy semi finalists 1978
FA Amateur Cup quarter finalists 1964, 1973
FA Cup third round 1936
FA Cup second round 1928, 1936, 1967
FA Cup first round 1912, 1927, 1928, 1932, 1933, 1934, 1936, 1946, 1953, 1967, 1969, 1972, 1975, 1977, 1986, 1990, 1994, 1995

As Spennymoor Town
Northern League 2005
Northern League Second Division championship winners 2007

Contents

Foreword by Eric Gates

Club history

Notes by the author

Chapter 1	"I'll find you somewhere to play"	9
Chapter 2	"Where have the crowds gone?"	33
Chapter 3	Laurie scores again – and so does Duggie	40
Chapter 4	At the crossroads	60
Chapter 5	The return to amateurism	64
Chapter 6	For whom the Bell tolls	72
Chapter 7	Give the ball to Kenny	81
Chapter 8	1977-78 season Bye Bye Wembley	99
Chapter 9	Getting itchy feet	104
Chapter 10	The return of the prodigal	120
Chapter 11	"Beggars at football's banquet"	134
Chapter 12	Officials' memories	145
Chapter 13	Fans' memories	180
Chapter 14	Players' memories	193
Chapter 15	Spennymoor Ladies Football Club	244
Postscript		245
Acknowledgments		246

Chapter One
"I'll find you somewhere to play"

Every football club can point to somebody in its history who was both a visionary and a great benefactor, and in Spennymoor United's case, the early development of football can be credited mainly to one man, Thomas Grant.

The roots of football in the town can be found way back in 1888, when churches set up teams. St Paul's played friendly matches on their pitch in Wood View – not to be confused with the Wood Vue where the Brewery Field is now - and in their first season competed in the Durham Challenge Cup, but were outclassed 13-0 by Sunderland Albion on January 19th 1889. Probably as a consequence of this, St Paul's realised that if they were to compete and be more successful they had to expand, so they combined in the summer of 1890 with another club in the town with a church background, St Andrew's, and called themselves Spennymoor Town.

The Town played friendly matches at first, and in 1896 at a meeting in "Mr Bassett's Crown Hotel" - presumably having decided that religion and alcohol weren't entirely compatible in working class Spennymoor - they set up two teams, one to compete in the Wear Valley League (the Albion) and the other in the Mid Durham League (the Juniors).

The Albion won the club's first honour in season 1899-1900, when on their Green Lane field they won the second division of the Wear Valley League which contained clubs such as Howden-le-Wear and Tow Law Reserves, and in 1902, despite losing 16-0 to Sunderland A in a Durham Senior Cup tie – they were 10-0 down at half time – the Juniors finished second in the Mid Durham League behind Cornforth.

There were several football teams already in the town when the Weardale Ironopolis club was formed out of the Weardale Coal and Coke Ovens company in 1900, with Councillor Thomas Grant, one of the bosses at the factory, the main benefactor. He believed that "young men in offices and shops following a sedentary occupation need some form of exercise at the end of their day's labour, and I can think of no more manly invigorating sport than either football or cricket." The footballers played their games on a pitch where the Leisure Centre is now.

John Mordue, an early Spennymoor Utd player who went on to appear for Arsenal, Sunderland and England

The "Nops" and the Town met in a Durham Amateur Cup tie on Jan 23rd 1904, and the Town won by a handsome 6-2 margin, with forward Alf Smith scoring a hat trick – a feat which earned him a pair of Tylers "TRYKIKS" football boots from a local shop. One of the first sponsorship deals, you could say.

Maybe that game was a catalyst, and discussions followed, presumably with Mr Grant's encouragement and backing, about forming a new, stronger team to represent the town of Spennymoor. But they faced a problem - where would they play as neither of their home pitches was suitable for football at a higher level?

The answer was supplied by the influential Mr Grant. He knew that Tudhoe Rugby Club, which played at the Brewery Field behind Durham Road, was struggling in many ways and was sadly close to extinction, so he used his contacts and after negotiations, arranged for the new football club to move there.

The facilities were much better at the Brewery Field, as during its 20 years' previous existence, the rugby club had erected a grandstand capable of holding at least a thousand spectators. It was called the Brewery Field simply because the field used to belong to the nearby Tower Brewery, and the dray horses used for pulling the beer carts, were stabled on the field. The players used to change in the County Hotel, which was situated diagonally opposite what is now the Salvin Arms pub at the top of Durham Road.

Boosted by the news that Mr Grant had arranged a ground – although there was some money to be paid - the members of the Nops and the Town held a meeting in July 1904, just a few days after the Rugby Club folded, to formally merge into one club which would live for over a century – Spennymoor United. The Durham Chronicle reported that "Mr Grant was heartily thanked for furthering the cause of a united team." Such was the interest in the town at this amalgamation that 60 players wanted to turn out for United, and the club advertised for "guinea and half-guinea subscribers" – the first season ticket holders. (A guinea was 21 shillings, or £1.05p now). The foundations were in place.

The generous Mr Grant emigrated to Canada in the summer of 1906, but his legacy was immeasurable. He left the club in very ambitious and

enthusiastic hands, and he would have been proud of its progress and glittering history – well, the vast majority of it anyway.
The first game United played was in the Mid Durham League against Bearpark on September 3rd 1904, Alf Smith scoring both goals – he scored a total of 21 that season - in a 2-2 draw. United finished sixth that season in the league, which was won by Eldon Albions. Gate receipts for the season were £269 2s 11d, which was enough to pay off some of the club's debts when they took over the Brewery Field.
The new club rounded off that inaugural season by reaching the club's first ever cup final, causing quite a buzz in the town.

Durham Aged Miners Cup final April 22nd 1905 at Kelloe
Spennymoor United 0 Ryhope Villa 1
Over 2,000 people attended the game at Kelloe, and it's fair to say that a good proportion of those would have made the journey from Spennymoor. The Cup attracted many entries from around County Durham, and United played seven games to reach the final, including two replays against Cockfield in the quarter final. There was also a 15-0 thrashing of Quarrington Hill along the way, a club record that stood for over thirty years.
Maybe, though, there were some cup final nerves amongst the players, as the report in the Durham Chronicle hinted; "Ryhope had the game nearly all their own way with a goal just before half time. The Spennymoor forwards never seemed to get going at all, and nobody except Alf Smith seemed to know where the goal lay." The nearest United came to scoring was a shot by Small, which was cleared off the line.
The Spennymoor team was; Hess, Dial, Franklin, Lancaster, F Smith, Hindmarsh, Robinson, Alf Smith, F Small, G Jenkins, Barrass.
At least the game didn't go to a replay, because at the annual meeting of Durham FA in 1902, there was a discussion about introducing extra time at the end of cup replays. The Northern Echo revealed that Mr Smith of Spennymoor opposed the proposal and reported him as saying that "if any Spennymoor players come by their death through over-exertion, we will sue the Association for compensation."
No doubt encouraged by Mr Grant before he left for Canada, the club took a huge step in 1905 by successfully applying for the Northern League of which Bishop Auckland, South Bank and Crook Town were members, as well as the A teams of Sunderland, Newcastle and Middlesbrough -- a good standard of football. United's first Northern League game on September 2nd ended in a 2-1 home defeat against Darlington St Augustines. The team that day was; Jimmy Kidd, T Reece, W Snowdon, T Wake, Fred Smith, R

Jones, W Davies, Alf Smith, T Higgins, J Shoulder, W Douglas. The visitors led at half time, but then Alf Smith and W Douglas combined "to convert a centre" from W Davies for the equaliser. However, Saints soon scored a winner.

United's first Northern League win was 3-0 at home to Scarborough a fortnight later, F Smith 2 and G Jenkins the scorers. The biggest home gate of that first season was against neighbours Bishop Auckland on February 17th 1906, when over 6,000 people saw the visitors win 1-0 – the first of many battles between the clubs in different competitions.

United finished the season in a respectable 8th place, with 22 points from 26 games, and gate receipts of £321 10s 2 1/2d. The league was won by Sunderland A, the reserve team of the Football League club. There was so much enthusiasm at the end of that first season, that a move from the amateur Northern League to the newly-formed professional North Eastern League was discussed, but United decided not to apply until the end of season 1907-08.

First of all, there was some cup business. United played their first FA Cup tie (or English Cup as it was called then) against Croft at the Brewery Field on September 15th 1906, Alf Smith scoring both goals in a 2-0 win. However, United lost to Saltburn in the next round.

Spennymoor United Football Club, 1906-07.
Back row: J. Heslop, E. Ridley, B. Smith, H. Bolton, E. Gill, J. Barret, W. Harle, T. Smith, H. Askew, and J. Goundry. Centre: R. Oughton, J. Brydon, J. Watson, W. Mitchell, R. Jones (Captain), R. McRea, J. Eltringham, J. Naisbitt, A. Hemming (Honorary Treasurer), and W. Bainbridge. Front: G. Fletcher, S. Slade, R. Nicholson, J. Kidd, T. Wake, F. Small, G. Barrett (Honorary Secretary), and T. Brabban (Trainer).

United played their first FA Amateur Cup tie on October 27th 1906 against Darlington St Augustines and won 1-0 thanks to a goal by R. Nicholson but then lost 2-1 at home to Stanley in a replay in the next round.

Also in 1906, Spennymoor lodged a protest to Durham FA against Leadgate Park, whom they claimed had fielded four ineligible players against them in a Durham Amateur Cup tie, plus that the linesman had made a bet on the result of the match and had made decisions against Spennymoor. The club soon withdrew the protest.

The start of the game between United and South Bank on September 1st 1906 was delayed for an hour by excessive heat. The summer had been particularly hot, and a drought had been declared in the town. The heat must have affected the Moors' players, because they lost 1-0.

Spennymoor United Football Club, 1908-09.

Once the Northern League heard of Moors' application to the North Eastern League in 1908, they were kicked out of the Northern League at the AGM by 5 votes to 4 for "alleged objectionable conduct." Fortunately, they were duly accepted soon after into the North Eastern League. United chairman Harry Askew, another who was to play a major part in the club, said at the club's AGM; "The rejected of the Northern League have become the accepted of the North Eastern League." Askew pointed out that during their Northern League days, the club had never been fined, and no complaints had ever been made against them.

The first game in the North Eastern League was against Darlington at Feethams on September 5th 1908, but it ended in a 1-0 defeat. The team was; Jimmy Kidd, Henderson, Eltringham, Eddy, T. Hall, McRae, E. Bell, Beckram, Jobling, Thompson, T. Phillipson. United finished tenth in their first season, forward Phillipson scoring 26 goals in total, and for the first time in the club's history, the total income passed £1,000 for the season. The club spent £40 on improving the Brewery Field, including the cost of new turnstiles, a cabin, and a press box.

The following season, 1909-10, justified their switch from the Northern League when they became the first non-Football League team to win the North Eastern League, just pipping Newcastle United A. On the way, Moors had some excellent results against the Football League outfits, beating Middlesbrough and Sunderland at home. It was a remarkable feat considering they had come from nowhere to champions in such a short space of time.

Spennymoor United Football Club, 1909-10.
Top row: R. Nicholson, E. Bell (Capt), W. Jackson, M. Turner, T. Hall.
2nd: R. Harrison, T. F. Phillipson (Vice-Capt), A. Harwood.
3rd: J. W. Thomas, J. T. Peacock (Sec), H. Askew (Chairman),
A. H. Hemming (Tresurer), E. Goode.
Bottom: P. Quinn, J. Kidd, J. Barrett (Trainer), A. McAllister, R. Sanderson.

The club was presented with the magnificent "Oxo" cup – it was donated by the Oxo company, has survived for over a century and is now the Northern League Second Division championship trophy with the word "Oxo" still inscribed on it – and thousands of people turned out for the parade through the streets of Spennymoor to see the club's most successful moment yet. The cup was taken to the club's headquarters, the good old County Hotel, where it was "filled with champagne and other well-known if less expensive liquids," and passed around the players and supporters. It would be the first of many celebrations over the years.

Moors – as they were progressively nicknamed – dropped just one point at home all season and won 24 of their 32 matches. They played thirteen games, eight of them away, in the last eight weeks of the season.

Unfortunately, Moors failed spectacularly in the defence of their title, and could only finish twelfth the following season. They actually failed to finish their fixtures because they were suspended by the FA for not paying one of their players, Alfred Harwood, his wage arrears. All the professional players except Harwood agreed to a reduction in their wages in October of that season, and the club agreed to release him. However, the club apparently didn't pass on the paperwork in time, and Harwood complained to the FA, who stopped the club from playing their last two games of the season, away to West Stanley and South Shields. The dispute was soon resolved, and before the start of the following season, Moors played friendly matches at West Stanley and South Shields as compensation.

A challenge for the North Eastern League never really materialised over the following years, but there was still something to shout about in 1912.

FA Cup run 1912-13

FA Cup fever came to the town for the first time when Moors battled all the way to the fifth qualifying round of the FA Cup, the equivalent of today's first round proper. The run started with a 5-0 home win over Grangetown – Jackie Thomas scored a hat trick – then Jackie scored the winner from the spot for a 1-0 replay win over South Bank, following a 1-1 draw. Jackie then scored another two in the 4-2 home win over Crook Town – "zeal gave way to foul play, and the referee ordered two Crook men off the field" reported the Northern Echo -- and Joe Nicholson got the winner away to Stockton in the fourth qualifying round.

Moors were paired with Southern League club Gillingham – some record books call them by their previous name of New Brompton -- at the Brewery Field, but then the Kent club, clearly a bit worried about venturing northwards into unknown territory in front of a passionate crowd, offered

Moors £100 to switch the game to the Priestfield Stadium, the best part of 300 miles away -- and there were no motorways then! Moors turned them down flat, naturally preferring to play the biggest game in their history to date at the Brewery Field. Their decision was justified, as they held Gillingham to a 1-1 draw on December 16th 1912. The Northern Echo wrote; "If desperate rushes from one end of the field to the other with every man going in for all he is worth constitutes what the scribes call typical cup tie football, then the 2,000 spectators ought to have been fully satisfied." In other words, it was a real blood and thunder game, not exactly one for the purists. Moors missed good chances through Jackie Thomas and George Bell, but Gillingham scored with a long distance shot by Wolstenholme. But Moors equalised near the end when Matt Turner was fouled, and Jackie Thomas scored with the penalty "amidst a sound of great excitement."

However, there was a note of caution in the report; "Spennymoor could scarcely have had a better chance to win for the undoubted cleverness of the southerners was heavily discounted by the conditions under which the game was played."

The replay was set for the following Tuesday, and in the meantime, the draw was made for the first round. The winners of the game were given a perfect incentive – a home draw against holders and First Division giants Barnsley.

The Spennymoor team for the first game was; Tommy Clough, Franks, Daykin, Lamph, Hall, George Bell, Matt Turner, Jackie Thomas, Rivers, Barton, Goodwin.

However, travelling to Gillingham in Kent was a much more difficult proposition in 1912 than it is now, and for most, if not all of the Moors' party, they would never have travelled such a distance previously in their lives.

Unfortunately and perhaps not surprisingly, Moors lost the replay at Priestfield by 3-0. Gillingham took the lead after 12 minutes through Taylor and never looked back. The Echo said: "Spennymoor, though playing pluckily, were a little outclassed, and only their hard working full backs and Clough in goal prevented a heavier defeat."

Moors had a good season in the league, finishing in sixth place for the second successive season, but that would be their best placing for several years to come.

Moors didn't achieve much at all in the years after the First World War. They finished in the bottom half of the table four years in a row as they struggled against re-election, but there was no respite in 1922-23, when they finished bottom of the twenty clubs, going nearly four months without a home win.

There was so much gloom and doom that the club considered dropping out of the North Eastern League and returning to the Northern League – assuming of course, that the Northern League would have had them following the nature of their departure previously. But a meeting of the club, no doubt with Harry Askew heavily involved in some way, decided to persevere in the North Eastern League – despite a big £350 loss for the season – and Moors were re-elected. Billy Gardner, a former England amateur international, was transferred to QPR, which brought a small sum of money to the club, while Mr Harry Cummings proposed that a supporters club should be formed to help the club raise funds.

The gloom was lifted a little when Moors reached the final of the Durham Benevolent Bowl in season 1923-24. After a 0-0 draw against Bishop Auckland at Crook on February 2nd 1924, they lost 1-0 to the Bishops in the replay six weeks later at Shildon. Moors keeper Bob Edwards was injured whilst trying to stop the winning goal and had to leave the field. A crowd of 2,625 saw the replay, with gate receipts of £136 11s 9d. "The Bishops deserved their win for they displayed greater dash whilst being equally as clever as their professional rivals," the Auckland Chronicle wrote. Bob Edwards had previously been at First Division Burnley and Durham City when they were in the Third Division North.

The club played two matches in the same day on March 8th 1924. One team drew 2-2 at home to Scotswood in the North Eastern League (Rodgerson scored twice) while the other lost 5-1 at Durham City Reserves in the Durham Senior Cup.

Sunderland legend Charlie Buchan played in Spennymoor's black and white colours in a friendly match against a team from Manchester University on March 31st 1924, Moors winning 3-2.

Despite the appearance of Buchan, Moors continued to struggle financially and also in the league, to the point that on March 10th 1925, a public meeting was called to discuss whether the club should fold with immediate effect, because they didn't have enough money to travel over the Pennines to Workington in the league the following Saturday. For various reasons, Moors hadn't played any home games for a month which didn't help their financial situation, and they had several more away games coming up. Treasurer Harry Cummings said: "The League hasn't considered our financial position one bit when re-arranging fixtures." Gate money was down £110 on the previous season, while the cost of running the club was reckoned to be £23 per week.

They managed to scrape the money together with the help of benefactors, and at the end of the season on May 11th 1925, they decided to continue, even though the club had debts of £300. Other clubs were apparently in worse condition, but Moors still finished the season second bottom. Despite the problems, they were re-elected to the league.

Moors won the Durham Benevolent Bowl, which was then played in the early part of the season, for the first time on November 20th 1926 by beating Stockton from the Northern League 3-2 in the final at Bishop Auckland. Ted Boustead and Ronald "Ronnie" Attley scored twice within five minutes in the first half, with Ronnie scoring another after half time.

"The great weight of the Spennymoor players coupled with their more robust tactics, proved too much for the amateurs," wrote the Northern Echo. It was a much better league season, Moors going all the way through to March unbeaten in the league at home, and they finished the season in 15th place, well away from the re-election zone.

Moors were kicked out of the FA Cup in season 1926-27 for playing a "wrong un" against West Auckland, whom they'd beaten 2-1. West protested because Moors fielded Percy Dolphin against them, and they claimed that he had signed for Crook, and Moors hadn't submitted the necessary fourteen days' approach. The FA upheld West's protests and re-instated them.

The improvement continued the following season, when Moors sampled some FA Cup glory for the first time in fifteen years, and they also reached the Durham Challenge Cup final for the very first time.

The FA Cup run 1927-28

Moors almost pulled off a giant killing act as the town really got behind them. They started the competition on September 3rd 1927 with a comfortable 5-0 home win over Northern League club Stanley with Teddy Boustead and Joe Nicholson scoring two each, then they won 4-2 in the next round at neighbours Ferryhill, Nicholson amongst the goals again.

That win gave Moors an away tie at Bishop Auckland on October 1st 1927, and there were celebrations in the town after Moors comfortably beat their

Secretary Charlie Sutton (left) with the Durham Benevolent Bowl

rivals 5-0, with Bob Kipling scoring a hat trick in the rout.

Tow Law were then beaten 3-1 at home, and Moors clinched a place in the first round proper for the first time ever (not taking into account the previous fifth qualifying round tie against Gillingham) by beating West Stanley 2-1, with goals by Jackie White and B Barker.

Moors were handed a home tie against Rotherham on November 26th 1927 and there was a genuine feeling in the town that they could cause a shock against the South Yorkshire club, because many thought that there wasn't that much difference in standard at the time between the Third Division North and the North Eastern League. Rotherham were in the bottom half of the Third Division North, above Durham City and Ashington. It was to be Durham's last season in the Football League, as they finished second bottom at the end of that season.

The shock result everybody in Spennymoor wanted nearly happened when Moors took an early lead, Ted Boustead heading in a Ronnie Attley centre. They missed several chances to make the game safe before Rotherham equalised with a fluke goal.

North Eastern League, 1927-28.
Officials: Mr. H. Cummings (Treasurer), Mr. C. Sutton (Secretary).
Players Back row: T. Wilkinson, T. Loughran, G. Blyth, J. Nicholson, B. Donkin, R. McFarlane, W. Gregson, J. Hastings, M. Gilmore.
Front: R. Attley, T. Boustead, B. Kipling, P. Dolphin, B. Barker.

The Sunday Sun wrote; "Spennymoor should have won .... Their attacks were so strong that Rotherham were compelled to pack their goal. It was sheer bad luck that Rotherham equalised. Blyth had saved from Hall, and Loughran in clearing, kicked the ball against Nicholson, from whom it rebounded into the net at a terrific pace. All the forwards played well, their attacks having much more method than the Rotherham line." There was a crowd of 4,776 at the game, and the gate receipts were £221 15s 9d.

Team; George Blyth, J T Wilkinson, Bill Donkin, Joe Nicholson, Tommy Loughran, J Hastings, Ronald Attley, Teddy Boustead, Bob Kipling, Percy Dolphin, B Barker.

Moors nearly completed the upset in the replay at Millmoor the following Thursday. They led through Ted Boustead from a Joe Nicholson free kick, and after Rotherham went 2-1 up, equalised with a goal by Bob Kipling. But Rotherham were fitter and stronger and won 4-2, all the goals coming in the second half.

The Northern Echo said: "The Moors fought back desperately hard when they saw the game going against them, and their pluck created much enthusiasm among a crowd of 5,000."

Team; George Blyth, J T Wilkinson, Bill Donkin, Joe Nicholson, Tommy Loughran, J Hastings, Ronald Attley, Teddy Boustead, Bob Kipling, M Gilmore, Percy Dolphin.

Joe Nicholson had signed for Moors during the summer, from Aston Villa. He had also played for Cardiff City in the 1925 FA Cup final, which the Welshmen had lost 1-0 to Sheffield United.

Despite the disappointment of losing to Rotherham, there was some consolation for Moors in the local competition every team wanted to win – the Durham Challenge Cup.

The Durham Challenge Cup run 1927-28

The Durham Challenge Cup always aroused a huge amount of interest in those days, and crowds of well over two or three thousand always watched the semi finals and final. Moors hadn't done very well at all in the competition previously – Sunderland Reserves were always the team to beat – but that run of bad form changed.

Moors were strong and powerful that season, beating Esh Winning away by 5-1, Craghead at home by 6-1, Consett at home by 2-0, and in the semi finals they beat Hartlepool Reserves 3-0.

The final against Sunderland Reserves in March 24th 1928 at Feethams ended in a goalless draw. "One could not help but admire the pluck and determination of Spennymoor. (Joe) Nicholson, the Moors captain, was superior to the remainder and was perhaps the best man on view," wrote

one reporter. The Auckland Chronicle wrote; "No one could deny that Spennymoor were full value for a replay."
Team: George Blyth, Bill Donkin, Higgins, Joe Nicholson, Tommy Loughran, J Hastings, Ronald Attley, R MacFarlane, Bob Kipling, Percy Dolphin, B Barker.
Another bumper crowd of 4,927 turned up for the replay at Bishop Auckland on April 21st 1928, but after Percy Dolphin gave Moors a shock lead in the 3rd minute, Sunderland hit back to win 2-1, although Joe Nicholson had a shot cleared off the line near the end. But there was plenty of honour in defeat, and the Northern Echo wrote; "Although showing signs of fatigue, Spennymoor endeavoured to save the game but without avail. The second half was Spennymoor's from beginning to end." The team was the same as it was in the first game.
However, there was some consolation for Moors when they won the Ferryhill Nursing Cup beating Shildon 2-0 in a replay with goals by Tommy Loughran and Ted Boustead after the first game had finished 1-1 when Barker scored for Moors.
Striker Tom Ruddy set an individual club scoring record against Moors on March 14th 1928. Ruddy, who later played for Moors in his career, scored all eight for Darlington Reserves in the 8-1 win. Moors were resting players ahead of their Durham Challenge Cup final against Sunderland Reserves a fortnight later.
Moors and many other clubs had to quickly bring in some new blood for the start of season 1928-29. The spring and summer of 1928 were chaotic because of a huge scandal (in football terms) which swept through the north east concerning illegal payments to amateurs. It all started with the infamous Crook Town affair --- Crook were suspended by Durham FA and their Northern League record was deleted. A huge total of 341 players were suspended by Durham FA, with many clubs deemed guilty of paying their amateur players too much. Spennymoor had all but two of their squad suspended, and incredibly even the much respected club chairman Harry Askew, who was also chairman of the North Eastern League, was banned from football. "Amateur football in the strictest sense of the ruling is dead except maybe in the case of a few well-to-do players in the south," he said. Amateurism wasn't to be abolished for nearly fifty years. Instead, the word "shamateurism" was coined as a result.
Despite the suspensions, Moors still had a good season in the cups in 1928-29.

The FA Cup run 1928-29
Moors' reward in reaching the previous season's first round was an

exemption in season 1928-29 to the later qualifying rounds, and they proved again that they were capable of competing against clubs higher up the ladder. This time, they pulled off one of their biggest giantkillings, beating their Football League neighbours Hartlepools on their way to the second round.

Moors started in the last qualifying round with a 2-1 away win at Chilton Colliery, where Harry Barkas and Hardy scored, setting them up with a home tie against Hartlepools United who were near the bottom of the Third Division North at the time. The old arguments about the standard of the North Eastern League compared to the Third Division North resurfaced again, and those that felt there was hardly any difference at all were vindicated.

Pools never stood a chance once Harry Barkas put Moors into the lead from a pass by William "Billy" Race after just three minutes. Joe Nicholson crossed for Alex Nicholson, who was being watched by Nottingham Forest, to score the second, and Barkas made it 3-0 before half time. He went on to score two more in the second half to finish off a 5-2 win, but surprisingly there was fewer than 2,000 in the ground – officially anyway -- to witness Moors' greatest Cup victory to date.

The Sunday Sun wrote; "The North Eastern Leaguers gave their best display of the season, their forwards, splendidly led by Barkas being a real live combined line which the Hartlepools half backs failed to hold."

Team; Purvis, Bill Donkin, Nichol "Nick" Pharoah, Joe Nicholson, Tommy Loughran, William Rose, William Race, Bartley, Harry Barkas, Alex Nicholson, Dinsdale.

Unfortunately, Moors came to grief in the following round at the home of Accrington Stanley, another Third Division North team who were in midtable at the time, by 7-0. From a Spennymoor point of view, it was an embarrassing first half, because they trailed 5-0 at half time, and near the end keeper Purvis was carried off injured after colliding with the post. To put it mildly, the defeat was a huge embarrassment after the heroics of the last round.

Moors went 2-0 down after 15 minutes, and the Sunday Sun wrote; "It was evident after the first quarter of an hour's play that Spennymoor were a beaten team. Up to then, their forwards had played well, but the halves were clearly not strong enough to deal with the fast and well-planned Stanley attacks."

Team; Purvis, Bill Donkin, Nichol Pharoah, Joe Nicholson, Tommy Loughran, William Rose, William Race, Harry Barkas, Alex Nicholson, McFarlane, Percy Dolphin.

North Eastern League Cup 1928-29

The North Eastern League Cup was a difficult competition to win, because of the presence in the league of the reserve sides of the north east big three, plus the reserves from Hartlepool and Darlington.

Moors started the competition by winning 3-0 at Durham City where Alex Nicholson scored twice, then they just edged out Dipton 4-3, with Alex Nicholson on target again. They had an excellent 3-0 win in the semi final over Newcastle United Reserves, with Winter scoring twice, and Joe Nicholson scoring the other.

The final against Darlington Reserves on May 4th 1929 ended in a 0-0 stalemate, although the referee didn't endear himself, giving one or two strange decisions. The Echo wrote; "Spennymoor suffered from some bad decisions by the referee, whose interpretation of the offside law brought loud protests from the crowd." Some things never change!

Team; George Blyth, Bill Donkin, Nichol Pharoah, Joe Nicholson, Tommy Loughran, William Rose, William Race, Winter, Harry Barkas, Percy Dolphin, Ronald Attley.

Because the season had officially finished, the replay was held over until the following season, and Moors won 3-1. Harry Barkas gave Moors the lead, but Jackie Hill, who later played for Moors, equalised. Percy Dolphin put Moors 2-1 up from Ronnie Attley's centre, and Harry Barkas scored a third. Moors were the first team from outside the reserve teams to win the competition, no mean feat considering that they beat hot favourites Newcastle United Reserves along the way.

Team; George Blyth, Jack Carruthers, Nichol Pharoah, Joe Nicholson, Hugh Richmond, William Rose, Ronald Attley, Young, Harry Barkas, Percy Dolphin, Billy Younger.

Moors also did well in the North Eastern League, finishing in fifth place, their best placing since 1913.

The 1929-30 season started controversially, because the FA wouldn't allow Moors to enter the FA Cup, claiming that they hadn't paid the fine regarding the amateur suspensions on time, but maybe that decision spurred Moors on to do well in the Durham Challenge Cup.

Durham Challenge Cup run 1929-30

Moors had by now developed a taste for Cup runs. They beat Consett 3-2 in the first round, and in the second round they pulled off a shock, beating a strong Sunderland Reserves side 3-2, with Percy Dolphin (2) and Teddy Boustead scoring. They beat Cockfield 3-0 in a replay after a 1-1 draw, and then won 3-0 at Annfield Plain to clinch a place in the final against Tow Law from the Northern League.

How the cartoonist from the Durham Chronicle saw the Annfield Plain v Spennymoor Durham Challenge Cup semi final in 1930.

The game, at Bishop Auckland on April 19th 1930 -- the day after Moors had drawn 3-3 with Sunderland Reserves in a North Eastern League game -- was a 1-1 draw but the game was played on a heavy pitch following morning rain which didn't help the flow of play. The Sunday Sun wrote; "Any attempt to play good football on such a day was doomed to failure." Moors scored through Teddy Boustead, his 19th goal of the season, after a mistake by Coe in the Tow Law goal.

Team; George Blyth, Jack Carruthers, Frank Chisem, John Armstrong, Tommy Loughran, William Rose, Ronald Attley, Teddy Boustead, Bob Kipling, Percy Dolphin, Billy Younger.

Moors won the replay at Hartlepool on May 10th 1930 (believe it or not, the date was considered to be "out of season") by a single goal, scored by Percy Dolphin after another mistake by Tow Law keeper Coe, but overall the game was poor. "Those who watched the game must have been disgusted with the fare served up," was one match report. Moors weren't grumbling though – after all, they'd won the Cup for the first time in their history!.

Team; George Blyth, Jack Carruthers, Frank Chisem, John Armstrong, Tommy Loughran, William Rose, Ronald Attley, Teddy Boustead, Lowes, Percy Dolphin, Billy Younger.

The Durham Challenge Cup win also completed a Cup hat trick. They won the Durham Benevolent Bowl at Kingsway on January 11th 1930, beating Chilton Colliery 3-1, with goals from Nichol Pharoah (penalty), Teddy Boustead and Bill Younger and they beat Cockfield 4-3 in a thrilling Ferryhill Nursing Cup final.

Unfortunately, the following season was a big let down. After pulling off some giantkillings themselves in previous seasons, Moors were on the receiving end of one in their Durham Challenge Cup defence, when they were beaten 3-2 by little-known Wearside League club Shiney Row Swifts in the first round, plus they also lost the Ferryhill Nursing Cup 1-0 against Evenwood. In October 1930, Moors inside right Jack Reed was transferred to First Division Wolves for "big help financially", but he played only one game for them before moving down the road to Walsall, where he played 134 games.

The following season was much better. After finishing in 14th place in the North Eastern League in 1931, Moors finished eighth in 1932, and they gave their fans something to shout about in the cup.

Durham Challenge Cup run 1931-32

Moors reached the Durham Challenge Cup final for the second time in three seasons, but they lost to fellow North Eastern League club Crook Town.

Harry Ridley scored twice in a 4-0 home win over Leslies from Hebburn, then Cook scored the only goal against Hebburn Colliery in the second round. Harry Ridley got the only goal away to Annfield Plain, and in the semi final W Tucker, signed from South Shields, scored a hat trick in the 4-2 home win over Easington.

Moors played Crook in the final on Easter Saturday, March 26th 1932, a day after they'd played Shildon in the North Eastern League. Crook, from the Northern League, won 2-1 after Scott had equalised for Moors, in front of a crowd of 6,793.

"Crook were much stronger in defence than their opponents, and Ridley the goal scoring winger was held in subjection," the Sunday Sun wrote. Team; Reid, Jack Carruthers, Tutin, Tommy Loughran, Turner, Robinson, M Cook, W Tucker, Scott, Harry Ridley.

Harry Ridley had returned to the club after five years with Aldershot and Nelson. He was the man to follow that season, scoring 47 goals in total, including six in a game against Gateshead on February 20th 1932.

North Eastern League cup run 1931-32

Moors played seven games to reach the final, because three games went to replays.

They started with a 0-0 draw at Wallsend, but comfortably won the replay 7-2, with five players amongst the goals. Harry Ridley scored one of the goals in a 3-3 draw with Hartlepool Reserves at the Brewery Field, and he scored again in the 2-1 replay win, Ronnie Attley scoring the other.

Moors then faced another replay against Newcastle United Reserves. They drew 1-1 with them at the Brewery Field, Harry Ridley scoring again, and then as underdogs they pulled off a great 2-1 win in the replay, Tutin and McKane scoring.

They played their fifth tie inside the month of March 1932 against Ashington, beating them 4-1, with McKane on the scoresheet.

However, they lost the final 3-0 against Middlesbrough in front of 4,515 fans – "outclassed and outplayed" was the Northern Echo's verdict.

Team; Reid, Jack Carruthers, Scott, Tutin, Tommy Loughran, Turner, Robinson, W.Tucker, McKane, Ted Boustead, Harry Ridley. One interesting feature of that match was that nobody from either team was pulled up for offside throughout the course of the game. Spennymoor fans would probably have argued that they didn't get close enough to the Boro goal to be offside.

Moors won the Durham Benevolent Bowl by beating Stockton 3-2 in the final on March 12th 1932 at Kingsway, Tommy Loughran scoring the winner.

Relationships between Spennymoor and Crook were strained that season. Moors were hauled in front of Durham FA on 23rd December 1931 after Crook complained of misconduct by spectators during their Durham Benevolent Bowl semi final. "A certain liveliness" was the Echo's headline. Crook claimed that the "shouting and catcalling to the Crook players before the game was calculated, and led to rough play." Missiles were allegedly thrown at the Crook keeper and full backs, and one of them, Harry Mitton – who signed for Moors a few years later – was supposedly hit by a stone. The Crook representative said: "Our players were so intimidated that several asked not to be selected to play against Spennymoor on Christmas Day."

The referee, Mr W Chambers, said that while there was a good deal of shouting, he heard "no language to which exception could be taken." Furthermore, he didn't think Mitton had been hit by a stone.

In retaliation, Spennymoor complained about an article in the Crook programme for a Northern League match the following week, which read; "The Spennymoor players were urged by the spectators to cripple our team. The match was almost a tragedy. I have never witnessed such a rough and vicious game." The referee came to Spennymoor's rescue again,

and said that he'd never heard the spectators shouting anything of the sort. Moors secretary Charlie Sutton also complained about the conduct of the Crook chairman Mr Bordman, whom he alleged in an argument had asked him to "go behind the stand to settle their differences".
Durham FA cautioned Moors about the future conduct of their spectators, and were instructed to post warning notices around the Brewery Field. They were told that "if the complaint had been made by the referee and not an opposing club, then the ground would have been closed." DFA expressed their "grave dissatisfaction" about the article in the Crook programme, and the "indiscreet remarks" made by representatives of both clubs did not warrant any action. The league game on Christmas Day passed without any repeat incidents, and presumably, without any Christmas cards.
Moors then withdrew from the Benevolent Bowl for season 1932-33 saying that they had a busy fixture schedule, especially when they had the FA Cup in mind.
The facilities at the Brewery Field were improved in 1932 when the club purchased and erected a grandstand from Catterick Racecourse. The housing estate had now been built next to the Brewery Field. Good old club president Harry Askew, now in his seventies, conducted the proceedings.

The FA Cup run 1932-33

Forward Harry Barkas, who later moved to Jarrow, Gateshead and then Liverpool, gave the fans in the new stand plenty to cheer on September 3rd 1932 when he scored seven of Moors' goals in their 10-1 thrashing of Dawdon in the FA Cup, five of them coming in a twenty minute spell. Moors scored goals galore in their run to the first round of the Cup in 1932-33, scoring 27 in six qualifying round matches.
In the next round, Harry scored twice in the 5-1 home win over Murton but soon after he left the club for South Shields. M Cook, who replaced Barkas, then scored twice in the 4-1 home win over Seaham, then Jackie Hill, who was to become a prolific scorer for the club, scored both goals in the victory at Wardley. Hill and Jackie Hope sealed the 2-0 win at Horden.
Moors had to travel away to Bridlington in the last qualifying round, a draw that was certainly less than lucrative. Bridlington had beaten Stockton at home in an earlier round, and the crowd was so low that Stockton only made £2 profit from the game after expenses had been deducted. There was talk of the game being switched to Spennymoor, but Bridlington, just like Spennymoor had done to Gillingham years previously, stuck to their guns and refused to switch.
Nevertheless, 200 Moors fans made the journey to East Yorkshire and saw

them win 4-2 on November 12th 1932, with M Cook scoring a hat trick, and Jackie Hill the other.
Unfortunately, Cook was stretchered off after a bad tackle near the end, and at the final whistle, some angry Moors fans ran towards Higgins, the Bridlington player involved, and one of them "had him by the throat on the ground, before he was rescued by police." Higgins escaped by running across the field at the back of the ground, and a Spennymoor fan was arrested.
Moors' reward was a trip to North Wales, against Wrexham, then in the Third Division North. But Moors' goalscoring ability completely dried up, and they lost 3-0, the first goal a penalty given away by Archie Brown.
The Sunday Sun report said: "The visitors fought hard all the way through, but they were not a very polished team." A crowd of over 6000 watched the game, with total receipts £287.
The Spennymoor team was; J Scott, Billy Coulthard, Archie Brown, W Harrison, Tommy Loughran, W Scott, A Heslop, M Cook, JT Hall, JC Thompson, Harry Ridley.

1932-33 Durham Challenge Cup run

Moors couldn't have asked for a better start in the campaign, winning 5-0 at Bishop Auckland, with each of their five forwards scoring a goal. Jackie Hill scored twice in the 4-0 replay win over Crook after the teams had drawn 1-1 at the Millfield, and then Harry Ridley scored with two spot kicks as Moors beat Annfield Plain 3-1 in the semi final.
Moors went into the final against Jarrow on April 8th 1933 at Kingsway as strong favourites. They were sixth in the table at the time, while Jarrow were struggling in third bottom place. But Moors learned that league form is thrown out of the window in cup ties, and Jarrow caused an upset, winning 2-1, Moors' second successive final defeat.
Moors actually took the lead through Jackie Hill from Harry Ridley's corner after just five minutes, but they relaxed and let Jarrow back into the game.
Team; J Scott, Billy Coulthard, Archie Brown, Drummond, Tommy Loughran, Turner, A Heslop, M Cook, Jackie Hill, Ronald Attley, Harry Ridley.
Harry Barkas, a Moors goalscoring hero from the past, played for Jarrow, but didn't score.
There was some consolation when Moors won the Sunderland Eye Infirmary Cup, beating Crook 3-2 in the final, and they also finished a good sixth in the North Eastern League, the defence conceding the fewest goals in the league – better even than the Football League clubs.

Moors improved again in the North Eastern League in season 1933-34, finishing in third place behind Sunderland Reserves and Jarrow, with their highest ever points total (52, one more than the season they won the league in 1910) and their highest ever goals scored, 114.
There was also another trip out, this time to the midlands, in the FA Cup.

Spennymoor United Supporters Club

1933-34 FA Cup run
As a reward for their exploits in previous seasons, Moors were handed an exemption from the early qualifying rounds of the FA Cup, and they came into the competition at the fourth qualifying round, in which they beat Stockton 2-1 in a replay at the Brewery Field with goals by Archie Brown and A Heslop, after a 2-2 draw.
Just like the season before, they were drawn away to a Football League club, this time Walsall from the Third Division North. However, they had to make a quick change to their team, because Jackie Hill went down with flu on the journey to the midlands, so he was replaced by Jack Oakes at centre forward. Moors held the Football League side for nearly an hour, but were furious over the first goal with the referee, who disagreed with a linesman's flag for offside and waved play on instead. Moors eventually went down 4-0, but they made a good impression on one local reporter.
"Spennymoor played football equal to that of some of the Third Division clubs who have visited Fellowes Park this season," wrote the Birmingham Mail.

The team was; J Scott, Billy Coulthard, Archie Brown, W Harrison, Tommy Loughran, Porter, A Heslop, Reg Siddle, Jackie Oakes, Billy Wyness, Sid Turnbull.
Defender Tommy Loughran, for so long a key part of the Spennymoor defence, left the club soon after, and he was replaced by defender Arthur Andrews, a former Sunderland centre half.
Moors must have wondered what they'd done to upset the FA, because they were drawn away again in the first round the following season!

1934-35 FA Cup run

Thanks to their continuing exemption, Moors didn't have to battle through the early qualifying rounds again, and with the help of the inspirational Arthur Andrews, they won 4-0 at Jarrow in the fourth qualifying round, with goals by Andrews, Holmes (2) and Harker.
The much wanted home tie still didn't materialise, because Moors were drawn away to Rotherham, who were struggling in the Third Division North. Moors again fancied their chances this time, but Rotherham hit them with two goals inside the first twenty minutes using unexpected "kick and rush methods". Moors went close a couple of times in the second half, but the damage was already done.
The team; Morgan, Sid Bott, Harry Hubbick, Reg Siddle, Arthur Andrews, Jackie Towers, Charlie Coates, Jackie Hope, Holmes, Tom Ruddy, Harker.
Tom Ruddy was the Darlington Reserves striker who'd scored eight against Moors in the league just a few years before. He didn't stay long at the Brewery Field, because he moved on to Irish club Linfield, but Moors made sure they got a fee for him! Linfield wanted to take the player for nothing, but Spennymoor secretary Charlie Sutton stuck to his guns, and squeezed £25 from the Irish club, who also paid Southampton, his previous club, £200. Full back Harry Hubbick came to the club from Blyth, and signed for Burnley along with Sid Bott on March 18th 1935.
The Durham Challenge Cup third round tie between Spennymoor and Blackhall on February 16th 1935 had to be abandoned because one of the Blackhall players collapsed because of exposure. There had been very heavy rain on the morning of the match, as well as during it, so much so that some of the lines, done with whitewash, were obliterated. The referee stopped the game for a few minutes in the first half to allow the wind and rain to ease, but after half time, the Blackhall keeper Jarps was injured, and then full back Jones collapsed. Moors drew the re-arranged game 1-1, and then lost the replay 3-2. On the same day, the Crook v Eden CW tie had to be abandoned because five Eden players left the field because of exhaustion.

The match referee scored for Spennymoor in their league game at Jarrow on April 4th 1935. Left half Jack Towers crossed the ball, and it bounced off the head of referee Bob Bowie into the net. The goal didn't matter, as Spennymoor still lost 3-1.
Moors' North Eastern League season still wasn't all that bad, but they slipped to seventh from third place.
Moors signed former Ferryhill forward James (Pimpie) Carr from Arsenal at the start of the 1935-36 season, and after five goals in six matches, he was soon on his travels again, this time to Leeds United.
The Crook goalkeeper, Peacock, scored the winner against Moors in a North Eastern League game at the Millfield on 20th April 1936. With the score 1-1 at half time, he swopped jerseys and went to outside right for the second half. According to the Echo report, "he ran almost half the length of the field before sending in a powerful right foot drive which left Heywood helpless."

However, despite all their success, crowds at the Brewery Field dwindled, and on January 18th 1936 the Auckland Chronicle reported that the club was considering a surprising return to the Northern League because "there are more people at the dog races -- they have taken away a large number of people. Local football of the professional type is being crowded out." At the time, there was a dog track less than 200 yards down the road from the Brewery Field, and was clearly a popular counter attraction.
There were fewer than 100 people in the ground for a North Eastern League game against Throckley late in the season, just to prove the club's point. The club finished in ninth place in the table, their fifth straight finish in the top ten – not bad going. Certainly the club was a strong force to be reckoned with, and had progressed a long way since its formation under Thomas Grant. But would the town sit up and take notice of the warning signs? Was the club's warning about the future a bluff? Everyone would soon find the answer in what turned out to be an extraordinary season, the most dramatic yet in the club's history.

Spennymoor United, 1935-36.
Back row: A. Moult, W. Foster, A. Heywood, K. Nimmo, J. Towers, A. Andrews.
Front: C. Coates, J. Fletcher, J. Hill, T. Dodds, E. Brain.

Chapter Two
Where have the crowds gone?

Moors enjoyed their finest hour when they played mighty West Bromwich Albion in the third round of the FA Cup – but within four months they almost went out of existence.
It was an incredible season for all sorts of reasons, and it is difficult to imagine how the club enjoyed one of its best ever seasons, made plenty of headlines and new friends, and then literally pulled the plug. It was simply unbelievable.
Moors certainly grabbed the limelight with their FA Cup run, playing nine matches before losing to First Division giants West Bromwich Albion in the third round – the best run in their history, either before or since.
Led by former Norwich defender Nichol (Nicky) Wall who had been signed from Crook and Billy Wyness who had returned from a spell at Shrewsbury, the run started way back on September 19th 1936 when they beat Willington 5-1 at the Brewery Field with five different players scoring, and then they won 4-0 at Dawdon where Jackie Hill scored twice. Moors then won a replay by 3-1 at Bishop Auckland in front of 5,270 after they drew 1-1 at the Brewery Field, and then in the third qualifying round went to town on Easington CW, hammering them 6-1, Brown scoring twice.
They just managed to pip North Shields 3-2 away from home to give them a place in the first round for the fourth time in five seasons – Jackie Hill was on target for the fifth successive game -- but imagine the Moors' disappointment when they were drawn away from home yet again, this time at Boston United from the Midland League.
But despite the four hour trip to Lincolnshire on November 28th 1936, Moors drew 1-1 with Jackie Hill scoring the goal, although Albert Heywood saved a penalty when Boston were leading 1-0. "Heywood earned the plaudits of everybody with a masterly display of goalkeeping," said the Echo.
The town rallied around the club for the replay on December 2nd, two local factories, Kenmirs and Coulson, closed for the afternoon so then the workers could attend the match, and full back Sid Bott – who had returned to the club -- managed, with a lot of persuasion, to get time off work from his job as a clerk at Craghead mine.

A crowd of 3,537 (receipts £175 8s) squeezed into the Brewery Field to see Moors win 2-0 with goals from Bill Wyness, a 10th minute shot that went through the keeper's hands, and Jackie Hill from a loose ball on 25 minutes after Sid Turnbull's shot was parried. "The home side established an early lead and never looked like losing it. The first half ran consistently in Spennymoor's favour. They got Boston on the run and kept up the attack with long sweeping movements," wrote the Echo.

The team for both matches was; Albert Heywood, Sid Bott, Billy Alderson, Reg Siddle, Nichol Wall, Jackie Towers, Charlie Coates, Jack Brown, Jackie Hill, Bill Wyness, Sid Turnbull.

The second round draw gave them the dubious pleasure of an overnight trip to East Anglia to play Ipswich Town, then a Southern League club. Full back Sid Bott couldn't play because he was needed at work and couldn't get time off, despite several pleas to his employers by club secretary Charlie Sutton.

Moors certainly caught Ipswich and most of the 12,491 crowd cold, scoring in just the second minute of the game when Sid Turnbull crossed for Billy Wyness to beat the Ipswich keeper. Ipswich equalised, but Moors got a magnificent winner on 72 minutes through Jackie Hill from a Charlie Coates cross.

The Sunday Sun reported; "Spennymoor changed like lightning from defence into attack. First time tackling, hard clearances and straight-for-goal methods when the occasion arose were features of their play."

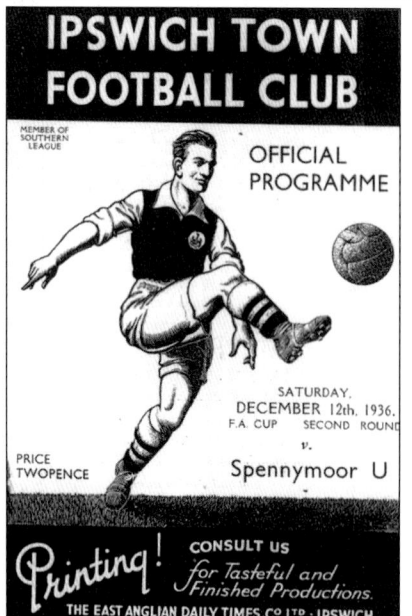

"Spennymoor had to be on the defensive for the greater part of the game, but so well did they play that the Ipswich forward line was made to look very mediocre," said the Echo.

The team; Albert Heywood, George Porter, Billy Alderson, Reg Siddle, Nichol Wall, Jackie Towers, Sid Turnbull, Bill Wyness, Jackie Hill, Jackie Brown, Charlie Coates.

There weren't many Spennymoor fans there at Portman Road to salute the victory, but there were plenty to welcome them home at Bank Top station in Darlington. It was probably one of Moors' best ever away performances in their history to give them a place in the third round draw of the FA Cup.

All the Moors' players were heroes and Cup fever gripped the town like it never had done before. Unfortunately, they didn't get a home draw in the third round that they were hoping for, but the mighty West Bromwich Albion, midtable in the First Division, was a pretty good consolation.

The spotlight was really on Moors leading up to the tie and for the first time in Moors' history the players were local celebrities. Unfortunately, the fairytale ended at the Hawthorns, when the First Division side scored three quick goals, and although Jackie Hill scored from a left wing cross – the 475th goal of his career -- the Albion scored four more goals to complete a 7-1 win.

Spennymoor United team and officials arriving at Birmingham New Street Station before their FA Cup tie at West Bromwich Albion

"Spennymoor were by no means disgraced," said the Sunday Sun. The Birmingham Post observed; "If the Spennymoor forwards had as good a notion of their job as their defence had of its duties, the game would have been not keener, but more interesting."

The team; Albert Heywood, George Porter, Billy Alderson, Reg Siddle, Nichol Wall, Jackie Towers, Charlie Coates, Jack Brown, Jack Hill, Bill Wyness, Sid Turnbull.

Straight after the game, keeper Albert Heywood joined Sunderland on the train northwards for a £150 fee, the end of a successful quest by the Sunderland scout, who had followed Moors to Boston and Ipswich waiting for them to lose before he could grab his man ahead of other clubs. Along with a healthy share of the gate receipts from a 23,781 crowd, the Echo headline said; " Spennymoor return from West Bromwich £600 richer than when they set out." They also came back with the match ball, autographed by members of both sides and a tribute from the West Brom chairman, Major E Wilson Keys; "It was a gallant fight by a plucky team and we are proud to have met you."

But despite a crowd of 3,537 for the Boston game, league attendances at the Brewery Field were disappointing, and secretary Charlie Sutton is supposed to have said that "there were more people at Bank Top station when we came back from Ipswich than there were to watch home matches." One fan who called himself "Never absent" wrote to the Echo and said; "The work done by Mr Sutton deserves better support." There was also a suggestion that the unemployed of Spennymoor should pay a reduced admission price of 4d instead of the usual 6d (just over 2p nowadays!).

There was plenty of speculation on the fate of the club. Charlie Sutton denied that Moors had applied to join the Northern League, and that the players had offered to appear without pay. "Neither I nor any of the officials of the club have any knowledge of a move to consider adopting amateur status. I cannot very well see how this move could be made until the future of the present club is determined. The report that our players have offered to play on a "no profit, no pay" basis is ridiculous. There is no need for them to do this because the club's finances have never been better." But the Echo still made the point that "public support is too meagre to support a North Eastern League club."

Charlie Sutton then submitted his resignation, and revealed that he was going to another North Eastern League club, Horden, before the start of the following season. "His ability to spot likely players and develop them for bigger clubs has brought playing success and financial gain to his club which as been largely responsible for Spennymoor maintaining a good reputation in spite of poor public support," the Echo pointed out. During his ten years in charge, Moors had reached the first round of the FA Cup four times.

Despite the growing turmoil off the field, the team somehow kept its concentration to win the non-reserve medals in the North Eastern League, but they had a very hectic fixture backlog, caused by their cup success. They recorded their biggest ever win in the North Eastern League on

February 5th 1937 when they hammered Eden CW 19-0. The newspapers didn't describe the goals in their match reports because they didn't have enough space, so they just listed the scorers with the times! Sid Turnbull and Wildsmith both scored four, with Jack Hill and Jackie Coates scoring hat tricks, Jackie Towers and Bill Wyness scored two each, with one own goal. It was 8-0 at half time.

They won thirteen league games in a row to catch their main rivals, Blyth and Workington, then a 3-3 draw at Annfield Plain after being 3-0 down on April 24th 1937, and a 2-0 victory at Workington sealed second place for them, behind champions Sunderland Reserves, and with it the non-reserve winners' medals. It was an excellent achievement, their best in the North Eastern League since 1910.

And then came the bombshell news. Under the headline of "Spennymoor withdraw from the North Eastern League" on May 6th 1937, Charlie Sutton revealed at a special members' meeting that the attendances were so low that the receipts were sometimes only £11 in total; "We have often been told that if we had a good team, we are sure to get support. That does not apply at Spennymoor." The Echo wrote; "The meeting provided yet another illustration of the football apathy which exists in the town for there was a very small attendance. Members of the committee intimated that they were not prepared to carry on and as there were no volunteers to take over the management, it was decided to apply to the league for permission to resign."

How sad Spennymoor president Harry Askew, the man who helped Moors so much in their early days, must have felt in his position as chairman of the North Eastern League when the resignation was accepted by clubs on May 21st 1937, but personally he was determined to keep the club in the league. Knowing that there was a possibility of a group of supporters battling to rescue the club, he pleaded to the AGM for a stay of execution, saying that "the league management committee had deferred consideration of Spennymoor's application to resign, and that to all intents and purposes they were still members." He also told the league of a forthcoming meeting to discuss the future of the club, and he knew of "twelve guarantors who expressed willingness to carry on."

However, the Spennymoor club officials who were present painted a different story. Harry Cummings said: "Football in the league was not a paying proposition. There had been talk in Spennymoor of a town meeting, but no one had come forward intimating willingness to carry on." Charlie Sutton chipped in; "The club had never been a paying proposition, and but for cup ties this year there would have been a deficit of £250. North Eastern League football in Spennymoor will not go."

The league secretary then produced a letter from the secretary of Spennymoor – who of course was Charlie Sutton -- which sealed its own fate. "Football was a dead letter and would need something sensational to revive it in the Spennymoor area," the letter read, adding that the club wished to resign from the league. The representatives from Sunderland Reserves and Blyth then moved that the resignation should be accepted, and in the vote that followed, ten clubs were in favour and five against. After thirty years' membership, a glorious run to the third round of the FA Cup and runners up in the North Eastern League the very same season, Spennymoor were out of the league. Of the other business that day, the league agreed to expand to twenty clubs. An innocuous decision at the time, but significant later.

Harry Askew kept battling away to keep the club afloat. At the club's AGM on May 30th 1937, a new committee was formed, and the decision was made to carry on as a club, although in what league had still to be decided. Harry also criticised the decision to resign from the North Eastern League. "That was an unwise decision. The old committee might have had certain good reasons for the step they took, but further enquiries should have been made to ascertain whether anyone else would step in to take control."

Charlie Sutton pointed out that in view of his twelve years' experience he and the club's committee were "fighting a bankrupt business." Gate receipts worked out at around £14 per week. Harry Cummings, in his report, said: "One or two seasons without a football club in the town would be the best tonic towards making any future club a self-supporting concern."

Two days later, the determined Harry chaired a meeting in Tudhoe and Spennymoor WMC, at which 300 supporters squeezed inside the hall, with more listening outside. Five more people were found to serve on the club's new committee, and with the help of Durham FA secretary Mr W Spedding, a supporters' club, nicknamed the Spennymoor Tigers, was formed with Mr W Nichol as secretary, and Coun B Franks as chairman. The revival had begun.

The question was; which league should Spennymoor play in? Harry Askew had already said his piece about trying to rejoin the Northern League at the club's AGM; "The whole situation as far as the amateur is concerned, is a very distasteful one." Moors couldn't go back to the North Eastern League, they didn't apply for the Northern League, but instead they successfully applied to join the Wearside League.

With the backing of the supporters, the club's renaissance gathered momentum. They clubbed together, set up a penny ticket scheme, and raised £24 to give it a good financial start.

Charlie Sutton moved to Horden, and guess who the football gods decided that Moors should play in the second qualifying round of the FA Cup on October 15th 1937? Yes, Horden, who came out on top by 3-2. What the thoughts were of some individuals involved in the preceding season's crisis were unrecorded, but it's fair to assume that there won't have been much handshaking going on.

Throughout that Wearside League season, support grew for a return to the North Eastern League, and on March 17th 1938 in the Wheatsheaf Hotel, the club's members decided by an overwhelming majority, to apply for their old place back after raising guarantees, £100 from the committee, and £50 from the supporters' club. The supporters felt that if they could raise another £100 to cover more guarantees, then they would have a good chance of success.

Moors finished second in the Wearside League behind Blackhall, but a well conducted campaign won them their place back in the North Eastern League, much to the relief of the ageing but hard working Harry Askew.

There were two places available in the league, one from Moors' departure a year previous, and a second because City of Durham had resigned, hoping to win a place in the Northern League. Consett had finished bottom and were seeking re-election.

Blackhall, the Wearside League champions, said they wanted a higher class of football, and denied that the club "had a policy of paying players ten shillings a match" which at the time was quite high. Consett stated that they had made a profit, and intended to "improve the ground, accommodation, and build a steel stand."

Secretary Mr G W N Smith represented Spennymoor along with Mr H P Schwartze, the deputy chairman, and said; "We started the season with a millstone of £50 but we cleared that off and are starting the new season with roughly £75, together with £100 promised by supporters and a further £100 which has been promised they will have at the beginning of next season - £275.

"Regarding our past record, this is quite good. We have been members of this league since the second year of its inauguration. It was through a misunderstanding that we withdrew last year."

Maybe those words were enough, maybe the fact that Harry Askew had given the league such long and devoted service was a big factor, but Moors and Consett both picked up 16 votes each, with Blackhall only receiving 6. Moors were back in the North Eastern League, and a highly dramatic two years were over. There would be similar drama later in the club's history, and no "misunderstandings" along the way.

Chapter Three

Laurie scores again... and so does Duggie!

The club's pre-war renaissance had plenty of momentum thanks to its supporters and the townspeople. The bank loan was quickly paid off, so were the outstanding debts and the membership list – the season ticket holders – increased from 25 to 145, with 21 of those applying for places on the committee.
Moors finished a creditable 12th on their return to the North Eastern League, and there was even a cup run to get excited about, with Moors capping their comeback season by reaching the final of the Northern Eastern League Cup on April 15th 1939 – they gained some satisfaction by beating Horden 2-0 - but centre half John Hands picked up an injury early in the game, and with substitutes more than twenty years away, Moors were handicapped and they lost 6-0 to Gateshead Reserves.
Team; Wright, Ryecroft, Emmerson, White, John Hands, Thornton, Walker, McDonald, Russell, Raw, Smart.
Moors' FA Cup first qualifying round tie at Stanley on September 30th 1938 was abandoned by the referee after he changed his mind about allowing Stanley a possible second goal. The Spennymoor players appealed for offside, and after the referee consulted his linesman, changed his decision. This prompted the crowd to run on to the field, and even though the ground was cleared, the referee refused to carry on and the match was abandoned. Moors wanted the tie awarded to them, but the FA ordered a replay which Moors won 3-2.
Sadly, Harry Askew, who had worked so hard for the club during its early days and also in the 1937 crisis, passed away that season aged 79. Many local football dignitaries attended his funeral.
The Second World War interrupted football and the North Eastern League was abandoned after just three games of the 1939-40 season, although the Tudhoe Orphanage Cup final was staged against Bishop Auckland on May 18th 1940 at the Brewery Field, the match finishing 1-1. Guest players were allowed in the war years, and several who went on to achieve fame turned out for Moors.

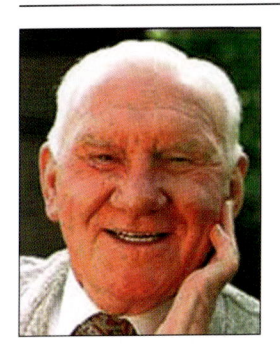

Laurie scores again... and so does Duggie!

Bill Nicholson    Bert Johnson    Tommy Dawson

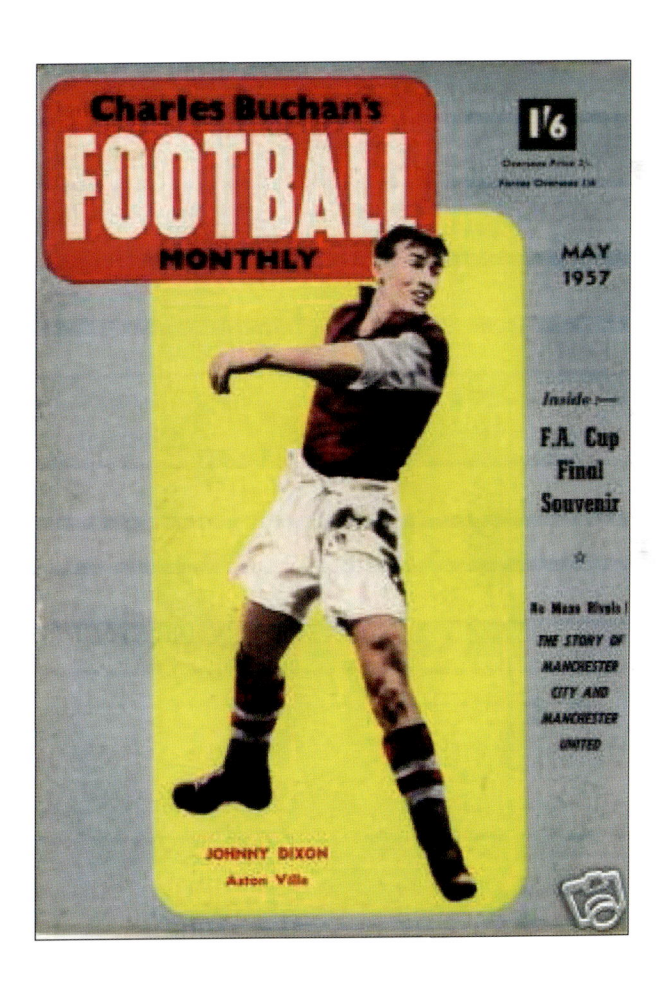

Charles Buchan's FOOTBALL MONTHLY

1'6

MAY 1957

Inside:—
F.A. Cup Final Souvenir

No Mean Rivals!
THE STORY OF MANCHESTER CITY AND MANCHESTER UNITED

JOHNNY DIXON
Aston Villa

41

Full back Bill Nicholson was one of the most well known as he later became manager of First Division giants Tottenham Hotspur in their heyday when they won the League and FA Cup double in 1961. He played in four games. Inside forward Tommy Dawson, who started his career at Spennymoor before moving to Charlton, returned to the north east and played several games. He returned to Charlton after the war and won an FA Cup winners' medal in 1947.

Charlie Wayman also appeared for the Moors after being signed from Chilton Colliery, and after the war finished, he signed for Newcastle United, and then went on to play for Southampton, Preston North End, Middlesbrough and Darlington, scoring over 250 goals.

Probably the most famous of them all was Johnny Dixon. Johnny inspired the Moors in the season after the war, so much so that instead of being called Spennymoor United, the club was nicknamed "Dixon United". He went back to Aston Villa when the Football League recommenced, and as captain, he lifted the FA Cup in 1957, and became one of their greatest ever players. He even had his own newspaper column! Unfortunately, he never gained any England caps, but he was made reserve for the game against Wales in 1952.

The team against Bishop Auckland was; Jack Clark, Norman Fowler (Middlesbrough), Bill Nicholson (Spurs), Kirtley, Ronnie Peart (Derby), Tom Callender (Lincoln), Young, Tommy Dawson (Charlton), Condron (Sheffield Wednesday), Bert Johnson (Charlton), Laurie Wensley (Sunderland).

Bert Johnson, a left half, played for Spennymoor before moving to the Valley for a £500 transfer fee before the war. He was chosen to play for England against Switzerland on May 11th 1946 and was also a guest player for Bolton.

Laurie Wensley was a free scoring forward, and scored a hat trick for Bishop Auckland in the 1939 Amateur Cup final – and what an impact he was going to make later for Spennymoor.

Moors didn't get involved in any sort of organised football again until season 1944-45, when the North Eastern League was revived. Moors were in the best position to take advantage of the restart of football with the exciting Johnny Dixon leading their team, and they were title challengers all the way through that shortened first season.

Guest players were still allowed, and one of them, Middlesbrough striker George Camsell scored a hat trick in a North Eastern League game against Reyrolles on 30th September 1944, and another was the famous amateur Bobby Hardisty in an 8-3 win against Hartlepool on New Year's Day 1945. Moors beat Darlington Reserves 3-2 on January 13th to complete their 22 league fixtures – every home gate was more than 2,000 -- and they had to wait nervously at the top of the table for Blackhall CW to play their last two, which were both against lowly Hartlepool Reserves. If Blackhall won them both, they were champions, but Hartlepool held them 2-2 in the first game to give Moors the league. No doubt there were celebrations in the town that night when the news came through! The team celebrated the win by having a dinner, and then going to watch the wrestling at St James Hall in Newcastle.

With the league in their pocket, Moors switched their attention to the Durham Wartime Cup, which effectively was the Durham Challenge Cup.

The Durham Wartime Cup 1945

Moors celebrated the return of Cup football by hammering Crook Town 10-2 away from home on February 24th 1945, Laurie Wensley scoring five of them.

Moors then had tough opponents in Horden, whom they beat 3-1 in a replay with goals by Johnny Dixon, Tommy Dawson and new signing Laurie Larner after a 1-1 draw in which Andy Donaldson scored. Horden keeper Dorman wore spectacles in the first game.

Port Clarence were hammered 7-1 thanks to a hat trick by Newcastle forward Andy Donaldson and two more from Laurie Wensley. A week after losing to Murton in the semi final of the North Eastern League Cup, Moors drew 3-3 with the same opponents on April 7th 1945, Laurie Larner scoring a last minute equaliser. In the replay, Blenkinsopp scored two and Johnny Dixon the other as Moors beat Murton 3-1 at the Brewery Field in front of 3,527.

Kingsway was packed for the final against Stanley, as the crowd turned out to watch the first Cup final for several years. Led by Johnny Dixon, Moors easily won the final 5-0 on May 12th 1945, all the Spennymoor forwards uniquely scoring in rotation – Ken Twigg, Johnny Dixon, Andy Donaldson, Laurie Larner and Laurie Wensley. Tom Blenkinsopp also missed a penalty. Team; Ray Lee, David Bell, Tom Blenkinsopp, D. Young, Bobby Shanks, Pop Welch, Ken Twigg, Johnny Dixon, Andy Donaldson, Laurie Larner, Laurie Wensley.

Ken Twigg had also played for Bishops before the war, and was rated by many fans to be the best outside right Moors ever had. He won an FA Amateur Cup winners' medal, along with Laurie Wensley, in the 3-0 win over Willington at Roker Park in 1939.

Laurie joined permanently from Sunderland in August 1945, and hit a phenomenal 63 goals in the 1945-46 season as Moors won the North Eastern League and the Durham Challenge Cup. Johnny Dixon chipped in

We'll Always Be United

Durham Challenge Cup Final 1944-45.
Spennymoor Utd 5 Stanley Utd 0
Back row: R. Dent, D. Bell (Derby County), R. Shanks (Crystal Palace), J. Dixon (Aston Villa), R. Lee (Newcastle Utd.), T. Blenkinsop (Grimsby Town), R. Welch, J. Kennedy. Front: K. Twigg, L. Larner (Blackpool), L. Wensley (Sunderland), A. Donaldson (Newcastle United), D. Young.

with another 39 – so in total the pair scored over 100 goals between them. Laurie scored the same number of goals that his father, Harry, had scored two decades earlier, and it's reckoned that Laurie deliberately missed a penalty in the last game of the season so then his father still had a share of the record.

The crowds turned out in force to welcome back some form of organised football after the war. Moors were flying in the North Eastern League in the first full season on the resumption of "official" football, and there was a real chance of a League and Durham Challenge Cup double.

Moors were prolific that season, scoring a mammoth 195 goals in all competitions, and they ran up double figures against Gateshead Reserves and Eppleton in league games.

The 1945-46 Durham Challenge Cup run

Moors started their Durham Challenge Cup run with a 6-2 home win over Darlington Reserves on December 22nd 1945 with Laurie Wensley scoring a hat trick, then Laurie, along with Wakenshaw both scored four apiece in a 9-0 hammering of Felling Red Star. Laurie helped himself to another hat trick when Moors won 6-2 at Easington, and then in the semi final, against his old club Bishop Auckland, Laurie scored the only goal of the game in front of an 8,000 Brewery Field crowd, which had to be made all ticket because of the huge interest in the game.

The final was staged at Kingsway against Brancepeth No4 ITC, a team based in the Army camp at Brancepeth who called on several professional footballers in service there, and Moors scored twice early in the game with shots by Laurie to set up a 2-1 win in front of a 6,924 crowd. It was Moors second successive win in the final.

Team; Tom Smith, Jimmy Minto, Joe Musgrave, Tommy Flockett, Bobby Shanks, Pop Welch, Ken Twigg, Pat Wood, Laurie Wensley, Charlie Purves, Charlie Duers.

Liverpool and Wales international keeper Cyril Sidlow played against Moors that day, and then signed for Moors the following season, playing four times.

Laurie had an amazing scoring sequence, scoring 34 goals in twelve games

Cyril Sidlow (Liverpool and Wales) - not exactly in front of a packed Kop!

like this; 3 v South Shields on December 8th 1945, 3 v Darlington Reserves on December 22nd, 4 v Gateshead Reserves on Dec 25, 4 v Eppleton on December 29th, 4 v Hartlepool Reserves on January 1st 1946, 4 v Felling Red Star on January 12th, 2 v North Shields on Jan 19th, 2 v Darlington Reserves on January 26th, 3 v Easington on February 2nd, 1 v Consett on February 9th, 1 v Darlington Reserves on February 16th and 3 v Eppleton on February 23rd. Annfield Plain finally managed to find a way of stopping him but he still had enough goals in him to score both the goals that beat Brancepeth No4 ITC in the final. In an amazing eight game spell between December 22nd 1945 and February 2nd 1946, Moors scored 63 goals, so no wonder the Brewery Field was packed as they went on to win the North Eastern League by a single point from Murton and Ashington. However, they had a touch of fortune, because Murton would have pipped them to the title if the colliery team hadn't had four points deducted. Nonetheless, Moors became the first club ever to win both the North Eastern League and Durham Challenge Cup in successive seasons.

Moors signed a Scottish international for the start of the 1946-47 season,

Supporters proudly holding "Nellie's flag" presented to the club by Nellie Downs

Charlie Thomson who had been at Sunderland, but a third successive League and Durham Challenge Cup double didn't materialise.

There was a buzz around the ground though on September 23rd 1946 when Charlton manager Jimmy Seed (left) watched forward Charlie Purves in the Durham Benevolent Bowl match against Annfield Plain, and a few weeks later, he signed him for £1250.

Three Spennymoor players appeared for Charlton in two FA Cup finals. Jack Oakes and Bert Johnson played in Charlton's 4-1 defeat against Derby County in 1946, then a year later Bert Johnson and Tommy Dawson were on the winning side against Burnley in the 1-0 win.

The 1946-47 FA Cup run
Moors started their run with a high scoring 7-2 win over Willington in the preliminary round, new forward from Halifax Town, Alan Niblo scoring four, with Laurie Wensley chipping in with another two. Then they beat Shildon 4-2 in a replay, with Charlie Purves and Laurie Wensley both scoring two apiece. Charlie Purves then scored again in a 2-0 home win over Ferryhill, and after he departed for Charlton, his replacement, Billy Fenton scored twice in the 4-0 win at Seaham CW, then he scored twice again in the 3-0 away win at South Bank.

To Moors' disappointment, they were handed an away tie in the first round at Lancaster City, then in the Lancashire Combination League, on November 30th 1946, but they didn't hit form at all, and went down to a 75th minute goal in front of a 6753 crowd.

The Spennymoor programme for the next home game didn't seem to have many grumbles about losing, and it complimented the referee. "One of the best features of the game was the splendid performance of the referee. It is many a day since his equal has been seen and a recommendation to the right quarters would be no more than his just reward."

Another match report said; "The visitors were lively in the first half, but the game was dying a bit in the second half when the decisive goal came."

Team; Frank Bell, Pat Wood, George Reeves, Charlie Thomson, Tommy Flockett, Pop Welch, Jackie Smith, Jimmy Cummins, Billy Fenton, Laurie Wensley, Ken Wilson.

Tommy Flockett moved to Chesterfield for an £800 fee, and made over 200 appearances for them in eight years.

Moors also lost their grip on the Durham Challenge Cup when their old rivals Horden beat them 4-1 in a second round replay following a 4-4 draw, and they finished an even more disappointing fourth bottom in the league. Perhaps Moors were missing their talisman, Johnny Dixon.

The 1947-48 season was a poor one as far as the league and FA Cup were concerned. Moors finished below midtable in the league, and they lost in the preliminary round of the FA Cup at Horden again, but they made up for it by reaching the Durham Challenge Cup final.

1947-48 Durham Challenge Cup run
Moors started the campaign by beating Easington 3-0 on December 20th 1947, with goals by Tommy Simpson, Jimmy Cummins and Joe Mullen, and then they went to town on Seaham in the next round, Laurie Wensley

scoring a hat trick in the 7-3 win.
Jimmy Cummins then scored a hat trick in the 5-0 win over Blackhall, then Laurie Wensley scored twice in the 3-0 semi final win over Murton.
That set up Moors for a final against North Eastern League colleagues Consett, but they were easily second best in the final at Roker Park on April 15th 1948 in front of 7,871, and lost 4-1.
"The Spennymoor defence which has been the mainstay of the side for the greater part of the season, had a most disappointing game and this weakness contributed in large measure to the defeat," said the Auckland Chronicle. "None of the Spennymoor team covered themselves in glory," said the Echo.
Moors actually took an early lead through John Smith, but then a series of mistakes in the Moors defence allowed Consett to win.
Team; Tom Smith, Val Thompson, Don Harnby, Jock Smith, Dick Morris, Jimmy Smallwood, Jimmy Cummins, John Smith, Laurie Wensley, Joe Liddle, Jimmy McCormack.
Some pride was restored when Moors won the Durham Benevolent Bowl by 2-1 at Kingsway on April 26th 1948, Ronnie Peart and Laurie Wensley scoring the goals. Moors played the last fifteen minutes with only ten men after Jock Smith went off injured.
Moors added to their facilities at the start of the 1948-49 season when they opened a new covered stand (where the main stand is now) that could

Spennymoor Utd, 1948-49
Back row: Flanagan, Smith, Farley, Morris, Flockett, Smallwood, Harnby.
Front: Moore, Feenan, Garbutt, Whaley, Humble.

accommodate 2,500 spectators, which meant there were now stands on two sides of the ground, and installed a new public address system, both paid for by the thriving supporters club. Moors finished fourth in the league, but only had success in the North Eastern League Cup, in which they reached the semi final before losing to Blackhall.

They were back on the Durham Challenge Cup trail in 1949-50, but again they lost to their bogey team Consett.

1949-50 Durham Challenge Cup run

Ray Garbutt, who had been signed from Manchester City, got the Durham Challenge Cup off to a flyer when he scored in the 4-1 win at Evenwood on

A cutting from The Auckland Chronicle, 1949.

December 10th 1949, then he scored four in Moors' 6-2 away win at Crook. In the third round new signing Duggie Humble scored both in the 2-0 home win over South Shields, and in the semi final Ray Garbutt and Benny Edwards scored one each to put Willington out.

But at a windswept Roker Park on April 8th 1950, Moors let their fans down and lost by the only goal of the game to Consett. "Consett deserved

We'll Always Be United

Duggie Humble

to win because they were the better balanced team" said the Sunday Sun's match report. The Moors' team; Bill Fletcher, Denis Eyton, Bill Keenan, Jock Smith, Ronnie Peart, Bobby Brabban, Duggie Humble, Peter Feenan, George Corbett, Alan Hogg, Benny Edwards. Centre forward Ray Garbutt had signed for Watford before the final. Duggie Humble was the new crowd hero after replacing Laurie Wensley, and he would become the scoring star of the fifties.

The financial alarm bells started to ring again in the summer of 1950 at the AGM, when the chairman, Mr Maxy Coia, spelt out the importance of transfer fees. "Spennymoor cannot exist as a North Eastern League club without transfers. It is not a crime to receive transfer fees and use them in the interests of

Spennymoor Utd, 1951-52
Back row: R. Brabban, G. Taylor, J. Smith, W. Chisholm, W. Rowley, R. Peart.
Front: J. Scott, R. Horner, D. Humble, T. Ward, J. O'Connor.

the club." Moors made £2,100 in transfer fees during the year, and spent some money on dressing room improvements. "Wet and weary players no longer have to queue up for a bath," said Mr Coia.

There was little to cheer about in the 1950-51 season – Moors finished midtable and never threatened to win any of the cups.

The 1951-52 season was better, possibly because of the return of inside right Tommy Dawson after spells at Charlton, Brentford and Swindon. Moors got past West Auckland (4-2), Shildon (2-0) and Crook (2-0) –8,000 watched the game at the Millfield -- in the FA Cup before they lost 4-3 at Goole Town in the final qualifying round. Full back Gordon Taylor was sent off, and Bobby Brabban put through his own goal, although several Moors fans thought that the winning goal should never have been allowed, as the referee ruled that the Spennymoor keeper Wilf Chisholm had dropped the ball over his own goalline.

Duggie Humble was popping the goals in quite nicely though, as he scored five in a Durham Challenge Cup tie at Shildon on January 5th 1952, but Moors lost in the next round to Tow Law.

Spennymoor Utd, 1952-53
Spennymoor Utd 3 South Shields 1
Back row: R. Brabban, D. Cudlip, J. Smith, W.Rowley, W. Chisholm, R. Peart, H. Gibson. Front: J. O'Connor, H. Milne, D. Humble, S. Nicholson, A. Fagan.

Nearly 14,000 people watched two FA Cup fourth qualifying round ties between Moors and Bishops in 1952. Bishops were the best amateur team in the country at the time, and it was decided to make the game at the Brewery Field all ticket, so the crowd was restricted to 7,400 who saw a 1-1 draw. Duggie Humble scored first for Moors, and then another 6,593 saw a late winner for Bishops in the replay at Kingsway. Former chairman Barrie Hindmarch remembers watching the game at the Brewery Field desperately holding on to a tree outside the ground!

The North Eastern League AGM in June 1953 contained a pivotal moment that ultimately would contribute to the demise of the league, and the strengthening of the Northern League a decade later. Spennymoor chairman Mr "Maxy" Coia proposed at the North Eastern League AGM that the word "professional" should be deleted from the rules, thus allowing amateur clubs to enter the league. Twelve clubs out of eighteen voted for it, but Mr W Tulip, the league president, used his vote to ensure that Moors' proposal couldn't be carried without a two thirds majority. Several Northern League clubs were thought to be considering a move into the North Eastern League at the time.

Moors signed former Portsmouth defender Norman Field in the summer of 1953 – he got a job working at Smart and Browns – and in the 1953-54 season Jackie Smith and Ronnie Peart were both granted benefit matches for their long service. Norman Field provided the strength which Moors needed to launch another cup run.

Spot your grandad - some of the fans at a Spennymoor game in 1953

The 1953-54 FA Cup run

Moors were handed five successive home ties in the 1953-54 competition. Ken Johnson scored a hat trick in a 6-0 home win over West Auckland, with Duggie Humble scoring two. Duggie then scored in each of the 2-1 home wins over Stanley and Willington, setting Moors up for a revenge tie in the fourth qualifying round against mighty Bishop Auckland at the Brewery Field.

Bishops were flying going into that match, as they were unbeaten since the start of the season, but Moors rose to the occasion in the battle of the local rivals and won 3-1.

"Bishops were swept right out of the game by a speedier and more workmanlike combination, and ended a well-beaten side," wrote the Echo. Bishops took the lead, but Moors came bouncing back in front of an 8,000 crowd somehow squashed into the Brewery Field with goals by Bob Brownlee and Duggie Humble (2) in the second half.

Moors were handed their first home tie against a Football League club since 1928, when they were paired with Barrow from the Third Division North on November 21st 1953, but they lost 3-0 in front of 6,557. The Cumbrians scored all their goals in the last fifteen minutes.

The Auckland Chronicle wrote, with maybe a touch of sarcasm; "Barrow were winners by three clear goals, but never once did they show any great idea of football, Spennymoor only had themselves to blame for their defeat."

The team; Wilf Chisholm, Jock Smith, Hylton Spedding, Norman Field, Ronnie Peart, Cecil Sands, Bob Brownlee, Ken Johnson, Duggie Humble, Mattie Armstrong, Jackie O'Connor.

Two Barrow fans cycled over the Pennines to watch the game, while the visiting fans put a toy wheelbarrow in the centre circle, which the Spennymoor fans tried several times to obtain themselves, without success.

1953-54 Durham Challenge Cup run

Spennymoor fans will remember the competition this season for a 6-1 home win in the semi final over Bishop Auckland when the amateurs were at their peak.

Bishops fielded a weakened side because they had more pressing commitments in the Amateur Cup, and they paid the penalty as Duggie Humble scored a hat trick, his sixth of the season at the time. It was only the second defeat of the season for Bishops – both of them against Moors.

In the first round, Moors beat Billingham Synthonia 4-2 in a replay after a 1-1 draw, then Duggie scored a hat trick in an excellent 6-2 home win over their bogey side Consett. After Bishops were despatched, Moors

*Spennymoor Utd, 1953-54. Durham Challenge Cup Winners
Back row: J. Flanagan, C. Sands, H. Spedding, W. Chisholm, N. Field,
D. Harnby, W. Miller. Front: D. King, B. Brownlee, D. Humble, J. Smith,
M. Armstrong, J. O'Connor, J. Scott.*

comfortably beat Blackhall by 3-0 in the final at Hartlepool on April 3rd 1954. Ian Scott scored from a Dennis King centre on 27 minutes, then he got the second before half time from a Duggie Humble flick. Dennis King scored the third from fifteen yards in the second half. The biggest surprise was that Duggie didn't score!

"Nobody could deny Spennymoor's authority, especially in the second half when Blackhall were scarcely in the picture," wrote the Auckland Chronicle. It was Moors' third Durham Challenge Cup win since the war.

Team; Wilf Chisholm, Jock Smith, Hylton Spedding, Walter Miller, Norman Field, Cecil Sands, Dennis King, Ian Scott, Duggie Humble, Mattie Armstrong, Jackie O'Connor.

Duggie Humble scored a total of 44 goals that season, a tally which included six against

> **EASY CUP WIN FOR "MOORS"**
>
> Blackhall C.W. 0, Spennymoor 3
>
> Spennymoor United had an easy victory in the Durham County Challenge Cup final, played at the West Hartlepool Victoria ground. They outplayed Blackhall C.W. and it was only splendid defensive play by centre-half Wilson and full back Blythe that kept the score down to three goals.
>
> Outside-left O'Connor was the star of the "Moor" forward line. He gave a pass to Scott for the inside man to put his team ahead after 30 minutes and just before the interval, Scott took a lovely pass from centre-forward Humble and shot past Gray for the second goal. Outside-right King got the third goal after 60 minutes. He put in a fast drive which went into the net with Wilson making a vain effort to clear.
>
> The only shot of note throughout the match for Blackhall came from Thomas (A.), who shot just wide from 20 yards. This was Spennymoor's third final win in six post-war appearances.

Hartlepool Reserves and a hat trick in the glorious 6-1 Durham Challenge Cup semi final win over Bishop Auckland.

The North Eastern League Cup run 1953-54

Moors started the campaign with a 2-0 home win over Horden, with Jock Smith and Duggie Humble scoring, and on March 27th they reached the final by beating Annfield Plain in the semi final, with Dennis King and Ian Scott scoring.

The two legged final against their old rivals Consett was played in a hectic period at the end of the season in April, and maybe the gruelling schedule told on Moors, because when they went to Consett for the first leg of the final on April 17th 1954, they lost 5-1, Duggie Humble scoring a consolation goal for them, but the Steelmen were deserved winners.

Team; Wilf Chisholm, Jock Smith, Don Harnby, Norman Field, Ronnie Peart, Cecil Sands, Dennis King, Duggie Humble, Ian Scott, Mattie Armstrong, Jackie O'Connor.

Moors, however, nearly pulled off the impossible ten days later, winning the return leg 3-0, just failing to score a fourth goal. Walter Miller, who had returned to the club from Luton, scored along with Duggie Humble and Jackie O'Connor.

Team; Wilf Chisholm, Jock Smith, Hylton Spedding, Walter Miller, Norman Field, Cecil Sands, Dennis King, Bob Brownlee, Duggie Humble, Mattie Armstrong, Jackie O'Connor.

However, Moors ran out of steam in the North Eastern League title race. They were locked in a battle with Sunderland Reserves and Middlesbrough Reserves at the top, but they had to play a hectic schedule of fourteen league and cup games between April 3rd and May 4th, including one gruelling spell of six games in six days. They lost to Darlington Reserves on April 26th, won the second leg of the North Eastern League Cup on April 27th – but lost on aggregate to Consett – beat Stockton 3-0 on April 28th, won 3-0 at West Stanley on April 29th, drew a crucial game against Sunderland Reserves 0-0 on April 30th, and then lost 1-0 to Middlesbrough Reserves on May 1st. Moors finished three points behind champions Middlesbrough Reserves, who won the title on goal average from Sunderland Reserves, and had to be content with the non-reserve medals. No wonder some clubs thought about erecting floodlights so then they could play midweek games during the winter.

Despite that good season, question marks were raised again over the level of the club's support. After finishing third for the second successive season in the North Eastern League in 1954-55, and again reaching the final of the North Eastern League Cup and the semi final of the Durham Challenge Cup, the club reported a loss on the season of £373, despite the efforts of the supporters club which raised nearly £1000. New chairman Joe Forrest said: "Unless the man in the street plays his part fully, there will eventually be no other option but to wind up the club." It was the old familiar story – a tale which would be even more telling in the next few years.

There were also criticisms of the Durham Challenge Cup. Earlier that season, Moors won 4-0 at Blackhall – Bobby Blair scored in the first minute and then went to hospital at half time with a broken collar bone – and after all the expenses had been taken into account, Moors' share of a £42 gate was just over £1. The clubs were unhappy at the cut for Durham FA.

It was also farewell to Duggie Humble, who retired at the end of the season following the game at Stockton on May 3rd 1955, and the club held a well-attended benefit match for him, 2000 people turning up on September 8th 1954 for a 2-1 home win over Crook Town.

The North Eastern League Cup run 1954-55

The competition was delayed, and the two legged final was held over until the start of the following season.

Moors started on August 23rd 1954 with a 1-0 home win over West Stanley, Matty Armstrong scoring, then Duggie Humble hit four in the 5-0 demolition of Annfield Plain, one of them when he charged the Annfield Plain keeper over the goalline.

Moors then needed three attempts to see off Workington in the semi final, Ray Wilkie getting the winner after 1-1 and 0-0 draws. But by then, it was the end of April, and the league decided to hold the final over, thus denying Moors the chance of an immediate double.

Bert Calland scored the winner for Moors in the first leg against Blyth at home on August 24th 1955, but they lost the second leg at Croft Park by 4-0 in front of 3155. The two clubs were to clash again several times some years later in the Northern League in similar circumstances.

Team; Wilf Chisholm, Don Harnby, Hylton Spedding, Walter Miller, Norman Field, Jackie Sands, Hector Clarke, Harold Houlahan, Bert Calland, Ray Wilkie, Jackie O'Connor. In the second leg, Norman Miller replaced Hector Clarke.

Ray Wilkie played for several clubs, and was manager of Barrow when they won the FA Trophy in 1990.

Moors also drew 1-1 with Bishop Auckland in a full blooded semi final of the Durham Challenge Cup in front of another full house on March 19th 1955 at the Brewery Field – 7,202 watched the game – but they lost 3-0 to

Harry Sharratt, the Bishop Auckland goalkeeper, clears from a Spennymoor attack.

the Amateur Cup finalists in the replay a week later. The games between the two teams certainly continued to grip the imagination of the local fans. Spennymoor were in trouble with the FA after they lost to North Shields in a North Eastern League Cup tie in 1956.

The crowd was upset at some of the decisions of referee W Robinson from Darlington, and on the final whistle, a spectator ran on the field and grabbed the referee, then other fans threw mud at him.

Spennymoor United, 1956-57. North East League Champions
J. Flanagan, J. Robson, G. Outhwaite, K. Carr, W. Chisholm, N. Field, H. Spedding.
W. Miller, R. Briggs, J. Spuhler, D. Carr, J. O'Connor, R. Bell, T. Johnson.

Moors won the North Eastern League for the fourth time in season 1956-57, as the interest of the professional clubs in the league started to wane. Former Middlesbrough winger Johnny Spuhler was appointed player-coach of the Moors in November 1956, and they lost only one league game between his appointment and March 23rd to put them in command at the top of the table.

They had another gruelling run in, playing seven games in the last fortnight of the season, winning five of them, but this time they had enough stamina and experience, and by the time they lost to nearest rivals South Shields in the last game, the league was already won.

Johnny Spuhler

However, they lost to Bishop Auckland in a replayed semi final of the Durham Challenge Cup in April 1957 by 3-0 at Kingsway in front of 6,100 spectators, the match spoiled by "petty incidents, back chatting and deliberate pushing" according to the Northern Echo report. Bishops won the Amateur Cup later that month with a 3-1 win over Wycombe Wanderers.

Later in the year, Moors were linked with former Middlesbrough great Wilf Mannion, but he didn't want to move back to the north from Cambridge Town. Maybe he had a good idea what was going to happen next!

Another Middlesbrough legend turned out for Boro reserves in a North Eastern League game at the Brewery Field on August 20th 1955 – centre forward Brian Clough, who later went on to make a legendary name for himself in management.

Moors signed a Hungarian inside forward Naghy in 1957, but he didn't turn up for training one night. When club officials managed to find him, he'd got on the wrong bus and ended up well away from Spennymoor. "I couldn't read the bus destination and travelled in the wrong direction," he told them. Presumably in Hungarian!

There was another warning about the club's finances in the programme for a game against

Brian Clough

Middlesbrough Reserves. "It is by no means certain that the club will be able to carry on another season unless more support is forthcoming and the finances can be subsidised from other sources." The supporters club donated £200 but it wasn't enough to pay off the bank overdraft and other creditors. The dark clouds were looming again – and not just over finances.

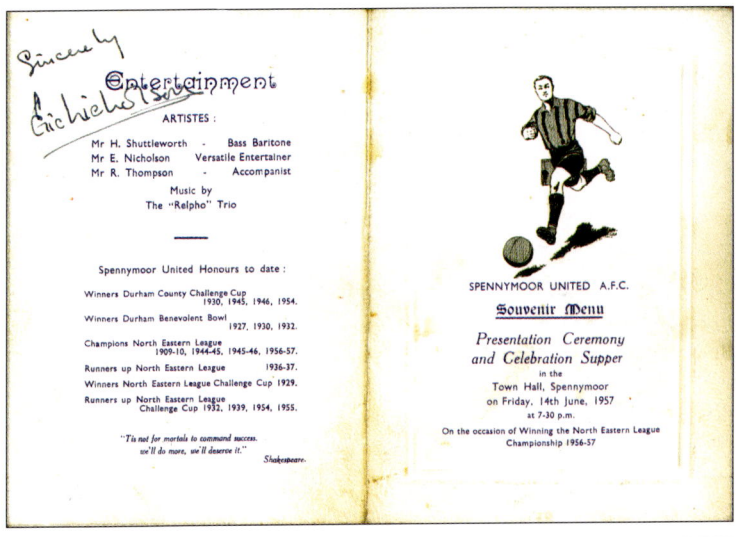

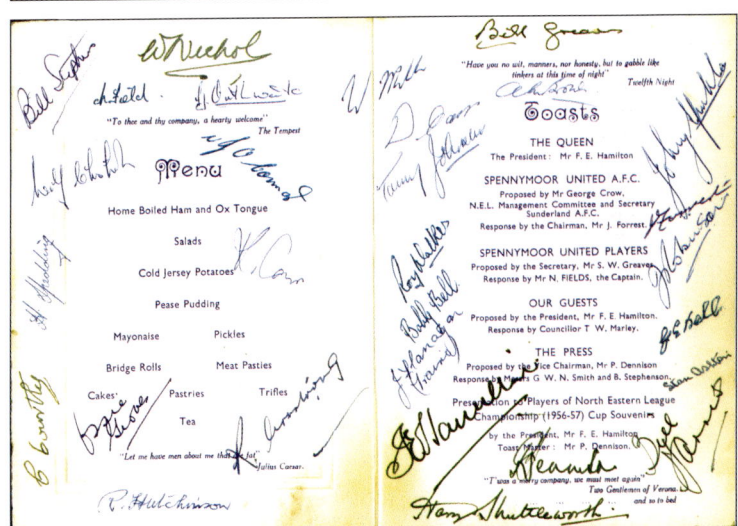

Souvenir Menu from 1956-57 North Eastern League Championship winning Presentation Ceremony and Celebration Supper

Chapter Four

At the crossroads

Moors had to think quickly and carefully about their future at the beginning of 1958 as the North Eastern League showed signs of falling apart.
The Football League clubs decided to pull out of the league, and at another meeting in York, decided to set up the North Central League for their reserve teams. Middlesbrough in particular had been trying for years to enter the Central League, which contained the reserve teams of Manchester United and Liverpool, but without success.
The actions of the Football League clubs caused confusion. The Moors committee proposed that their club should apply for the Northern League, but those against amateurism suggested the Midland League instead, and got their way at a special annual meeting of the club by a large majority. Most of the other North Eastern League clubs were heading the same way, effectively folding the league at a stroke.
Club chairman Mr Joe Forrest said: "I hope and trust everything comes out all right. I hope everyone in the town will support us and make this decision justified. We must have good support." Several other clubs also left the North Eastern League for the Midland League, which it was hoped, would reduce the travelling difficulties. The decision not to allow amateur clubs, taken earlier in the decade, had come back to haunt the North Eastern League. Moors' last North Eastern League game was against Carlisle United Reserves on May 3rd 1958, Arthur Gardner scoring in a 1-1 draw. Moors finished the season in 12th place.
Whilst the borders of the North Eastern League stretched across to Carlisle and Workington and only as far south as Darlington and Middlesbrough, the area covered by the Midlands League was suddenly much greater. Peterborough United, way down in Cambridgeshire, were members, along with Grantham and Skegness. The Midland League had a very distinct north and south look about it, the other member clubs were; Ashington, Blyth, Consett, Horden, North Shields, South Shields, Stockton -- all ex-North Eastern League -- plus Sutton, Peterborough, Frickley, Scarborough, Denaby, Scunthorpe Reserves, Gainsborough, Grantham and Skegness.

Spennymoor United, 1958-59. Midland League.
Back row: K. Chisholm, W. Miller, R. Ward, E. Bygate, H. Rich, T. Johnson, R. Thompson. Front: A. Robinson, N. Field, R. Clegg, T. McGuigan, A. Gardner.

The new league briefly captured the imagination of the Spennymoor public, and 3,500 fans, one of the biggest ever for a league game at the Brewery Field, turned up for the first Midlands League game against Skegness. Moors led 2-1 with goals by Harry Rich and Arthur Gardner – who was watched by several Football League clubs -- until Skegness equalised in the last minute.

Team; Ron Ward, Eric Bygate, Ray Thompson, Walter Miller, Norman Field, Tommy Johnson, Alan Robinson, Ray Clegg, Harry Rich, Tommy McGuigan, Arthur Gardner.

However, gates steadily decreased to around 500 as the interest faltered after that first day, and with travel expenses and hotel bills to places like Peterborough and Skegness a major factor, Moors' finances were badly hit. Moors felt that they needed to form a reserve team to help them in what was a stronger league, but they couldn't afford to set one up. They had to sell their ground to Spennymoor Urban Council to help them pay some mounting debts, and pressure mounted on the club from the fans to apply for the Northern League.

They finished the first Midland League season in a disappointing 14th place, with Stockton the only former North Eastern League team below them. There was some consolation with a Durham Benevolent Bowl victory by 2-1 against West Auckland at Shildon, Melvyn Osmond and Burridge, who ran half the length of the pitch, scoring.

The straw that broke the camel's back came on January 30th 1960, when the crowd was so poor for the home game with Sutton Town that the gate receipts came to only £12. Three weeks later, Moors decided to revert to amateur status, and applied to join the Northern League.

The supporters seemed to have tired of the Midland League, and in a letter to the Northern Echo, one fan wrote; "How much longer are the long suffering supporters of Spennymoor going to wait before they are given something to shout about? There is only one course left, to join the Northern League." The fan claimed that the Supporters Club had given United £20,000 over the previous years, the club cost £100 per week to run, and the club could only rely on Spennymoor supporters for home gates, because not many visiting fans travelled to the Brewery Field at all.

The Midland League called an emergency meeting of clubs, in the words of Scarborough chairman Arthur Marriner, "to try and establish a new unity among non league clubs designed to avoid the break up of long established leagues caused through clubs breaking away to join new competitions. If such a scheme was carried out on a regional basis, it will help to improve

Spennymoor United, 1959-60. Midland League.
Back row: N. Field (Coach), F. Stansfield, J. Folwell, A. Greenwood, K. Walton, A. Rich, W. Blenkiron, J. Flanagan (Trainer). Front: H. Dobbie, R. Young, H. Bell (Capt.), T. McGuigan, M. Lawson, D. King (Res.).

the standard of non league football as well as eliminating the need for long journeys." Nearly fifty years on, those arguments still rage! There was also dissatisfaction with some fixture congestion, caused by clashes with County Cups, which took precedence over league matches on Saturdays.

The club took a risk by quitting the Midland League, because it was by no means certain that they would be accepted into the Northern League. Moors played their last Midland League game on May 4th 1960 against Denaby United at the Brewery Field, winning 4-0, to give them a finish in ninth place. Peterborough United won the league for the second successive season by three points from North Shields, and later managed to win election to the Football League.

It was a real cliff hanger at the Northern League AGM as Moors pushed their application. Five clubs chased just one vacancy in the league – Moors, Stockton, Annfield Plain, Cockfield and Redcar Albion. One league official said beforehand; "It is very open, the voting will be close." It certainly was – the first vote gave Moors and Stockton six votes each, Annfield Plain four, Cockfield one and Redcar Albion none. After more debate, Spennymoor won the second vote 10-7, so they were elected.

Spennymoor representative Billy Longstaff was given credit for persuading the other league clubs to accept Moors. "I have wanted a good amateur side on the town for ten years," he said. Maybe he was jealous of the success of Bishop Auckland and Crook in the FA Amateur Cup?

Club chairman Billy Weatherill gave another viewpoint: "Competing in the Midland League was financial suicide. We had decided to become an amateur club whatever league we took part in. It is much nicer to be in a local amateur competition and I am sure all the derby games will arouse interest in the town."

Chapter Five

The return to amateurism

Northern League football was embraced by Spennymoor supporters, as they could look forward to games against clubs from the local area, especially Bishop Auckland, Crook and Shildon.
Coach Harry Bell brought in some new players to replace some of the professionals who left the club in the previous summer, and the team he built held its own in the Northern League, without launching a strong title challenge.
Moors' first game back in the Northern League was at Willington on August 20th 1960, but it was a far from auspicious return, as they lost 4-0. The team was; Ken Matthews, Alan Iceton, Gordon Newton, George Ramshaw, Walton, Billy Blenkiron, Norman Jubb, Melvyn Osmond, Derek Dowson, Ken Pearson, Don Laverick.
The following week, Moors played Bishop Auckland in the first league game between the two clubs since 1908, and Moors won 2-0, both goals scored by Norman Jubb in front of a 3,000 crowd. "It is obvious that it will take time for Moors to settle down in their new surroundings," the match programme observed.
Being amateurs again, they were allowed to enter the FA Amateur Cup, and their first campaign for over 50 years went well. They just managed to scrape past Highgate United from the Northern Combination by 2-1 thanks to a late penalty by Derek Dowson, then Dowson, along with Don Laverick both scored two apiece in the 4-1 win at Langley Park.
They were starting to dream of a really good run when they thumped South Bank 5-2, with Norman Jubb scoring twice, but they were hammered 5-1 at home by Stanley in the fourth qualifying round. Moors never really threatened to win the league and finished sixth, but the club was sure it had made the right move.
The following season, Moors finished sixth again, one of their highlights the 10-2 home win over Tow Law in the league on September 16th 1961. Keith Walklate scored four, with all round sportsman Billy Blenkiron – he also played cricket for Warwickshire – scoring another three. Ken Bainbridge (2) and Ken Todd got the others.

After seven years without a cup final to get excited about, Moors ended their barren run by reaching the Durham Challenge Cup final in May 1963 at Hartlepool against Horden.

The 1962-63 Durham Challenge Cup run

Moors got off to a flier in the first round, beating Kibblesworth 7-1, with Len Walker, later to become Aldershot and Darlington manager, scoring two of the goals.
They scored another seven in the next round, this time against Swalwell, with Alwyn Juniper scoring four, and Len Walker again on the scoresheet. Moors then beat Billingham Synthonia 3-0 with a promising youngster called Kenny Banks amongst the goals, and in the semi finals they again ran riot, this time hammering the old foes Bishop Auckland 6-0, with Kenny Banks scoring twice.
After scoring 23 goals in the games leading up to the final, Moors found goals harder to come by against Horden on Easter Monday 1963, but they still managed to win with a Len Walker penalty.
The team; Bobby Ellen, Alan Iceton, Brian Berryman, Len Walker, Gordon Newton, Trevor Atkinson, Keith Walklate, Ron Fryer, Alwyn Juniper, John Brown, Ken Todd
Their league position was also an improvement on the previous two seasons, finishing fourth, ten points behind champions Crook Town.

The 1963-64 FA Amateur Cup run

Moors thought they had their best chance to win the Amateur Cup since they had turned amateur four years previously. At one stage, there was the possibility of an all Northern League final, with four Northern League teams in the last eight, but unfortunately despite having home advantage, Moors missed out on a semi final place.
Moors started the competition with a goalless draw at Durham's Ferens Park on October 12th 1963, but they hammered City in the replay by 7-0, John Brown scoring a hat trick. After a hard fought 2-1 win at Langley Park, Moors thumped Stockton 6-2 away from home, Derek Fawell scoring four. Billingham Synthonia put up a tough fight in the last qualifying round before they went down 2-1, Derek Fawell and Brian Morris scoring.
That win put Moors into the national draw, and in the first round they beat Stratford Town 3-0, with Derek Fawell, John Brown and Jim McGeorge, later to sign for Leyton Orient, scoring with 1200 watching.
There was 2,077 inside the Brewery Field when Moors beat Leytonstone 2-1 on February 1st 1964, Derek Fawell scoring in the dying minutes after Jim McGeorge's 52nd minute goal had been cancelled out. Brian Berryman, the

Back row: J. Flanagan (Trainer), A. Iceton, G. Defty, P. Joyce, R. Ellen, A. West, B. Berryman, J. Brown. Front: B. Morris, J. McGeorge, H. Bell (Manager/Coach), D. Fawell, K. Banks.

Spennymoor left back, was the man of the match. Leytonstone had reached the semi finals the previous year.

Moors had a long trip in the last sixteen to Isthmian League club Wycombe Wanderers, and they did well to come away with a 2-2 draw after being two goals down at one point in front of a 7,000 crowd. Brian Berryman conceded a penalty for the first goal, then Wycombe scored a second. But Alan West pulled one back before half time, and then Derek Fawell equalised from a Brian Berryman free kick.

"The teenage inside trio of Kenny Banks, Derek Fawell and Jim McGeorge produced a brilliant short passing combination which often bewildered the home defence," said the Echo report. 400 supporters made the journey to Wycombe, and Alan Iceton, the Spennymoor captain, said: "Things certainly looked black for us when we were trailing 2-0, but thanks to some magnificent vocal support, we were able to fight our way back into the game."

Moors, average age 20, then pulled off one of the best Amateur Cup wins in their history in the replay, when they beat the Wanderers 2-1 at the Brewery Field, with 4,900 inside the ground, the biggest crowd since the Durham Challenge Cup games against Bishop Auckland in the fifties.

"If Wycombe had concentrated on playing good football – of which they are quite capable – they might just have upset the home men," wrote the Echo.

Moors were well on top in the first half and took the lead through John Brown from a penalty on 26 minutes, then after Wycombe equalised, Brian Morris got the winner just before half time. According to the Echo, Spennymoor's right half and captain, covered every inch of the pitch – hence the headline "Iceton keeps cool". Moors were now in the quarter finals for the first time in their history.

The Northern League clubs thought they were invincible, and the Echo wrote; "The southern clubs are in fear of the northern challenge for honours."

Oops! Moors made a right mess of their quarter final against Barnet, and lost 5-2. Peter Joyce had a header cleared off the line, but then the defence failed to cope with Barnet's long balls, and the visitors went 3-0 up, all of them coming from Roger Figg. Derek Fawell pulled one back, but then Figg scored two more before Kenny Banks replied in the last minute.

"The Moors turned in their worst display for months," said the Echo. "The slippery surface did not help the home side, who seemed to have lead in their boots."

Team; Bobby Ellen, Graham Defty, Brian Berryman, Alan Iceton, Peter Joyce, Alan West, Brian Morris, Jim McGeorge, Derek Fawell, Kenny Banks, John Brown.

Local lad Peter Joyce, a centre half, became a kingpin of the Spennymoor defence and was to become one of the most highly rated players in that position in amateur football.

While Barnet waited for their train back to London from Bank Top station, the Barnet players stood Roger Figg against the blackboard which was used for giving out public information, and drew his outline around him in chalk.

Despite the exit, the club felt that they had been vindicated in switching back to amateurism. Kit Courtly, the club treasurer, said: "Amateurs put more into the game then professionals and the game is much keener, " and another committee man, Jack Meggeson pointed out; "When we were in the North Eastern League, there was nothing to look forward to except a brief time in the FA Cup. In the Northern League we have hopes of winning the FA Amateur Cup."

Barnet were beaten by eventual winners Crook in the semi final.

Whitby Town twice ended Moors' hopes in the other cup competitions. The seasiders beat Spennymoor in an FA Cup second qualifying round replay by 2-0 at the Brewery Field, but Moors weren't helped by the non-arrival of

Brian Morris and Ken Todd, whose car broke down on their way to the game. And later in the season, Moors lost 2-1 in a Northern League cup semi final replay after a 2-2 draw at the Brewery Field. They also played and lost to Whitby in a Northern League game which started half an hour after their league cup tie ended. Inside forward Kenny Banks played in both games – and earlier in the day he had turned out for his college team Durham Johnston.

Moors dropped a real clanger at the end of the 1963-64 season – they forgot to enter the following season's FA Cup. Moors were concentrating so much on the FA Amateur Cup that they forgot to submit their entry forms. Moors appealed to the FA, but their application was kicked out because it was received after the deadline.

After thoughts of Wembley in the previous season, Moors suffered a huge embarrassment in the 1964-65 Amateur Cup. After beating Skelmersdale 3-0 at home in the first round on January 2nd 1965 – Ken Banks, Ken Todd and Tommy Searle scored -- three weeks later, Moors suffered one of their worst ever defeats losing 11-2 at Kingstonian, their nervous stand-in keeper George Carney having an absolute nightmare after conceding a soft first minute goal through his hands.

There was some consolation for a midtable finish in the league when Moors reached the Northern League Cup final.

The 1964-65 Northern League cup run

The 1964-65 season dragged on so long because of postponements, that Moors had to play the final against Whitley Bay the following season.

The run started with a 3-0 home win on September 26th 1964 against Whitby, who would lose in the Amateur Cup final that season, with Brian Morris scoring twice, and he also scored the winner against Bishop Auckland in the second round. Moors drew 0-0 at West Auckland in the semi final on November 28th 1964, but they didn't stage the replay until February 20th 1965, when West were beaten 5-1, Kenny Banks scoring two. The final was played on April 5th 1965 against Whitley Bay at North Shields, the teams drawing 1-1. Moors defender Chris Thompson cleared one off the line, before Whitley took the lead when Brown scored direct from a corner after 82 minutes, but Ken Todd nipped in for the equaliser. The ball burst during the game when one of the Whitley players took a corner kick.

The team; Brian Chicken, Chris Thompson, Graham Defty, Alan West, Peter Joyce, John Gatens, Malcolm Clark, Kenny Banks, Tommy Searle, John Brown, Ken Todd.

The replay was held over until August 23rd 1965, again at North Shields, and this time Moors lost 3-1. "A ragged Spennymoor team were lucky to keep the score to three goals against them," said the Echo. Kenny Banks scored for Moors midway through the second half, but by then the game was well lost.

The team; Brian Chicken, Chris Thompson, Graham Defty, Alan West, Shanley, Ralph Wright, K Thompson, Kenny Banks, Phil Moreton, Tommy Searle , John Gatens.

But Moors bounced back to lift the League Cup the following season, although there was an element of controversy of their semi final victory over Crook.

The 1965-66 Northern League cup run

They drew 2-2 at Evenwood in the first round where John Gatens and Kenny Banks scored, and in the replay Kenny scored again in the 3-0 win.

They beat Bishop Auckland with ten men in the second round, Ted Lawson scoring the only goal at the Brewery Field, but Colin Richardson was sent off for swearing.

Moors drew 1-1 with Crook in the semi final on May 7th 1966 at the Millfield, but they protested to the league that Crook had fielded Keith Hylton, who had appeared in unaffiliated Sunday football, which was against County FA rules at the time. The league carried out an investigation, and instead of kicking Crook out of the competition as Moors had hoped, they fined Crook £10 and ordered a replay, which Moors won with a goal in extra time through Michael Maley.

Moors met Penrith in the final at Shildon on May 23rd 1966 and beat them 2-1, the first time they lifted the Northern League Cup. Penrith took the lead, but Alan West equalised with a 30 yard free kick on 52 minutes, and three minutes later Sowerby scored from a Brian Newton free kick.

Team; Brian Chicken, Graham Defty, Colin Summerson, Alan West, Billy Lovejoy, Ralph Wright, Kenny Banks, Brian Newton, Michael Maley, Clark, J Sowerby.

The league campaign, however, took a long time to get going, with Moors not recording a win in the league until late October when they beat West Auckland 3-2, although they eventually finished sixth.

Moors were involved in an explosive Amateur Cup tie against Leyton on January 8th 1966, when two players were carried off, two more were sent off, the referee got injured, and the Leyton keeper had a fight with a Spennymoor supporter in front of the main stand as Moors lost the game 4-1.

The following season, Moors couldn't stop their neighbours Bishop Auckland from completing the treble of Northern League, Northern League Cup and Durham Challenge Cup.

The 1966-67 Durham Challenge Cup run

Spennymoor United, 1966-67. Northern League.
R. Bell, D. Crampton, G. Defty, C. Richardson, R. Wright, W. Lovejoy, A. West, J. R. Sowerby. Front: M. Robson, K. Storey, M. Maley, K. Banks, J. Gatens.

Forward Keith "Porky" Storey – who played as an emergency keeper once for Moors – scored a hat trick as Moors hammered Boldon CW 7-0 on January 28th 1967, and then a week later Kenny Banks scored the only goal of the game against Gateshead, who were then in the North Regional League.

Kenny was again on target on February 18th 1967 as Moors just managed to squeeze past Tow Law 3-2, Michael Maley and Johnny Gatens getting the others. In the semi final, Moors won 2-0 at Blackhall, Michael Maley and Alan West scoring the goals.

But in the final on April 17th 1967, Bishop Auckland were too strong for Moors, and won 2-1.

The Moors team; Brian Chicken, Graham Defty, Colin Richardson, Alan West, Billy Lovejoy, Ralph Wright, Phil Craig, Kenny Banks, Michael Maley, John Gatens, Brian Newton.

Also in 1967, the club greatly improved the Brewery Field. Floodlights were erected, the supporters' club opened a snack bar on the corner of the ground, and the club purchased Darlington's old PA system. Their timing couldn't have been better.

The return to amateurism

Just like Moors in the 1967 Durham Challenge Cup final, this picture has faded a little!
Back row: C. Summerson, B. Chicken, C. Richardson, G. Defty, B. Lovejoy, R. Wright, A. West, R. Morgon (mascot).
Front row: B. Newton, J. Gatens, M. Maley, K. Banks, P. Craig.

Chapter Six

For whom the Bell tolls

Moors appointed Bob Bell as their new manager in 1966, and Bob steadily built a team that was capable of winning trophies – and many thought that he laid the foundation for the next fifteen years.

The 1967-68 season was the best for almost two decades, with the team playing some bright football, using a system which Bob had learned on an FA coaching course at Lilleshall. Just like Bishops the previous season, Moors pulled off the treble -- the Northern League, Northern League Cup and Durham Challenge Cup - as well as reaching the second round of the FA Cup. The smiles were back on the faces of Spennymoor supporters!

Bob revolutionised Moors with his coaching ideas, ditching the orthodox 2-3-5 formation, and introducing the 4-4-2 system which helped England win the World Cup in 1966. The goals flowed as opponents struggled to get to grips with Moors.

Moors won the Northern League title for the first time with a record number of points – they dropped just seven points in 34 league games.

They lost just once in the league all season, against Shildon in August 1967, and had good wins by 3-1 against champions Bishop Auckland at Kingsway, and a 7-0 home win over Blyth Spartans. In a hectic finale to the season - -a backlog caused by their cup successes -- they won four games after the start of May, with John Tobin scoring at least one goal in each of them -- Evenwood 5-0, Crook at home 7-2, Ferryhill 2-1 and Crook away 2-1.

The 1967-68 FA Cup run

Moors' run in the FA Cup lasted for four enjoyable months.

Kenny Banks scored a hat trick in the preliminary round, two of them penalties, in the 5-0 home win over Boldon CA on September 2nd, Stan Summerill scoring the other two, and Kenny scored another two against Stockton in the 3-0 first qualifying round win. They drew 0-0 just up the road in Ferryhill, beating their neighbours 4-2 in the replay, Kenny scoring, along with John Tobin, Stan Summerill and Alan West.

John Tobin was the hero in the fourth qualifying round, scoring the only

For whom the Bell tolls

goal of the game against Morecambe, the Lancashire Combination champions, at the Brewery Field. Even though John was struggling because of flu, he scored in the opening two minutes of the game, to put Moors into the first round for the first time since 1953.

Moors played Goole Town from their old league, the Midland League, in the first round. Memories of Moors' previous visit there in the previous decade when they lost to a controversial goal, were revived.

Spennymoor Utd. team who defeated Morecambe in The FA Cup. Back row: R. Bell (Coach), G. Defty, C. Richardson, D. Crampton, B. Lovejoy, P. Joyce, R. Wright with R. Morgan (Mascot). Front: S. Summerill, K. Banks, J. Tobin, A. West, J. Wilkinson, I. McPherson (Sub).

They drew the first game 0-0 on December 9th 1967 away from home on a frozen pitch, wearing Sunderland's red second strip because of a colour clash. Moors defender Graham Defty cleared a shot off the line, while John Tobin limped off through injury at the start of the second half.

Team; Dave Crampton, Graham Defty, Colin Richardson, Billy Lovejoy, Peter Joyce, Ralph Wright, Stan Summerill, Kenny Banks, John Tobin (sub John Wilkinson), Alan West, Alan King.

Moors took a stranglehold on the replay in the second minute, when Stan Summerill scored from a Graham Defty free kick, then the Goole keeper Knowles pushed a Stan Summerill corner into his own net after 7 minutes.

BLACKBURN ROVERS
Football & Athletic Co Ltd

GROUND: EWOOD PARK

SECRETARY: D. J. GRIMSHAW

MANAGER: E. Quigley
~~J. G. MARSHALL~~

REGISTERED OFFICE
EWOOD PARK
BLACKBURN

TELEGRAMS 'ROVERS' BLACKBURN
TELEPHONE NUMBER 55432
RESIDENCE PRESTON 55898

ALL COMMUNICATIONS TO BE ADDRESSED TO THE SECRETARY

Blackburn Rovers Football & Athletic Company Limited hereby promise to make a donation of £500.0.0d.(Five hundred pounds) to Spennymoor United Football Club upon player David Crampton signing as a Professional player for Blackburn Rovers and also promise to make the further donations of:-

£500.0.0d. (Five hundred pounds) when the player has made 10 first team appearances.

£500.0.0d. (Five hundred pounds) when the player makes an appearance for the England Under 23 or Full International Team.

£500.0.0d. (Five hundred pounds) should the player play in the Football Association Cup Final for Blackburn Rovers.

And we further agree:-

1. That in the event of the player being transferred by the Blackburn Rovers Football Club for a fee Spennymoor United will be paid a further sum calculated at the rate of 1% of the fee received.

2. That permission is hereby given for the player D. Crampton to tour Holland with Spennymoor United in June 1968.

3. That Blackburn Rovers will send a Team to play against Spennymoor United in a Friendly Match.

For and on behalf of the Blackburn Rovers Football & Athletic Company Limited. ....Secretary

For and on behalf of the Spennymoor United Football Club. ....Secretary

Dated this ...7th..... day of February, 1968.

Copy of the transfer deal that took Spennymoor keeper Dave Crampton to Blackburn Rovers. Stan Bradley signed on behalf of Spennymoor.

Wagstaff pulled one back for Goole, but Colin Richardson hit a 30 yard free kick – he was a free kick specialist -- that hit the bar, bounced off the keeper and into the net for the third to send the 3,900 crowd wild.
The Echo wrote; "Goole never gave up, but against a magnificent home defence in which left half Ralph Wright was outstanding, their forwards never looked like finding a loophole."

Team; Dave Crampton, Graham Defty, Colin Richardson, Billy Lovejoy, Peter Joyce, Ralph Wright, Stan Summerill, Kenny Banks, John Tobin, Alan West, John Wilkinson. Sub Alan King.

To their disappointment, Moors missed the Football League clubs in the second round draw, and instead were drawn against another non league side, Macclesfield from the Cheshire County League, at Moss Rose on January 6th 1968.

Unfortunately, they went behind after 13 minutes to a goal by Taberner, and then Denis Fidler got the second after 50 minutes, but Moors were very unlucky not to force a replay.

Macclesfield manager Keith Goalen said: "Spennymoor were harder to beat than Third Division Stockport who we knocked out in extra time in the previous round. I am glad we didn't have to face them away from home." One of the Macclesfield papers wrote; "Macclesfield keeper John Cooke earned his bonus the hard way."

Goalkeeper Dave Crampton

Team; Dave Crampton, Graham Defty, Colin Richardson, Billy Lovejoy, Peter Joyce, Ralph Wright, Stan Summerill, Kenny Banks, John Tobin, Alan West, John Wilkinson.

Ralph Wright made a good impression though, and several Football League clubs kept a check on his progress.

The 1967-68 Durham Challenge Cup run

*Durham Challenge Cup Winners, 1967-68.
Back row: R. Bell (Coach), R. Wright, C. Richardson, A. King, A. West, E. Hulme, A. Hickman. Front: S. Summerill, G. Defty, P. Joyce, J. Tobin, J. Wilkinson, K. Banks.*

In an exciting and hectic season, Moors lifted the Durham Challenge Cup for the fifth time in their history.

Their first tie was at Gateshead on February 10th 1968, where a young Albert Hickman scored in the 1-1 draw, but Moors moved up a gear in the replay, winning 6-1, with John Tobin and John Wilkinson both scoring two apiece.

After beating Eldra United – a team setup by former Spennymoor manager Billy Bell -- on February 21st at Kingsway by 2-0 with goals by Kenny Banks and Ian McPherson, Moors then had a great tussle with holders Bishop Auckland, beating them 3-2 at the Brewery Field on March 2nd with Alan King scoring twice.

That set up Moors for the final against Horden at Feethams on April 19th 1968, although the kick off was delayed for twenty minutes because the Horden team coach and referee Mr R Griffiths from Consett were held up in heavy traffic.

Only one goal decided a hard fought game, on 73 minutes from John Tobin, who scored from a pass by John Wilkinson. "That was the hardest game of

the season," said a relieved Bob Bell. The Auckland Chronicle wrote; "It was a hard fought affair and there is no doubt that although the standard of football didn't rise to a great height, both clubs covered themselves in glory as a result of their all action displays."
The squad was: Eric Hulme, Graham Defty, Colin Richardson, Billy Lovejoy, Peter Joyce, Alan West, Kenny Banks, John Wilkinson, John Tobin, Ralph Wright, Alan King, Stan Summerill.
And to cap a memorable season, Moors also won the Northern League Cup.

The 1967-68 Northern League Cup run

Moors started the competition on September 23rd 1967 when they beat Crook Town 3-1, and for the second time in a cup competition that season, they beat Ferryhill, this time by 3-0, with Stan Summerill scoring again. Peter Joyce was also on target.
In the semi final, John Wilkinson scored twice as Moors pulled off a good 3-1 away win at Whitby Town. The final, against Whitley Bay at Crook on April 27th 1968, was a dull goalless draw, with very few chances.
The team; Eric Hulme, Graham Defty, Colin Richardson, Billy Lovejoy, Peter Joyce, Ralph Wright, Ian McPherson, Kenny Banks, John Tobin, Alan West, Alan King.
But in contrast, the replay at North Shields on May 7th 1968 was a real thriller. Alan King opened the scoring with a shot that went in off the post, although Whitley claimed that the ball hadn't crossed the line. Ray Wrightson equalised for Whitley, and after Moors keeper Eric Hulme saved a penalty, Moors went 2-1 up with a shot by Ralph Wright. Whitley equalised again through Neale Walton's header, but Alan West got the winner with a shot through a crowd of players.
Team; Eric Hulme, Graham Defty, Colin Richardson, Billy Lovejoy, Peter Joyce, Alan West, Kenny Banks, John Wilkinson, John Tobin, Ralph Wright, Alan King.

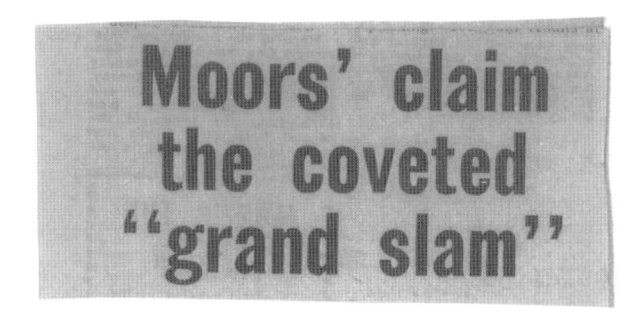

Moors' claim the coveted "grand slam"

The only disappointment that season was the unexpected exit from the FA Amateur Cup. After Alan West scored the winner in a tough game at Skelmersdale in the first round on January 20th 1968, Moors fell at the next hurdle against unfancied Prestwich Heys. They drew 1-1 at the Brewery Field, Kenny Banks scoring, then they lost 2-1 after extra time in Manchester, Prestwich scoring a wind assisted goal for the winner.

But despite that FA Amateur Cup exit, the club still covered itself in glory, and they had finally established themselves as a Northern League force. At the end of that glorious season, Moors were honoured with a civic reception by the Town Council.

Unfortunately, the 1968-69 season was an anticlimax. Moors finished a disappointing seventh in the defence of their title, they lost 4-3 to Blyth in the first qualifying round of the FA Cup, and they lost their grip on the Durham Challenge Cup after losing 2-0 to Consett after two drawn games. In the league cup, Moors needed four games to beat Billingham Synthonia – the tie lasting from December 21st 1968 to March 12th 1969, but they lost to North Shields in the semi final, Albert Hickman putting through his own goal.

Spennymoor United, 1969-70. Northern League.
Back row: Johnson, M. Bailey, G. Defty, C. Richardson, E. Hulme, G. Parker, P. Joyce, B. Robson, B. Bell (Coach). Front: A. Kell, D. Crosby, J. Tobin, K. Smith (Mascot), A. Harding, A. White, T. Strong.

Moors improved in 1969-70, but they could only finish fourth in the Northern League, and they finished trophy-less, losing to Whitby in the final of the Northern League Cup.
However, they had a good run in the FA Cup, and reached the competition proper again.

The 1969-70 FA Cup run

Moors reached the first round proper by winning all four qualifying round ties by the odd goal.

They left it late in the first qualifying round, John Tobin scoring in the last minute to beat South Bank at the Brewery Field, and after a 2-2 draw at Gateshead, who were then in the Northern Premier League, Doug Crosby, who had scored in the first game, scored the winner in the replay at the Brewery Field. Alan Harding, who later went on to play for Darlington, Lincoln and Hartlepool, scored the decider to put out Whitley Bay in a 3-2 win in the third qualifying round. And when the late Geoff Parker scored the winner against Tow Law on November 1st 1969, that meant Moors had gone unbeaten in fifteen games in all competitions.

Moors were given a really attractive home tie, against runaway high scoring Fourth Division leaders Wrexham, in the first round, but there was disappointment in the size of the crowd at the Brewery Field, as only 2,241 turned up, especially as Moors had turned down an offer to switch the game to the Racecourse Ground where there could have been a crowd of 14,000.

"The Brewery Field lads appeared to be overawed against their opponents, who had specialists in all positions except goalkeeper, who wasn't too happy under pressure," said the Sunday Sun.

Wrexham were leading 2-0 when Moors scored their goal, Kenny Banks curling the ball home direct from a corner, with Wrexham keeper David Gaskell helping it in. Ian Moir, a former Busby Babe, destroyed the Spennymoor defence. The Echo said that the star of the match was Graham Defty "who treated this game as he would have done a Northern League encounter." So did Moors full back Billy Robson -- he clashed with Wrexham inside right Bobby Park, who was stretchered off.

Team; Eric Hulme, Graham Defty, Colin Richardson, Doug Crosby, Peter Joyce, Billy Robson, David White, Geoff Parker, John Tobin, Allan Harding, Kenny Banks. Sub; Alan Kell.

Keeper Eric Hulme was later chosen for the FA representative XI, and later joined Nottingham Forest.

The 1969-70 Northern League cup run

Moors reached another Northern League Cup final, but this time they lost to Whitby Town by 4-1 at South Bank, with Kenny Banks scoring in every round.

Unusually for him, Kenny missed a penalty in the 2-0 home win over Shildon on September 27th 1969, but he didn't miss from the spot in the 3-1 home win over Tow Law. Kenny converted another penalty in the 1-0 away win at Crook, but his successful free kick in the final against Whitby was nothing but a consolation as Moors were out of the game by then.

Team; Nattrass, David White, Colin Richardson, Alan Kell, Peter Joyce, Billy Robson, Ian McPherson, Geoff Parker, John Tobin, Kenny Banks, Doug Crosby. Sub Watson.

Kenny, who made his debut for Moors in the early sixties was a massive hit with the Spennymoor fans because of his all round ability, and he became a key man for more reasons than one in the seventies.

Chapter Seven

Give the ball to Kenny

The seventies was a golden era for Spennymoor, and many people say that the team which carried all before them in that era was probably one of the best they'd seen at non league level. If it wasn't for another Northern League team, Blyth Spartans, hitting their peak at the same time, then Moors would have achieved much more than they did.
The Spennymoor teams of the seventies had all the necessary qualities to win championships and trophies. They had leadership, skill, determination, teamwork and character, but most of all they had excellent team spirit and camaraderie.

Bert Elliot (left) and Manager Bob Bell (right)

Manager Bob Bell left in 1971, and he was replaced by Billy Bell, who had just guided Evenwood to the Northern League title. Bob, who used more and more ideas from his FA coaching courses, appointed a fitness coach for the start of the 1970-71 season. Bob brought in Derek Priestman, an athletics

coach, to assist with Moors' pre season preparations. Bob said at the time; "I have always had a good response to the players from training and I feel they will react to it well." Priestman said; "There is more to training than jogging and exercises, or running round a football field."
Moors finished fourth in 1970 and eighth in 1971, but they bounced back in season 1971-72, winning the Northern League title for the second time in style.

Spennymoor United, 1971-72
Back row: T. Butterfield, J. Heaviside, B. Robson, G. Simpson, P. Joyce, A. Hickman. Front: G. Parker, A. Kell, K. Banks, B. Roughley, T. Cochrane, K. Storey, Smith (Mascot).

They got off to a great start on the first day of the season, beating Blyth 4-3, after leading 3-0 at half time. New striker Tommy Cochrane was amongst the goals, and then they hammered Tow Law 10-2 at the Brewery Field, Geoff Parker (4), Tommy Cochrane (3), Geoff "Butch" Simpson, John Heaviside and Kenny Banks on the mark. That set the mood for the season. Moors lost only three times in the league, against Shildon, Tow Law and Ferryhill, scoring a century of goals in the process.
Unfortunately, Moors couldn't make it a league and league cup double, losing to North Shields in a replay on May 15th 1972.
There was a good strong backbone in the team, which would be a huge platform for the years ahead. Geoff "Butch" Simpson and Peter Joyce at the back, midfield general Kenny Banks and utility man Albert Hickman, who could play just about anywhere. Kenny, who was an England Amateur international, was the man who pulled the strings for Moors, and the players were told "Give the ball to Kenny."

Peter Joyce, the Spennymoor captain, is chaired by members of the team after receiving the Northern League championship trophy.

The 1971-72 Northern League cup run

Outfield player Keith Storey played as an emergency keeper, and finished on the winning side against Blyth in the semi final on March 22nd 1971. Blyth finished second in the league that season, nine points behind Moors. Kenny Banks and Tommy Cochrane both scored two apiece in the 4-1 win.

Despite his heroics, Keith didn't get a place in the starting line up for the final against North Shields on May 10th 1972 at Blyth, which ended in a goalless draw.

Team; Ian Robson, Tony Butterfield, John Heaviside, "Butch" Simpson, Peter Joyce, Ian Kirkpatrick, Kenny Banks, Albert Hickman, Tommy Cochrane, Geoff Parker, Eric Shaw. Sub Keith Storey.

Keith Storey, emergency keeper against Blyth

Moors surprisingly lost the replay at Ferryhill five days later, Butch Simpson scoring in the 2-1 defeat.

Team; Ian Robson, Tony Butterfield, John Heaviside, Butch Simpson, Peter Joyce, Ian Kirkpatrick, Kenny Banks, Albert Hickman, Tommy Cochrane, Geoff Parker, Eric Shaw. Sub Alan Kell.

Geoff "Butch" Simpson was a local lad, who went on to establish a reputation as a tough, no nonsense defender, and would play a major part in Moors' seventies success.

Amateur Cup success still eluded Moors, and they lost in the second round on January 29th 1972 at Wycombe Wanderers, who gained revenge for their defeat at the hands of Moors in the competition some years earlier.

Teenager Eric Gates (left), who went to school in Staindrop, made his debut for the Moors, in the 4-0 home win over Ashington on March 24th 1971. Eric would later to go on to play for Ipswich, Sunderland and England.

There was also an individual honour for Moors midfielder Brian Mulligan, who was chosen to play for the National Civil Service XI against the RAF and the Army. Brian worked at the Department of National Savings in Durham at the time, and later became assistant manager at South Bank and a Northern League management committee member.

Billy Bell left in the summer of 1972, and the club appointed Kenny Banks as their new team coach – he was a qualified FA coach anyway.

The 1972-73 season saw the emergence of another player who would excite the fans for several years to come. Kevin Reilly, a quiet, unassuming lad signed from Byers Green, exploded onto the scene with some breathtaking skill and outstanding goals. But also up front was goalgetter John Davies, who himself would set a goalscoring record, and in midfield Brian Mulligan linked up with Kenny Banks.

Moors had some thrilling cup action in 1972-73. They had their best ever run in the FA Amateur Cup, when they reached the quarter final, only to lose at home to Walton and Hersham in a replay. They easily won the Durham Challenge Cup, beating Wearside League club Wingate 3-0 in the final, and they also reached the final of the Northern League Cup against Blyth, who themselves were starting to emerge.

The 1972-73 FA Amateur Cup run

Moors were so near to an FA Amateur Cup semi final place, but they lost at home in a quarter final replay.

In the first round they beat local rivals Shildon 1-0 with a goal by Len Walker, and then travelled to London and beat Leyton on January 6th 1973 with first half goals from Geoff Parker (2) and Peter Joyce.

Spennymoor United, 1972-73.
Back row: R. Burlinson, R. Adamson, P. Joyce, G. Simpson, B. Nicholson, T. Cochrane, A. Hickman, J. Heaviside. Front: K. Reilly, A. Kell, R. Nattrass, D. Bradley (Mascot), K. Banks, B. Mulligan, K. Walker, P. Adams.

There was controversy in the third round game against Hayes at the Brewery Field, when the Spennymoor defence heard a whistle, stopped playing, and Hayes ran through to equalise – the whistle was from the crowd and not the referee. Undaunted, Butch Simpson got the winner late in the game.

Moors had a tough away game in the quarter final. They pulled off a good 0-0 draw at Walton and Hersham, who included Dave Bassett (left), later to be Wimbledon manager, in their side.

But they lost the replay by a solitary goal a week later. The turning point for Moors was on 25 minutes when Brian Mulligan's header was headed into the Walton net by a defender.

The referee gave a goal, but the linesman spotted a handball in the build up. Kieron Somers scored the all important winning goal, with a header after 30 minutes.

Walton and Hersham manager Allen Batsford said: "It was all a matter of application. They got frustrated because we denied them the space to take us on and we even found the time to pressurise their own back four."

The Moors team; Dickie Adamson, Geoff Simpson, John Heaviside, Kenny Banks, Peter Joyce, Albert Hickman, Len Walker, Geoff Parker, John Davies, Kevin Reilly, Brian Mulligan. Sub Eric Shaw (for Kevin Reilly, 85 minutes) The gate money from an attendance of 3,800 was briefly stolen by a man at the end of the game, but after a scuffle, police made an arrest and all the money was quickly recovered.

The 1972-73 FA Cup run

New signing Tommy Cochrane scored in every qualifying round to help put Moors into the first round proper of the FA Cup. He scored a hat trick as Moors easily beat Stockton 5-1 in the first qualifying round, then he scored the winner at neutral Crook as Moors needed two replays to see off North Shields.

Moors then played their fourth FA Cup tie inside a fortnight when they comfortably won 4-0 at Gateshead, Tommy again on target, and on

Spennymoor United v Shrewsbury Town, FA Cup 1972.
Back row: B. Nicholson, G. Simpson, D. Adamson, A. Kell, P. Joyce, A. Hickman, K. Banks. Front: G. Walker, J. Parker, J. Davies, T. Cochrane, B. Mulligan.

November 4th 1972, Tommy and John Davies both scored the goals in the 2-0 win at Willington.

Moors were handed an attractive home tie in the first round proper, against Third Division club Shrewsbury, but a crowd of just 1,818 turned up for the 1-1 draw, a big disappointment to club officials. Secretary Stan Bradley said; "We have not made a penny out of the FA Cup so far. I don't know what you have to do to attract people these days." There was no prize money in the FA Cup then, the only money clubs made was from crowds. The gate receipts for the game were £474, and from that, Shrewsbury had to take out their expenses.

Moors did themselves proud by bouncing back from a goal down to earn a replay. Peter Dolby put Shrewsbury ahead on 70 minutes, but Kenny Banks equalised from a John Davies free kick.

Team; Dickie Adamson, Butch Simpson, John Heaviside, Kenny Banks, Peter Joyce, Albert Hickman, Geoff Walker, John Davies, Geoff Parker, Tommy Cochrane, Brian Mulligan. Sub Alan Kell.

Moors were unlucky in the replay at Gay Meadow, keeper Dickie Adamson was hurt in a first half collision and suffered slight concussion, Albert Hickman had to leave the field briefly for treatment, and Geoff Parker also carried a knock for most of the game. John Davies was unlucky three times with shots and Shrewsbury keeper Ken Mulhearn also pulled off a great save from him, before they were opened up by Shrewsbury midfielder Ian Moir, who scored from 35 yards. Substitute George Andrews added two more, but Shrewsbury knew that they had been in a battle well before John Davies pulled a goal back near the end. Maurice Evans, the Shrewsbury manager, complimented Moors on their style of play. "Spennymoor set out to match us with football skills and not as so often happens in these amateur-professional clashes, with more brawn than brain."

The Northern Echo wrote; "Their late goal brought them a standing ovation from Shrewsbury's largest crowd of the season."

Team; Dickie Adamson, Butch Simpson, John Heaviside, Alan Kell, Peter Joyce, Albert Hickman, Geoff Walker, John Davies, Tommy Cochrane, Geoff Parker (sub Brian Mulligan), Kenny Banks.

Moors wore a new yellow "Brazil" strip that night. But the referee wouldn't allow them to wear the blue shorts because of a colour clash, instead they had to wear white shorts, which spoiled the effect slightly.

The 1972-73 Durham Challenge Cup run

Moors ran riot in the first round, banging nine past Houghton, with John Davies, Geoff Parker and Paul Adams all scoring two apiece.

Peter Joyce scored the only goal of the game against fierce rivals Bishop Auckland, and in the third round Tommy Cochrane scored a hat trick in a 5-0 home win over Willington.

They needed two replays to see off Ferryhill, but that was only thanks to a last minute equaliser by John Davies in the first game at the Brewery Field. After a goalless draw in the second replay at Ferryhill, Geoff Parker and John Davies put Moors into the final – a total of 300 minutes of play.

Action from the 1973 Durham Challenge Cup Final

Wingate, one of the top Wearside League clubs, were Moors' opponents in the final at Feethams on April 23rd 1973, and Moors eventually managed to overcome them with three second half goals. Wingate defender Gerry Walker deflected a Kenny Banks shot past the Wingate keeper for the first goal just after half time, then Butch Simpson headed the second from an Eric Shaw free kick. Geoff Parker scored the third after the Wingate keeper spilled Tommy Cochrane's shot. It was the sixth Durham Challenge Cup win in Spennymoor's history.

Team; Dickie Adamson, Butch Simpson, John Heaviside, Alan Kell, Peter Joyce, Eric Shaw, Kenny Banks, Geoff Parker, Tommy Cochrane, John Davies, Brian Mulligan. Keeper Dickie Adamson was advised to retire from playing at the start of the following season because of injury. Unfortunately, Moors didn't win the Northern League Cup to round off a good season.

The 1972-73 Northern League cup run

Moors lost in the final for the second season running against another team from north of the River Tyne.

Peter Joyce scored the only goal of the game in the opening round at Penrith on October 28th 1972. Moors then beat Bishop Auckland, who were league runners-up that season, by 5-1 in a second round replay at Kingsway, Brian Mulligan and Geoff Parker scoring two apiece, and they really hit form again in the semi final, beating Whitley Bay 4-0 at the Brewery Field, with Geoff Parker scoring another two.

But Moors lost 2-0 to Blyth in the final on May 7th 1973, the Northumbrians completing a league and league cup double.

Team; Dickie Adamson, Butch Simpson, John Heaviside, Alan Kell, Peter Joyce, Eric Shaw, Kenny Banks, Geoff Parker, Tommy Cochrane, Kevin Reilly, Brian Mulligan. Sub Paul Adams.

Moors and Blyth were neck and neck in a thrilling title race in 1974, but Moors just managed to make up the ground and win their second title of the seventies. By now, Moors had added striker Geoff Hart and defender Billy Robson, for his second spell, to their squad, signings which helped them edge out Blyth.

Geoff Parker

The 1973-74 Northern League play off title decider at Ashington. Blyth 1 Spennymoor 2

Blyth and Moors finished level on 64 points at the end of the season, both having won 30 league games and drawn four – these were the days of two points for a win. League rules stated if two teams finished level on points then a play off should decide the title, but if goal difference had been the deciding factor, then Blyth would have won the league with a difference of

+63, while Spennymoor's was +50.

Moors' dogged determination kept them on Blyth's heels, and going into the last day of the season they were a point ahead of Blyth having finished their fixtures, but Blyth were surprisingly held to a 1-1 draw by Penrith, thus forcing the play off. Plenty of Spennymoor people were at the game cheering on the Cumbrians.

In the play off, Kevin Reilly gave Moors a vital lead when he scored from a cross by Kenny Banks after nine minutes, then a mistake by Blyth keeper Varvill let in Peter Joyce, who set up Geoff Hart for the second. Des Jardine pulled a goal back for Blyth, but it was too late.

Team; Jimmy Goundry, Butch Simpson, John Heaviside, Alan Kell, Peter Joyce, Billy Robson, Kenny Banks, Kevin Reilly, John Davies, Geoff Hart, Albert Hickman.

The 1973-74 Durham Challenge Cup run

Moors only played one home game on their way to the Cup.

John Davies and Peter Joyce scored in the 2-0 win at Annfield Plain in the first round, then Moors came back from 1-0 down at home against Wearside League club Easington to win 2-1 with goals from Peter Joyce and Alan Kell.

Kenny Banks delivers his team talk before the 1974 Durham Challenge Cup Final

John Davies then scored both goals in the 2-1 away win at Billingham Synthonia, and his striking partner Kevin Reilly fired a second half winner at Willington in the semi final.

In the final at Darlington on April 16th 1974, Durham City led Moors with a goal by Charlie Knott after 51 minutes, but Moors equalised through Kevin Reilly from Brian Mulligan's cross. The Evening Despatch wrote; "Spennymoor looked far from a team challenging for the Northern League title and it was midtable Durham who looked the surer and sharper side."

Team; Jimmy Goundry, Butch Simpson, John Heaviside, Alan Kell, Peter Joyce, Albert Hickman, Kenny Banks, Kevin Reilly, John Davies, Geoff Hart, Brian Mulligan. Sub Billy Robson.

Moors were better in the replay at Crook on April 23rd 1974. Peter Joyce got the winner after 27 minutes from Kevin Reilly's right wing corner to give Moors the cup for the seventh time.

The Evening Despatch wrote; "Moors played with method and understanding, which Durham lacked. Spennymoor's attack was more dangerous than Durham's, which did not get in one real serious shot."

Team: Jimmy Goundry, Butch Simpson, John Heaviside, Alan Kell, Peter Joyce, Billy Robson, Albert Hickman, Kenny Banks, Kevin Reilly, John Davies, Geoff Hart.

Moors also won the Vaux Floodlit League Cup, with a Kevin Reilly penalty against Consett.

That season was the last in the Amateur Cup as far as Moors were concerned, but to their disappointment, they couldn't get past the last sixteen, losing 2-0 at home to Sutton in a third round replay, after they had beaten Emley and Southall. The Southall game was played on a Sunday because the Government wouldn't allow floodlights to be used because of power cuts. Moors would now enter the FA Trophy, after the FA ended the long running distinction between amateur and professional players. It was the end of "shamateurism."

Moors lost their grip on the title in season 1974-75 to a very good Blyth team, who went through the full 36 game league season unbeaten. The first day of the season when the sides met was vital, and it was Blyth who gained an early advantage by winning the game after Peter Joyce gave Moors an early lead. Moors finished runners up to Blyth, winning 27 of their 36 matches.

The Northern League clinched its first sponsorship by agreeing a deal with Rothmans. With it, the league introduced three points for a win, goalscoring bonuses and a sportsmanship scheme. They were groundbreaking ideas where non league football was concerned.

Moors soon had an indication of the standard they would have to reach if they were to make an impact in the FA Trophy in their first match in the competition, when they were easily beaten 5-0 at their old foes Goole Town in the third qualifying round on November 30th 1974.

In October 1974, Spennymoor full back Billy Robson was suspended by the club for three weeks for two bookings in the first two months of the season, against Tow Law on August 20th and Ashington on October 12th. The committee felt that they "had to support the sportsmanship scheme that sponsors Rothmans have introduced." Rothmans set up a scheme which gave prize money to clubs with the least amount of bookings and sendings off – a scheme that is still around now in the Northern League. At the same time, Tow Law released full back Vic Hillier after he had been booked twice in two months.

Moors kept tight hold of the Durham Challenge Cup for the third year in succession to provide some consolation.

The 1974-75 Durham Challenge Cup run

Moors played three Wearside League clubs in the early rounds. Charlie Gott, later to manage Crook Town, scored two of Moors' goals in the 6-2 win over Murton, and after a 2-2 draw at home to Annfield Plain, Moors won a tricky replay 2-0 thanks to an own goal and one from Brian Mulligan.

Wingate, a really strong Wearside League club, gave Moors another tough game, before they were overcome 3-2 with John Davies (2) and Albert Hickman the scorers.

Moors nearly went out in the semi final at Willington – coached by former Moors player Brian Newton at the time – as the home side led 2-0 until late in the game, but Billy Robson and Kevin Reilly pulled goals back. Moors won the replay 5-3, even though they had Billy Robson sent off, along with his former team mate Tommy Cochrane. John Davies scored a hat trick, with Geoff Simpson and Geoff Hart scoring the others in a real thriller.

Moors beat Tow Law for the second time

John Heaviside with the Durham Challenge Cup

in a cup tie that season – they'd already beaten them in the FA Cup – when they won 3-2 at Crook in the final.
Billy Robson and Albert Hickman scored from Kevin Reilly corners to put Moors 2-0 up with the wind at their backs (anyone who has been to Crook on a windy day will know what it's like), but Tow Law, coached by Peter Feenan, came back and levelled by the 53rd minute through Bobby Hall and David Jones. But Geoff Hart brought the Durham Challenge Cup home to Moors when he beat three men and fired the winner near the end.
The Spennymoor squad was; Dickie Adamson, Butch Simpson, John Heaviside, Alan Kell, Peter Joyce, Billy Robson, Kevin Reilly, Eric Shaw, Albert Hickman, Kenny Banks, Geoff Hart, John Davies, Brian Mulligan, Neale Walton.
Spennymoor secretary Stan Bradley said: "I thought in the second half as the game wore on, our greater experience told."
The 1975-76 season saw one of Moors' greatest moments in their FA Cup history, when they defeated Football League club Southport 4-1 at the Brewery Field with some excellent football which gave them a deserved victory. It was their first win over a Football League club in the FA Cup since they beat Hartlepool way back in 1928.

The 1975-76 FA Cup run

Moors pulled off one of the shocks of the first round of the FA Cup but they very nearly stumbled out of the competition in the first qualifying round against Crook Town. Geoff Hart scored a late equaliser at the Millfield in a 1-1 draw, and then Kevin Reilly scored an extra time winner in the replay.
Moors then beat fellow Northern League side Penrith 2-0 with second half goals by Alan Kell and Butch Simpson, followed by a good 3-0 home win over Northern Premier League club Netherfield, with Kenny Banks, Albert Hickman and Geoff Hart scoring.
It was an all Northern League clash against Tow Law in the last qualifying round, and Kenny Banks scored two second half goals at Ironworks Road to put Moors into the first round proper, in which they were drawn against Southport, bottom of the Football League at the time.
Moors watched the Fourth Division side in action at Northampton before their big match, and the homework paid off. Southport led early on with a goal by Tom O'Neill, but Kenny Banks fired an equaliser, then Bill Gates set up midfielder Tony Rosethorn, whose shot hit a defender and ran for Brian Mulligan to run through and score. Kenny Banks made it 3-1 with another sweet volley from an Albert Hickman free kick, and Kevin Reilly cracked in the fourth near the end. Player coach Kenny Banks said: "We really stretched them at the back, although I didn't expect them to make so many

We'll Always Be United

Spennymoor v Southport: Kenny Banks takes aim...

...and the ball sails over the head of keeper Thomas for Moors' third goal.

Moors scorers v Southport - Brian Mulligan, Kevin Reilly and Kenny Banks

mistakes. Once we drew level, we had the measure of Southport and never relaxed our grip."
Moors midfielder Tony Rosethorn was part of the Tow Law team that thumped Mansfield 5-1 eight years previously, and he said; "It was like Tow Law all over again."
The team; Steve Rowell, Butch Simpson, Albert Hickman, Alan Kell, Bill Gates, Billy Robson, Tony Rosethorn, Kenny Banks, Kevin Reilly, Geoff Hart, Brian Mulligan.
Centre half Bill Gates had started his career at Spennymoor, before going to play for Middlesbrough for a decade. Tony Rosethorn had moved to London with his work, and on his return to the north east, signed for Spennymoor from Dagenham.
Moors would have loved another home tie, but instead they were drawn away to Third Division Bury in the second round.
Moors started the game well, and there was a chance of another shock until Bury scored just before half time through Keith Kennedy, only seconds after Moors had taken a corner at the other end. George Buchan and a Paul Adams own goal completed the scoring, while Butch Simpson went off injured with a broken arm to be replaced by youngster David Curry, who had made his Moors debut only a fortnight earlier..
"We let Bury off the hook in the dying seconds of the first half," said Kenny Banks.
Bury forward Derek Spence was kind in his after match comments; "Spennymoor played better than some of the Third Division sides we've met this season, and deserved better luck."
Team; Steve Rowell, Butch Simpson (sub David Curry), Paul Adams, Alan Kell, Billy Robson, Albert Hickman, Tony Rosethorn, Kenny Banks, Kevin Reilly, Geoff Hart, Brian Mulligan.
After the match, Bury made an enquiry about Kevin Reilly, and he later turned them down. Kevin said: "I went to Bury for a trial, but I was told the basic wage was only £40 per week when I was talking with international Derek Spence. As a production controller it simply wasn't financially viable to switch to full time football." Several more clubs made enquiries about Kevin, but all were unsuccessful.

The 1975-76 Durham Challenge Cup run

The Durham Challenge Cup was now virtually Moors' own property, as they comfortably held on to the trophy.
They had their usual tough game against Consett in the first round on January 3rd 1976, just beating them 2-1 with goals by Billy Robson and Kevin Reilly, and in the second round, Geoff Hart and Ray James scored the

Spennymoor United, 1975-76.
Back row: R. Adamson, G. Simpson, A. Kell, B. Robson, T. Rosethorn, W. Gates, K. Banks. Front: P. Adams, A. Hickman, K. Reilly, G. Hart, B. Mulligan.

goals in the 2-0 home win over Boldon CA.
Kevin Reilly and Geoff Hart scored in the 2-0 win at Crook, and in the semi final Geoff Parker and Geoff Hart scored in another 2-0 win, this time against Tow Law at the Brewery Field.
Moors easily won the final, by 4-0 against Willington in front of 1100 fans at Shildon on April 10th 1976, and became the first club since Sunderland A in the early 1900s to win the competition four seasons in a row. It was their tenth win in total.
Geoff Hart put Moors ahead after 4 minutes, then he pounced on a mistake to score the second after 40 minutes. He then set up Kenny Banks to fire the third just after half time, and Kevin Reilly rounded off the scoring.
Secretary Stan Bradley said: "It was the easiest of the four finals. We expected a much harder game. It was disappointing because we know Willington can play much better than they did."
Team; Keith Wakefield, David Curry, Paul Adams, Alan Kell, Bill Gates, Billy Robson, Albert Hickman, Kenny Banks, Kevin Reilly, Geoff Hart, Brian Mulligan. Sub, Geoff Parker.
Another Reilly burst on the scene for Moors in the competition – Gerry, Kevin's brother.
Moors almost won the league, but they just failed by a point. At one stage,

Moors thought they had a good chance of winning the title again, but Blyth won their last eight games to clinch the title, and Willington won seven out of their last nine to finish above Moors having scored more goals. Moors' away form let them down. They won all but three of their home games – they beat Blyth and Willington – but they lost five away games.

The first Rothmans Knockout Cup was introduced that season, which involved teams from all the Rothmans-sponsored leagues -- the Hellenic, Isthmian and Western, plus invited teams from the Channel Islands – but Moors didn't make much of an impact, losing to Ilford after beating First Tower of Guernsey. Albert Hickman and Kevin Reilly were both chosen for a Rothmans National XI tour of Jersey and Guernsey, Moors secretary Stan Bradley also accompanied them.

But then Blyth had to hand over the Northern League title, as Moors hit a real purple patch, to dominate the Northern League scene for the next three years.

Again, they had to come from well behind to catch up to Consett, who had already beaten Moors three times in different competitions during the season. One of those matches was in the Durham Challenge Cup, Consett winning the semi final 4-2 to loosen Moors' grip on the competition. It was Moors' first defeat in 26 Durham Challenge Cup matches.

Moors' dreams of reaching Wembley in the Trophy were dashed, even though their campaign got off to a great start when they beat one of the competition favourites Northwich Victoria 2-1 at the Brewery Field. In that season's FA Cup, Northwich had beaten Football League clubs Rochdale, Peterborough and Watford.

Moors captain Albert Hickman said: "It was a great win. While it is difficult to single anyone out in this wonderful all round team victory, I thought Alan Kell did a marvellous job in snuffing out danger man Frank Corrigan."

Moors went a goal down on 8 minutes, but Billy Robson headed the equaliser from a Kevin Reilly corner on 11 minutes, and Geoff Hart fired the winner on 71 minutes. Northwich manager Paul Ogden said: "I couldn't have grumbled if we had been beaten 5-1."

The Moors fans put the pressure on Northwich keeper John Farmer. "I've played on a few grounds in my time and been under pressure, but this was something special. With the supporters virtually standing on my back and nothing but black and white shirts in front, I was in the middle of a pressure cooker." But in the second round it all wrong, and Moors lost 1-0 at Nuneaton.

The Northern League title boiled down to one match, a winner takes all title game at Willington.

The 1976-77 Northern League title play off at Willington May 9th 1977 Spennymoor 3 Consett 0

Spennymoor and Consett finished the season level on points, and just like three years before when Moors and Blyth played off for the title, they had to do the same again. Both teams had 76 points, three points for a win having been introduced when Rothmans became sponsors. If the championship was decided on goal difference, then Moors' difference would have been better by 8 goals – +34 against Consett's +26.

Moors had a scare – an understatement when you read his memories later in this book -- before the game when star striker Kevin Reilly reported to the ground with a gash in his head sustained in the previous day's all England Sunday Cup final playing for Langley Park Rams' Head, but he passed himself fit.

Moors never looked back after going ahead on 11 minutes through Kevin Reilly who pounced on a mistake by a Consett defender, then Butch Simpson scored the second from a Kevin Reilly corner, the referee ruling that the ball had crossed the line before a defender headed it away. Butch Simpson got the third with a glancing header to give Moors the title. They won the league with the lowest winning points total since the three points for a win rule started three years previously, and hadn't lost a league game since November 6th, a run of 22 matches. They picked up ten points out of their last four games, their best performance a 5-0 win over Whitley Bay when Kevin Reilly scored four. It was tough on Consett, who had beaten Moors three times during the season.

The effect of Sunday football was the main issue afterwards, and Moors' player coach Kenny Banks said: "We lost vital points in the championship run in because of players turning out in Sunday football. Kevin Reilly was injured on Sunday and shouldn't have played today. But if he had been out, it would have been a real body blow to us."

Consett secretary Alan Shearer had some harsh words for his players. "A whole season's work was jeopardised by Sunday football."

Team; Steve Rowell, Butch Simpson, Neale Vickers, Alan Kell, Billy Robson, Albert Hickman, David Curry, Kevin Reilly, Kenny Banks, Geoff Hart, Brian Mulligan.

Chapter Eight

The 1977-78 season – Bye Bye Wembley

Some would argue that the 1977-78 season was the most exciting in the club's history, others would argue that it was the most disappointing.
While Moors kept hold of the Northern League title with a six point advantage over their old foes Blyth, they were tantalisingly in sight of an FA Trophy final place at Wembley, but it was agonisingly snatched away.
The name of Leatherhead still sends shivers down the spine of those who were in the Brewery Field that April day for the second leg of the semi final against the Isthmian League side, and players who were regarded as tough and devoid of emotion still shake their heads when they remember the second forty five minutes.
Before the drama of the Trophy, Moors had a great run in the FA Cup.

The FA Cup run 1977-78
Even though they had beaten a Football League club just two seasons before, Moors were denied exemption to the first round proper. They played seven games to reach the first round. Moors were given a tough starter at Horden in the preliminary round, where Albert Hickman salvaged a replay with a last minute equaliser. Moors won the replay 3-1, with 17 year old prospect Mattie Pearson, who replaced Tony Rosethorn in the team, on the scoresheet.
Kevin Reilly scored twice in the 4-2 win at Ferryhill in the first qualifying round, then a last minute own goal gave Moors a 2-1 win at Durham City. Moors then had to battle hard to draw 2-2 at Whitley Bay, and then John Davies, who had scored in the first game, was on target twice to give Moors a 4-1 replay win.
That gave Moors a home tie against Bangor in the fourth qualifying round, whose manager Dave Elliott said before the game; "We play in a superior league and should be too strong for them." Maybe that was the incentive Moors needed, because they won 2-1, with goals by Butch Simpson and John Davies, both set up by Kevin Reilly.
Moors were handed a home tie in the first round proper, against their old foes from Goole, whom they had beaten ten years previously at the same

stage, and were now in the Northern Premier League.
However, there was a snag for Moors, because star man Kevin Reilly was getting married the same day but fortunately, with his understanding wife Ann staying at the reception, he still played, albeit with minutes to spare. He had a blinder, as Moors won 3-1.
Kevin left the reception at 2.30 to change at his mother-in-law's, put his strip on, then a club car whisked him to the ground just before the start. "I have a reputation for missing team talks, so it will be nothing new for me to arrive late," Kevin told one of the papers.
John Davies scored from the penalty spot after Kevin was fouled after 22 minutes, then Mattie Pearson set up Brian Mulligan to turn and score. Brian provided the cross for John Davies to head in. Goole, who included striker Tony Galvin, later to play for Tottenham, scored a late consolation, and the Evening Despatch wrote; "For ninety minutes, the Spennymoor players ran their hearts out in their bid for further Cup glory and they deserved their success."
Team; Alan Porter, Butch Simpson, Neil Vickers, Albert Hickman, Billy Robson, David Curry, Alan Kell, Mattie Pearson, Kevin Reilly, Brian Mulligan, John Davies.
Moors didn't do themselves justice at Third Division Rotherham in the second round, and they lost 6-0, although new keeper Keith Wakefield, in for the injured Alan Porter, couldn't be blamed for any of the goals. John Davies hit the post direct from a corner early on, but Moors went behind after 17 minutes, and after that it was one way traffic. Trevor Phillips scored a hat trick for Rotherham. Kenny Banks said: "When I watched them a fortnight ago, Rotherham looked an ordinary side. So I was astonished to see them play so well."
Team; Keith Wakefield, Butch Simpson, Neil Vickers, Alan Kell, Billy Robson, Albert Hickman, Mattie Pearson , Kevin Reilly, John Davies, Geoff Hart, Brian Mulligan.

1977-78 FA Trophy run

Considering that Moors were unstoppable in the Northern League and had reached the second round of the FA Cup, they really fancied their chances of reaching Wembley for the first time.
In the first round, Kenny Banks scored a late winner for a 2-1 victory over Gainsborough, but in the second round against Whitby on February 4th 1978, Moors were 2-0 behind and then 3-2 down with eight minutes left until they fought back to win 5-3, with late goals by Butch Simpson, Geoff Hart and Kenny Banks.
Moors then beat Atherstone 2-1 in the fifth minute of injury time at the

Brewery Field, Geoff Hart scoring the winner to make them the first Northern League club to reach the quarter final of the Trophy. Moors had been a goal down at half time, before Geoff equalised with a diving header.

All eyes on the ball as Moors attack the Atherstone goal

The Atherstone manager was less than happy with the amount of time added on at the end of the game.

Moors had vital home advantage in the quarter finals against Dagenham from the Isthmian League, and beat them 1-0 in front of a 1,863 crowd. The Despatch wrote; "Moors are through after a display of doggedness and sheer determination which refused to lie down." The decisive goal came seven minutes before half time, when Brian Mulligan's goalbound header was put into his own net by Dagenham defender Norman Welch. Moors keeper Alan Porter pulled off several good saves, and Albert Hickman cleared another effort off the line.

Player-manager Kenny Banks said; "We were forced to defend instead of going at them. Now I feel we're really on our way."

Moors were drawn against Leatherhead in the two legged semi final, and really believed that they could battle through to Wembley, despite the formidable presence of Leatherhead striker Chris Kelly, who had scored winning goals against Football League clubs in the FA Cup in the previous three seasons.

Moors were caught out in the away leg on April 8th in the first twenty minutes, with goals by John Cooper and Dennis Malley, but they held on

well to give them a great chance still of going through.
The team at Leatherhead; Alan Porter, Butch Simpson, Neale Vickers, Alan Kell, Billy Robson, Dennis Ward, Mattie Pearson, Kevin Reilly, John Davies, Geoff Hart, Kenny Banks. Sub; Brian Mulligan.
Skipper Albert Hickman, who missed the game because of a broken ankle sustained at Evenwood a week before, said; "If we can get an early goal in the second leg, it will be a completely different game. We won't let Leatherhead attack us the way they did down there."
Kenny Banks sounded a cautious note; "Two goals is a big start to give any side, but we're not dead yet." Indeed they weren't, and by half time in the return leg, they had played some great football, as Albert had suggested, and they had clawed back the two goal deficit.
Everybody thought that they would go through at half time. Billy Robson headed Moors in front from a Brian Mulligan corner on 17 minutes, then John Davies made it 2-0 from a Billy Robson pass on 39 minutes.
But Leatherhead stunned everybody by getting the winner on aggregate through Johnny Baker in the second half after Moors failed to clear a corner. Moors were distraught, and the newspapers carried pictures of Geoff Hart, Kenny Banks and Kevin Reilly all in tears, and a simple headline captured everybody's feelings; "Bye, Bye Wembley."
Kenny Banks said: "The lads did everything I asked in the first half, then we went out to a sloppy goal." Keeper Alan Porter held his hands up; "I dropped the bloody ball on the goal line," he said. At least that's what he was quoted as saying, anyway.
Team; Alan Porter, Butch Simpson, Neale Vickers, Alan Kell, Billy Robson, Brian Mulligan, Mattie Pearson, Kevin Reilly, John Davies, Geoff Hart, Kenny Banks. Sub; Dennis Ward.

The failure to finish off Leatherhead was discussed at length for many years afterwards, as Moors reflected on a missed opportunity. Nevertheless, no Northern League club has reached the same stage of the FA Trophy since,

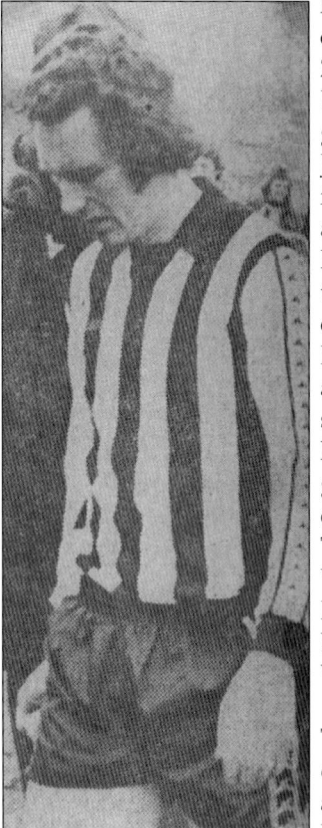

A dejected Kenny Banks

and are unlikely ever to now that the Northern League is restricted to the FA Vase.

It was a tribute to the determination and durability of the players that they managed to regroup and win the Northern League. They recovered from the dejection of the FA Trophy exit to win fourteen successive league games, but in their last game, with the title won, they were beaten 6-1 by Blyth. But Moors still finished six points ahead of their old foes.

Spennymoor United, 1977-78.
Back row: A. Porter, G. Simpson, K. Banks, B. Robson, N. Vickers, A. Kell, D. Ward. Front: M. Pearson, K. Reilly, A. Hickman, G. Hart, B. Mulligan.

Chapter Nine

Getting itchy feet

Moors dropped a bombshell in October 1978 when they announced that manager Kenny Banks was leaving, only months after they had won the Northern League title for the fourth time and reached the semi finals of the FA Trophy with him managing and playing in the side.
It was undoubtedly an unexpected decision, certainly for Kenny, who had gone to a meeting expecting to discuss just routine business, but instead he was surprised to be told he was being relieved of his managerial duties, and that secretary Stan Bradley would be replacing him, helped by Albert Hickman as coach.
Only weeks before, Moors missed out on a first round FA Cup place when they were beaten by Runcorn, who like them, had also lost in the semi finals of the FA Trophy the previous season. In the first game, Runcorn had made it difficult for Moors – "they wanted the game flat" said Kenny Banks – and the Northern Premier League side won the replay at Canal Street on November 7th 1978 with a goal by Kenyon just two minutes from end, after John Davies had equalised for Moors. In their next league game, Moors hammered Evenwood 9-1 with Kevin Reilly scoring a hat trick, but soon after the club stunned their fans and many Northern League followers by deciding to "relieve Kenny Banks of the managership, but we are hopeful that he will remain at the club as a player." Kenny decided to make a clean break and eventually he joined Ferryhill, therefore ending his long association spanning nearly two decades with the club.
The quest to go one better in the FA Trophy didn't materialise, as Moors lost 1-0 at Witton Albion in the second round on February 10th 1979 after beating Horwich RMI 1-0.
The title race became a real close run affair with Bishop Auckland favourites to win the league at one point because of their games in hand over the Moors. But Moors kept their nerve and dropped only seven points in their last fifteen matches. On the last Saturday of the season, Moors needed to beat South Bank and hope that Bishops slipped up in one of their last two matches against Crook and Horden.
Moors did their bit when Kevin Reilly scored with a powerful shot for a 1-

0 win against South Bank, and just a few miles away, Bishops missed a penalty and lost 1-0 to Crook Town to hand Moors their third successive title.

The 1978-79 Durham Challenge Cup run

John Davies and Kevin Reilly both scored two apiece in a comfortable 4-1 away win at Willington on December 9th 1978, and in the second round Moors came back from 2-1 down in the replay to beat Billingham Synthonia 3-2 after a goalless draw at Central Avenue.

Six different players got their names on the scoresheet when Moors hammered Washington 6-1 in the third round, and in the semi final Moors were irresistible in their 5-1 away win at Durham, Kevin Reilly scoring a hat trick.

Moors' free scoring mood was halted in the final against Horden at Feethams. Horden took a third minute lead through Jackie Hather, but Terry Hunter equalised from the penalty spot on 30 minutes.

Team; Alan Porter, Butch Simpson, Billy Robson, David Curry, Alan Kell, Derek Ward, Albert Hickman, Kevin Reilly, Terry Hunter, Geoff Hart, Chris Pickford.

Moors played better at Hartlepool in the replay, which was just days after they won the Northern League title for the third successive season.

Chris Pickford, playing only his third game for the club, put Moors ahead with a shot that went through the Horden keeper's hands, and after Horden levelled through Chris Cain, Pickford crossed for David "Kid" Curry to head the winner on 49 minutes.

Moors just missed out on a Northern League Cup final appearance, going out to Consett in the semi final, after leading 3-1 at one point.

It was during the summer of 1979 when Moors were informally sounded out about the possibility of joining the newly-formed Alliance Premier League along with their northern neighbours Blyth Spartans. Barrie Hindmarch, who was vice chairman at the time, says; "There was nothing formal about it, we were just sounded out. I know Jackie Smith and Jack Meggeson both said that we didn't have the resources, and we didn't pursue it. I think we erred on the side of caution."

Moors had some rebuilding to do in 1979, because the long serving John Davies left for Crook Town, and Geoff Hart left for Gateshead only to return after a month. There had been a suggestion throughout the season that some of the Moors players were getting too old, and needed to be replaced even though they had won three successive Northern League titles. However, others pointed out that there was still plenty of life in the legs when Moors beat Blyth 1-0 in a league game in December 1979.

Bobby Elwell was appointed manager in March 1980, after Stan Bradley resigned because of work commitments. Barrie Hindmarch, who had been become chairman just before Stan's announcement said: "It is most disappointing, Stan was beginning to get things right as far as the team is concerned." The popular Stan had been connected with the club as secretary and then manager for over a decade, and was an integral part of Moors' success during their heyday, persuading players such as Albert Hickman and Kevin Reilly to join the club. Moors eventually finished second in the table seven points behind Blyth and won the Northern League Cup, but they were knocked out of the FA Cup 3-2 by Northern Alliance club Brandon and they were very surprisingly beaten 2-1 at home by struggling Wearside League club Wingate in the Durham Challenge Cup at the Brewery Field after a 1-1 draw. They went out of the FA Trophy in the second round by 3-1 at Northern Premier League champions Mossley. Were the cracks starting to appear?

The 1979-80 Northern League cup run

Alan Gates, another of the footballing brothers, was in the first round Moors team that beat Willington 2-0, Tommy Cochrane scoring both goals. In the second round, Moors needed extra time to beat Crook 2-1 with Mattie Pearson, who had returned from a year in Australia, and Tony Richardson scoring the goals. Moors defender Butch Simpson and Crook midfielder Tony Butterfield were both sent off by the referee in what was described in the following day's Northern Echo as "an ugly incident."

Kevin Reilly and David Curry scored the goals that put out South Bank in the semi final and give them a place against North Shields in the final at Consett on May 3rd 1980.

David Curry, who had just been voted the league's player of the year, and Geoff Hart scored the goals in the 2-1 victory.

Team; Alan Porter, Butch Simpson, Billy Robson, Alan Kell, David Curry, Albert Hickman, Mattie Pearson, Kevin Reilly, Tommy Cochrane, Geoff Hart, Kenny Heslop. Sub Ian Stamp.

David Curry, Geoff Hart and Mattie Pearson were all picked in the Northern League XI that played the Scottish Junior XI at Bo'Ness on Friday May 23rd 1980. The League was now sponsored by Drybroughs, who had taken over from Rothmans.

Those who thought that Moors were on the slide had more ammunition because they crashed out of two cup competitions at home. They were beaten 2-1 in the FA Cup by Horden on October 4th 1980, and even though they topped the Northern League at the time, they lost 4-3 at home to

Wearside League club Reyrolles in the Durham Challenge Cup on December 7th 1980. However, they redeemed themselves somewhat on the cup front by winning the Turney-Wylde Northern League Cup, beating their old foes Consett 2-0 in the final at Blyth.

The 1980-81 Northern League cup run

Moors' first two matches were both away from home. They won 2-0 at Willington, where Geoff Hart and Terry Hunter scored and 3-0 at Tow Law with Butch Simpson scoring two. Butch also scored the only goal of the semi final against Penrith on March 11th.

Moors beat Consett 2-0 in the final at Blyth on Tuesday April 21st 1981. Kevin Reilly scored from a Kenny Heslop cross on 11 minutes, and recent signing Paul Main scored the second from a loose ball. Newcastle legend Jackie Milburn presented the trophies.

Team; Tommy Fenwick, Butch Simpson, Billy Robson, Alan Kell, David Curry, Tommy Gosling, Mattie Pearson, Kevin Reilly, Geoff Hart, Paul Main, Kenny Heslop. Sub Derek Watson.

Keeper Tommy Fenwick, who was signed from Peterlee, was chosen for the Middlesex Wanderers party for a three week tour of Australia, New Zealand and India in the summer. Although nobody knew it then, this was also Butch Simpson's last appearance in a final before he decided to emigrate to Australia in 1982.

Moors had a real head to head battle against their old foes Blyth in the league, agonisingly finishing just a point behind them as the power battle continued between the pair. Moors put them under pressure and nearly caught them up, especially as Blyth lost twice to Shildon in the last month of the season. However, Moors couldn't quite capitalise on Blyth's mistakes, dropping points at Ferryhill and Horden, and even though Moors hammered Ferryhill 6-1 in their last match – six different players scored including Kevin Reilly, who as it turned out was playing his last league game for the club – Blyth just managed to hold on with a 5-0 win at Crook, the gate boosted by many Spennymoor supporters who were Crook fans for the night.

There were still an individual honour though as striker Kevin Reilly was picked for the Northern League XI that drew 1-1 with the Scottish FA at Blyth on May 2nd 1981. Moors changed their manager at the end of the season, their old player John Heaviside replacing Bobby Elwell.

Moors lost in the Trophy to Altrincham in January 1981, but the game almost didn't take place because of a problem with the strips. The match referee ruled that Moors' strip had too much white in it, and clashed with the Altrincham strip, even though both clubs had agreed the colours beforehand and both managers were happy. The referee suggested that Moors try the nearest sports shop, but chairman Barrie Hindmarch pointed out; "Will you let us play without numbers on the back of the shirts?" The referee replied; "Of course not!" Barrie then pointed out that shirts weren't sold with numbers on, so Moors had to wear the Altrincham reserve team strip that had been used in a game that morning.

Moors broke new ground during the summer of 1981, when Joyce Hindmarch, wife of chairman Barrie, became secretary of the club, the first female club secretary in the Northern League, and one of the few female administrators anywhere in football at the time. Joyce got off to a good start, seeing Moors, as league cup winners, beat champions Blyth 5-4 on penalties in the inaugural JR Cleator Cup. The match itself finished 2-2, Mattie Pearson and David Curry on target for Moors. However, it took 18 penalties for the issue to be decided!

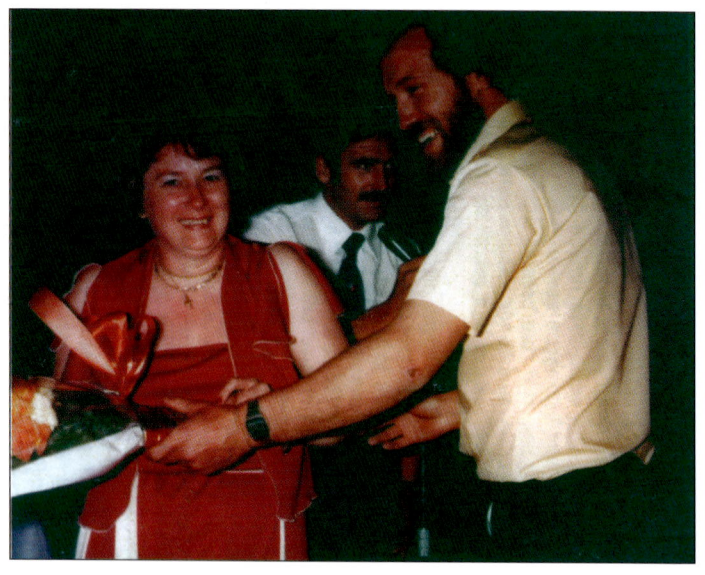

Joyce Hindmarch with Butch Simpson.

"Joyce's appointment was pretty well received," said Barrie. "She was involved in administration already in our business, so she was already very competent. Gordon Nicholson, the Northern League secretary, gave her tremendous help, and when she got the job, he said to her; "If you want any help, I'm on the end of the phone."

"Gordon used to say that she was spot on as a secretary and he pointed to her as an example. She was interviewed on television about her new job, and she said that her husband was football mad, her eldest son was football mad, so it was a case of if you can't beat them, join them." Joyce also filled the role of treasurer for a period, and was also secretary of the club when it moved into the Northern Counties East League. Sadly, she passed away in 1995.

She got on very well with the players, and she made the national papers one season after she played a practical joke on them. "The team was going through a bad patch, and Joyce joked that if they didn't start winning games, then she'd have their pants off them," remembers Barrie.

"So one day she went into the dressing room, pinched the players' underpants, and replaced them with frilly knickers. Joyce told the players that they could keep them if they wanted. You can imagine the uproar with some of the players we had at the time. One or two seemed tickled pink, though.

"We travelled away somewhere for our next match, and before we set off back, Joyce had put a clothes line up along the middle of the bus, and pegged the players' underpants on there! Alan Kell said that he couldn't see his, because there were no skidmarks on them! That was an example of the great camaraderie and spirit we had at the time."

Moors played three replays in the 1981-82 qualifying rounds of the FA Cup. They beat Northern Premier League Gateshead 3-0 after a 1-1 draw in the first qualifying round, Chester-le-Street 1-0 after a 1-1 draw, and North Shields 5-1 after a 2-2 draw. But Moors lost 1-0 at home to Runcorn in the fourth qualifying round in front of a 780 crowd on October 31st 1981.

Moors could only finish fifth in the table, their lowest position since 1972-73, behind Blyth, Whitby, South Bank and Tow Law, and they were knocked out of the Durham Challenge Cup in the second round by up and coming Peterlee Newtown. They were out of all the cup competitions by the end of January, an embarrassing failure, plus striker Geoff Hart, who had been an integral part of Moors title success, had moved on to Blyth. Was the golden era nearly over?

Certainly, the golden era as regards Northern League championship wins seemed to have gone, as other clubs overtook Moors in season 1982-83. They slipped further behind Blyth in terms of strength, and finished 19 points behind champions Blyth in fifth place. It was Blyth's fourth straight title win.

But they had much better fortune in the cups. They reached the fourth qualifying round of the FA Cup with a good 3-2 away win over Alliance Premier League club Frickley after two draws – Butch Simpson scored the winner in extra time -- but they lost to another Alliance club Scarborough by 4-2 in the last qualifying round, even though they led by a Paul Brown goal at half time.

Because of their lack of progress since the 1978 semi final, Moors lost their exemption to the first round proper of the FA Trophy, and they came into the competition at the third qualifying round against Southport, now in the Northern Premier League. Moors beat them even more comfortably than in their 1975 FA Cup tie, beating them on a frozen pitch by 5-0. Moors, who forced 18 corners in the game, wore Astroturf boots while Southport borrowed footwear from their supporters! After beating Bilston 2-1, Moors lost to a controversial goal in a replay at Telford, claiming handball for the deciding goal. The first game was a 0-0 draw at the Brewery Field, and Paul Brown had Moors in the lead at the Bucks Head before the Alliance Premier League side fought back. Butch Simpson had a testimonial match between past and present Spennymoor sides, the past team winning 4-2.

Moors held an unusual raffle in 1983, the winning prize of which was to start the demolition of the Bessemer Park flats. It was the idea of new club president Ken Newell, who also had the idea of organising another raffle with a car the main prize. The car was taken to several functions and shows during the year, and people from many countries, not just in England, bought tickets. The effort was worthwhile, as several thousand pounds was raised.

The 1982-83 Durham Challenge Cup run

Moors played eight matches to win the Cup, three of them replays.

Paul Main gave them a draw at Durham City in the first round on December 4th 1982, and a week later six different players, including new signings striker Dennis Foster and centre half Jackie Sheekey, scored in the 6-2 replay win at the Brewery Field.

Dennis Foster scored again in the 2-0 win at Washington in the next round, and David Curry scored twice at Chester-le-Street in the 3-0 win after the two teams had drawn 0-0 at the Brewery Field. Moors drew 1-1 in the semi final with Tow Law – Alan "Tinker" Jones scoring – and in the replay, goals by Robin Gill and Kevin Berry put them through to the final.

Peterlee were founder members of the second division and had won the title by three points from Gretna, but they had several players with Northern League experience.

Moors beat Peterlee 2-1 in the final at Darlington on May 18th 1983 with goals by Paul Brown and Jackie Sheekey in the space of five minutes in the second half. Stephen Gilroy replied for Peterlee right at the end

Team; Tommy Fenwick, Derek Watson, Paul Gibbon, David Curry, Paul Brown, Jackie Sheekey, David Hodgson, Robin Gill, Dennis Foster, Kevin Berry, Kenny Heslop. Sub Gerry Johnson. "I knew it wouldn't be easy, and it turned out that way," said Moors chairman Barrie Hindmarch. "The cup

is going home."
But the 1983-84 season was dreadful, Moors' worst for many years. They parted company with John Heaviside on November 12th 1983, and appointed Billy Bell for his second spell as manager. For the first time since 1964, they finished in the bottom half of the Northern League, and were out of all the cups by January 7th. They finished in the bottom half of the table again in 1984-85, lost to Ryhope CA in the first qualifying round of the FA Cup and to Peterlee in the Northern League Cup, but they nearly won the Durham Challenge Cup, losing in a final replay to Bishop Auckland at Shildon.

1984-85 Durham Challenge Cup run

Former Boro player Billy Woof scored one of the goals in the 3-0 win at Billingham Synthonia, and in the second round Micky Bartlett scored in the 4-0 win at Ushaw Moor on a snow-covered pitch. John Grady scored the winner at Chester-le-Street, and he was on target again in the 2-1 semi final win over Sporting Club Vaux.

That set up Moors for a showdown against Bishop Auckland at Shildon on May 6th 1985. Andy Toman put Bishops ahead from the penalty spot after a foul by Robin Gill, and they got a second from Brown. But Moors hit back against the Northern League champions, John Nicholson scored with a powerful shot, and then John Parnaby equalised from a Paul Riley cross.

Team; Kelvin Ross, Robin Gill, Paul Gibbon, Alan Hughes, Tommy Mason, Jackie Sheekey, Arthur Graham, John Nicholson, Paul Riley, Micky Heathcote, Stephen Storey.

Moors took the lead in the replay, Micky Heathcote scoring with a header after 23 minutes, but Andy Toman equalised just before half time, then he scored the winner from the penalty spot after 77 minutes.

Team; Kelvin Ross, Robin Gill, Paul Gibbon, Alan Hughes, Micky Heathcote, Tommy Mason, Arthur Graham, John Nicholson, Paul Riley, John Parnaby, Stephen Storey.

Micky Heathcote, unearthed from junior football, made his debut that season for Moors – he could play both as a defender and a striker -- and was later to play in the Football League for Sunderland, Shrewsbury and Plymouth.

Another defender, Steve Vickers, played some games in 1984-85, before moving on to Tranmere and Middlesbrough. He was

Steve Vickers

transferred for over £1million in his Football League career.
Moors and Bishops met in the Durham Challenge Cup final again the following season – there was a false rumour doing the rounds at the time that the draw was seeded – but again, Bishops came out on top.

1985-86 Durham Challenge Cup run

Moors recorded one of their biggest ever wins as they thrashed South Shields 13-0 in the third round of the Cup. Barrie Fowler scored five of them before half time, the first player to score five in a game since Duggie Humble way back in 1954. Sub Andy Walker came on and scored a second half hat trick. It still wasn't Moors' biggest victory, which was the 19-0 against Eden CW way back in 1937 in the North Eastern League.

The difference in the game, according to the Shields Gazette, was that "Moors were kitted out in Astroturf pimple soled boots which proved to be ideal in the conditions."

Barrie Fowler also scored twice in the 4-1 home win over Ferryhill in the first round, and again in the 3-1 away win at Chester-le-Street the round after. After the hammering of South Shields, Moors beat 1984 winners Coundon Three Tuns 2-1, with newcomer Micky Heathcote and Paul Haley scoring.

Moors lost 3-1 in the final to Bishop Auckland at Shildon on May 5th 1986 in a game interrupted for twenty minutes because of crowd trouble. Mark Lawrence put Bishops ahead after 8 minutes, then former Spennymoor player John Grady got the second from a Colin Barker throw. Barrie Fowler pulled a goal back, but Phil Linacre made it 3-1 from the spot.

Team; Aidan Davison, Robin Gill, Barrie Fowler, Jackie Sheekey, Tommy Mason, Arthur Graham, Ian Mohan, Stephen Storey, Gary Lowes, Wayne Dobson, Paul Haley. Subs Kevin Dinning, Glen Dixon.

But the Durham Challenge Cup run simply glossed over another poor season, Moors finishing a lowly 14th in the table, their third successive finish below halfway.

Northern League secretary Gordon Nicholson helped to clear the snow from the Brewery Field, and the match against Billingham Town on February 22nd 1986 was given the thumbs up by referee David Oliver. Moors won the game 4-1, with new signing Paul Haley from Tow Law scoring on his debut.

The 1986-87 season, under new manager Tony Monkhouse, was much better than the previous three years. Moors put together a long unbeaten run of 22 matches which lifted them into third place in the Northern League, behind Blyth and Bishop Auckland, plus they had two good cup runs.

The 1986-87 FA Cup run

Moors reached the competition proper for the first time since 1977, but they were denied by one of football's great entertainers.

Forward Dennis Foster returned to Moors after a spell at Crook, and scored one of the goals in the 2-0 win at Tow Law, and then he scored a hat trick inside 15 minutes when Moors beat Evenwood 5-0. Midfielder Ian Mohan clinched the win over Peterlee in the third qualifying round, then Dennis Foster and Barrie Fowler scored a goal apiece in the 2-0 fourth qualifying round win over Scottish club Gretna – who in 2006 reached the Scottish FA Cup final!

Frank Worthington

Moors were given a home tie on November 15th 1986 against Fourth Division Tranmere, who were then managed by former Leicester and England striker Frank Worthington. By then, the changing rooms had been moved into the old tea hut in the corner of the ground, because the old Catterick Racecourse stand had been condemned following the Bradford fire disaster just a few months earlier. Tranmere refused to play under the Brewery Field floodlights, so the game had to kick off at 2pm, and chairman Barrie Hindmarch said; "The fact that they refuse to, suggests that they're not confident of playing us."

Rothmans, the club sponsors, nearly fell foul of the cigarette advertising laws on television. Barrie said: "When we agreed the sponsorship deal with Rothmans, they stipulated that we mustn't allow the name Rothmans to be shown on television. I must admit, that I forgot to tell our kit man, and on the day, the television cameras showed our players walking down the steps onto the pitch wearing the Rothmans shirts.

"Sure enough, Monday morning, the phone rang first thing, and it was Rothmans wondering if we still wanted the sponsorship deal. Fortunately, I calmed them down, apologised, said it was my fault, and changed the style of the logo on the shirts. Rothmans were fantastic sponsors for the club and the end of their sponsorship when the factory closed was a factor in the club's financial struggles later."

Barrie Fowler headed Moors into the lead from a Paul Bryson free kick, but Fourth Division Tranmere levelled from an Ian Muir penalty after a blatant handball by Micky Heathcote – he pushed the ball over the bar -- and Muir scored another penalty following a foul by Marc Irwin, although the Spennymoor defender protested his innocence. Moors levelled just 40 seconds into the second half through Ian Mohan, but Muir pounced to

Robin Gill (left), Jackie Sheekey (centre) and Micky Heathcote (right)

score his hat trick with a low shot after a mistake in the Moors defence. Spennymoor manager Tony Monkhouse said: "Our lads did us proud. They battled well but luck was against them and they gave away three bad goals."
The team; Aidan Davison, Robin Gill, Marc Irwin, Ian Mohan, Micky Heathcote, Jackie Sheekey, Stephen Gilroy, Paul Bryson, Barrie Fowler, Dennis Foster, Tommy Mason. Sub; Arthur Graham.
Aidan Davison later signed for Billingham Synthonia after refusing to sign a new contract, and went on to play over 300 games in the Football League for several different clubs.

Aidan Davison

The 1986-87 Northern League cup

Moors won their fifth Northern League Cup, beating Easington 2-1 in the final at Shildon. Easington had just been promoted from the Second Division in the previous season.
Centre half Micky Heathcote scored twice in the 3-1 win at Bedlington, then Dennis Foster scored from the spot to give Moors a good win at their old foes Blyth in the second round.
Former Tow Law winger Stephen Storey scored both goals in the quarter final win at Brandon, and he also got the only goal of the game at home to Chester-le-Street in the semi final.
In the final at Shildon, Dennis Foster put Moors into the lead with a second minute penalty, and they missed several chances to increase the lead before Dave Evans equalised for Easington in injury time at the end of the 90 minutes. But Barrie Fowler got the winner early in extra time.
Team; Aidan Davison, Robin Gill, Tommy Mason, Ian Mohan, Micky

Heathcote, Marc Irwin, Stephen Storey, Paul Bryson, Barrie Fowler, Dennis Foster, Gary Lowes. Subs; Andy Nobbs, John Tweedy.

Dennis Foster cracked a hat trick against Blyth as Moors ran riot in a 6-1 win at the Brewery Field on October 18th 1986, spurred on by a less than complimentary remark that he resembled "The Fridge", the nickname for a huge American footballer at the time.

Moors won the Northern League curtain raiser for the 1987-88 season, the Cleator Cup, by 3-1 against Blyth at Croft Park on Tuesday August 11th 1987, Paul Bryson, Barrie Fowler and Stephen Storey scored the Moors goals. It was Micky Heathcote's last game before his five figure transfer to Sunderland, who were then in the old Third Division.

But they didn't get close to any more silverware. They only finished midtable in the Northern League, lost to Whitley Bay early in the Northern League Cup, and were beaten by South Bank just as early in the FA Cup.

They had a good run in the Durham Challenge Cup, and in their second round replay against Billingham Synthonia, keeper Kenny Dodds scored the winning penalty in the shootout. They eventually lost 3-2 at Bishop Auckland after extra time in the semi final.

Moors had their best run for nine years in the FA Trophy, before going out 3-0 at Isthmian League Wokingham in the third round on February 13th 1988. Tony Monkhouse said; "We froze. Their aerial power was too much for us."

The ground was situated below the flight path to Heathrow airport, and during the game, one Moors player – who'd best be nameless – stopped running, pointed skywards and said to a teammate; "Is that Concorde?"

Moors sold midfielder Neil Wilson to a Belgian club in 1988. Newcastle had signed the player once for £500, but chairman Barrie Hindmarch returned the cheque. "I sent them a note saying that they must need the money more than we did. He was worth more than that, considering what we'd already spent on him.

"He went to a Belgian club for £5,000, and to be honest, I couldn't get his clearance faxed quick enough. The daft thing was, that his contract would have run out in a few weeks, and they could have got him for nothing!"

By then, the face of the Northern League was beginning to change. Bishop Auckland, Whitley Bay and North Shields all left to join the pyramid, of which the Northern League weren't members, and Moors were getting itchy feet. "Ideally, we would like to be part of the pyramid through the Northern League, but if there is no change of policy soon, we will make the same move as Bishop Auckland and Whitley Bay in the near future. After spending £250,000 improving facilities, it is the only course open to us," Barrie said at the time.

The Northern League voted to join the pyramid in 1990, but wanted to feed into the Vauxhall Conference, alongside the Northern Premier League, and a stalemate ensued. Moors could wait no longer, and they submitted their resignation from the league.

Barrie said at the time: "We feel that after nine months no progress has been made as a body. We have been keen on the pyramid for a number of years, and we see it as the way forward for non league football. In recent years, the league's ambition has not matched our own, with too much consideration being given to the small thinking of certain clubs whose ambition goes no further than Scotch Corner. One of our fans said that the Northern League is getting left behind, and is trying to gatecrash a New Year's Eve party at four in the morning."

However, there were no vacancies in the Northern Premier League – of which Bishop Auckland and Whitley Bay were members -- so instead Moors applied for the Northern Counties East League, of which North Shields were also members.

The Northern League AGM, ironically, was held in the Brewery Field clubhouse – it had been arranged well before Moors announced their resignation – and Barrie was obliged to leave his own clubhouse when the club's resignation was officially accepted.

However, just as they were way back in 1960 after the ill-fated Midland League years, Moors were then in limbo, because it was still possible that the Northern Counties East League wouldn't accept them, but their gamble paid off when they were admitted at a meeting in Worsbrough Bridge in June 1990.

The club played its last Northern League game against Billingham Synthonia on April 27th 1990, and lost 2-0. The team; Geoff Ward, Geoff Young, Michael Connor, Billy Lees, Jackie Sheekey, Gary Lowes, Ian Potts, Jason Ainsley, Paul Ross, David Ross, Stephen Storey. Subs; Peter Johnson , Paul Cooper.

Jason Ainsley was signed from Guisborough Town juniors by manager Ray Gowan, and would go on to be a popular and long serving player in three different leagues as well as becoming manager in May 2007.

Strangely, in the reverse fixture between Moors and Synthonia earlier in the season, three referees officiated. The game started with Eric Pickersgill in charge, but he was injured, so senior linesman Ken Gilpin from Whitby took over. However, Mr Gilpin declined to continue at half time, claiming verbal abuse from the touchline, and he was replaced by John Baronowski, the junior linesman.

The 1990-91 season began by Royal appointment, when Moors played a pre-season friendly against the Coldstream Guards at Buckingham Palace.

They had played Uxbridge in another friendly the previous night. Their first game in the Northern Counties East League, which was sponsored by the Weekly Wynner newspaper at the time, was at Guiseley, who were then managed by Frank Worthington on August 25th 1990. Moors couldn't have got off to a better start in their new surroundings, winning 3-1, with goals by David Ross, John Elliott and Gary Robinson.

The team was; Steve Toth, Ian Potts, Andrew Strong, Gary Robinson, Ged Hartley, John Elliott, Jason Ainsley, Derek Ord, Gary Boagey, David Ross, Stephen Storey. Subs; David Gray, Don Peattie.

Moors were distracted from their new venture by becoming the first team from the Northern Counties East League to reach the first round of the FA Cup.

The FA Cup run 1990-91

Moors started with a game in the first qualifying round on 15th September 1990 against Stockton, who switched the game to the Brewery Field because of development work. Gary Boagey scored both goals for Moors in the 2-0 win.

Moors had to come from a goal down at half time to beat Esh Winning in the next round, with Stephen Storey, Micky Sell and Jason Ainsley scoring. Jason scored again, along with Don Peattie, in the 2-0 home win over Northallerton, which set them up for a very difficult away tie at Northwich Victoria from the GM Vauxhall Conference.

But Moors caused an upset by drawing 1-1 at the Drill Field, Micky Sell equalising from a Stephen Storey pass. "I believe we didn't give a good account of ourselves, even though we drew," said Moors boss Ray Gowan. Moors went behind again in the replay at the Brewery Field on October 31st 1990 to a Paul Maguire goal, but they equalised after a long spell of pressure through Paul Ross six minutes from the end. Vics then had two players sent off, before Matthew Hanchard headed into his own goal in the last minute of extra time to put Moors into the first round proper against Fourth Division Chesterfield at Saltergate.

In front of a big and good humoured visiting contingent, Chesterfield took an early lead, but Don Peattie equalised after John Elliott's shot was blocked. However, by half time Chesterfield moved up a gear and went 3-1 up, but the second half saw a Moors revival, with Gary Boagey pulling one back with a left foot shot from the corner of the box – some of the 500 or so Spennymoor fans at the game thought it was one of Moors' best ever goals. Try as they might and dominating possession, Moors couldn't force an equaliser, and they fully deserved the standing ovation by the fans from both clubs. There was plenty of honour in defeat.

The team; Steve Toth, Ian Potts, Colin Blackburn, Gary Robinson, Ged Hartley, John Elliott, Jason Ainsley, Don Peattie (sub Paul Ross), Gary Boagey, Derek Ord, Stephen Storey.

However, the league season didn't go as well, and a 2-1 home defeat against Guiseley on April 3rd 1991 put them out of the running. They finished third, behind champions Guiseley and their old Northern League friends North Shields.

Moors sampled the big time on Monday August 19th 1991 when one of the most famous clubs in the world, Manchester United, came to the Brewery Field to officially open the new stand.

The link was manager Ray Gowan, who had forged a relationship with United when he had sold winger Paul Dalton from Brandon to the Old Trafford giants three years earlier. The crowd of 2,550 weren't to know it then, but a little known youngster called Ryan Giggs in the United team was going to be a huge star.

Spennymoor United v Manchester United, 19th August 1991.
Spennymoor Utd back row: G. Boagey, T. Mason, K. Dinning, M. Wilson, P. Owers, D. Ross, S. Pidgeon, G. Dobson, G. Walton. Front: C. Blackburn, N. Hoban, J. Ainsley, G. Corkain, C. Wrigglesworth (mascot), B. Liddle, G. Hartley.

Man Utd back row: M. Gordon, N. Whitworth, B. Carey, J. Leighton, J. Lydiate, G. Pallister, L. Martin, D. Brazil, S. McAuley. Front: R. Giggs, M. Robins, P. Wratten, R. Beardsmore, P. Sixsmith, K. Toal.

United won the game 3-1, with goals by England international Gary Pallister – who played in midfield -- Mark Robins and Lee Martin. Moors presented United with a plaque to commemorate their visit, and the memento is now on display in the museum at Old Trafford.

The teams; Spennymoor; Phil Owers (sub Martin Wilson), Neil Hoban, Bryan Liddle, Tommy Mason, Ged Hartley (sub Steve Pidgeon), Glen Corkain, Jason Ainsley, Ged Dobson, Kevin Dinning, Gary Walton (sub Frank Robinson), Colin Blackburn.

Manchester United; Jim Leighton, Lee Martin, Shaun McAuley, Paul Wratten, Brian Carey, Gary Pallister, Russell Beardsmore, Jason Lydiate, Mark Robins, Ryan Giggs, Paul Sixsmith. Subs; Neil Whitworth, Derek Brazil, Mark Gordon, Keiren Toal.

Jim Leighton, the Scottish international keeper, took out his dentures in order to eat his post match meal – then a photographer suddenly took his photograph. "You should have seen the look on his face – he was like Dracula," said one fan.

But there was soon to be something tasty that the Spennymoor fans could well and truly get their teeth into.

Jim Leighton

Chapter Ten

The return of the prodigal

The prodigal son, Mattie Pearson, returned to the club for the third time in November 1991.
Mattie, a tough and nippy midfielder, had already enjoyed two spells at the club during which he had picked up several Northern League and cup winners' medals, and indeed he was one of the club's youngest players when he made his debut at the age of 16 at Crook in 1975.
In between successful spells in Australia, he came back to Moors, but resisted the temptation for a third time, preferring to play and then manage Ferryhill. But when the call came from chairman Barrie Hindmarch to take over as manager from Ray Gowan, he didn't need much persuasion.
The club made its move with Moors lagging thirteen points behind the early leaders in the Northern Counties East League table, so they replaced Ray with Mattie on November 27th 1991 – a move that proved to be a major turning point. Ray briefly became general manager, but quit three weeks later; "I don't like the way things have worked out," he said.
Mattie brought in several new players from his previous club Ferryhill and started to build a team that would win promotion. There was a touch of understatement in Mattie's first programme notes for the game against Glasshoughton on December 14th 1991, when he wrote; "Even if the gamble doesn't pay off, at least we will be able to say that we gave it a go."
Unfortunately, Moors never threatened runaway leaders North Shields that season, and they finished in fifth place, a mammoth 37 points behind.
Moors were kicked out of the Durham Challenge Cup in December for playing an ineligible player, Colin Blackburn, in the 3-3 draw with Murton. The 1992 close season saw Mattie aim for the quality players which he believed would win promotion, and he signed highly rated pair Brian Healy and Craig Veart from Gateshead.
The season started well, and Moors won every game they played in league and cup competitions, a run of ten matches, until they were thumped 7-0 at home by Gateshead in the third qualifying round of the FA Cup on October 10th 1992.
They had a good win in the FA Trophy by 6-2 in the third qualifying round

Spennymoor United, 1992-93. Back row: D. Beamson (Com.Man.), D. Heads. A. Nichol, D. Bostock, J. Nutt (Asst.Sec.), T. Ardle (Groundsman), B. Anderson, J. Norman (V.Chair), I. Thompson, B. Maughan, S. Barrass, P. Coombes, M. Whitehouse (Comm.Man.). Middle: J. Lumley (Physio), T. Bainbridge, A. Shaw, G. Powell, B. Healy (Capt.), G. NcNarey, B. Richardson, K. Gorman, G. Cowell, G. Ramshaw, S. Cuthbert, D. Barton (Asst.Man.). Front: R. Petitjean, T. Mason, M. Pearson (Manager), T. Beaumont (President), B. Hindmarch (Chair), J. Hindmarch (Sec.), L. Tucker, M. Hewitt, I. Bellamy, M. Seymour.

at Emley who were two leagues above them at the time and Moors reached a century of goals in all competitions when Keith Gorman scored in the 2-1 home defeat by Boston in the FA Trophy first round on January 5th 1993. However, the cup competitions were always secondary, as promotion was by far the top priority.

Moors were top of the table at Christmas, and gave themselves some breathing space when they beat closest challengers Pickering 5-0 on February 17th 1993, but they started to wobble when they lost the reverse game 2-0 at Pickering six weeks later. They played badly in a 2-0 defeat at Liversedge, but they just managed to recover and eventually they picked up the point they needed in a nail-biting goalless draw at the Brewery Field against Winterton to pip Pickering on goal difference on the last day of the season. Mattie, who played in the game, said: "We were very nervous and very uptight, and tried to settle the players before the game." It was the first time in the club's history Moors had won any sort of promotion.

Moors made it a league and cup double when they also picked up the League Cup – after they had won the title of course.

Northern Counties East League Cup run 1992-93

Moors were behind in the first three ties. They comfortably won 6-1 at First Division Selby Town in the first round, with Steve Cuthbert and Brian

Healy both scoring two apiece. For the second game in a row, Moors went behind, this time against Maltby, but won 4-1, "Snapper" Shaw scoring twice.

Moors beat Stocksbridge in the semi final 2-1 after the visitors took an early lead, "Snapper" and Marty Hewitt scoring.

Moors won the Cup on May 4th 1993 when they beat Thackley in the final at Ossett Town. "Snapper" put Moors into the lead, and even though Thackley equalised when they were down to ten men, Mattie Pearson fittingly crowned the promotion-winning season when he cracked the winner with a volley from outside the box.

Team; Gareth McNary, Mattie Pearson, Lee Tucker, Terry Bainbridge, Gordon Ramshaw, Brian Healy, Craig Veart, Jason Ainsley, Andrew Shaw, Marty Hewitt, Gary Cowell.

Keith Gorman, who didn't play in that game, ended the season as the club's top scorer with 33 goals. In total, Moors scored 168 goals in all competitions.

The 1993-94 season was probably the best season in terms of success and excitement for sixteen years. With a strengthened squad, Moors launched an attack on several fronts. "Our first target is to win the Northern Premier League First Division," said Barrie Hindmarch.

Before the season got under way, long serving full back Tommy Mason was

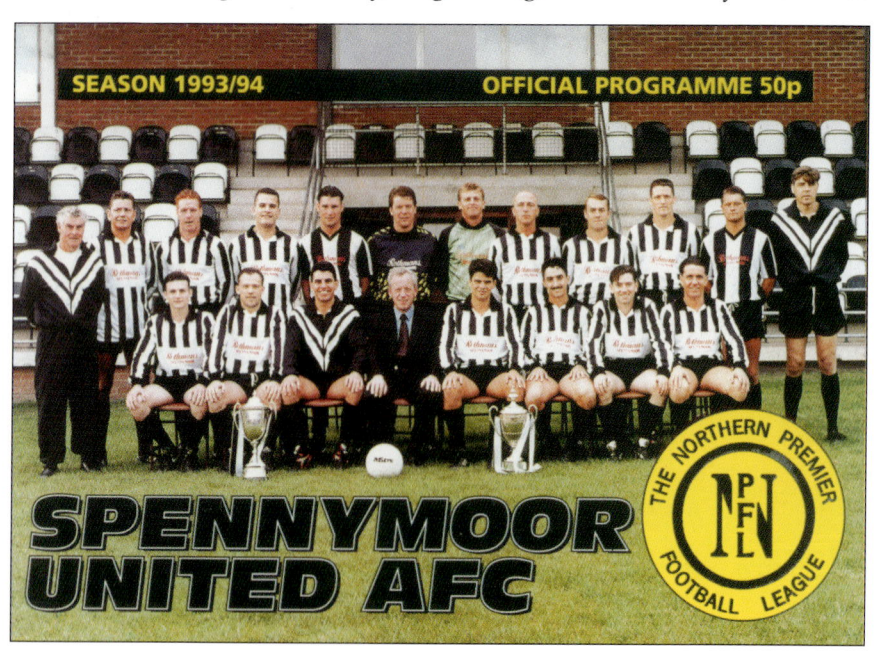

The return of the prodigal

given a testimonial against Newcastle United, Moors winning 2-0 with Craig Veart and Barry Wardrobe scoring the goals. Steve Harper, Robbie Elliott and Liam O'Brien were in the Newcastle team.

Moors however, lost their first Northern Premier League game, to a last minute goal by 2-1 at home to Warrington Town, summer signing John Cooke putting Moors ahead.

Team; Gareth McNary, Dean Gibb, Ralph Petitjean, Kenny Goodrick, Gary Powell, John Cooke, Craig Veart, Jason Ainsley (sub Lee Tucker), Andrew Shaw, Barry Wardrobe (sub Marty Hewitt), Brian Healy.

Moors lost their next two games as well, but then they won 2-0 at Bamber Bridge on September 4th 1993, with goals by Brian Healy and Craig Veart. Mattie also made another new signing who would play a major part in the club's fortunes, former Newcastle centre half Wes Saunders. But on his debut he was pressed into service as an emergency keeper at Bamber Bridge because Gareth McNary suffered a head injury. Wes had endured five knee operations, and pointed out; "I find it very difficult coming downstairs on a Sunday morning after a game."

The team blended together, and by the end of November was on top of the table. On New Year's Day 1994, another Moors keeper, Marc Hopkinson, went off injured when Moors were losing 3-1 against Workington, but defender Gary Powell went in goal and helped Moors to a 5-3 win.

Mattie won the divisional manager of the month award for two successive months as Moors stormed up the table and advanced in the cups with a 23 game unbeaten run, which ended with a 3-2 defeat at Ashton United in the First Division Cup on February 7th 1994. They still put together an unbeaten 17 game run in the league, but had a nervous end to the season, especially when Brian Healy was sent off for having a heated row with team mate Keith Gorman at Congleton.

The season climaxed with a promotion decider against Ashton United at the Brewery Field on the last day of the season. A draw was enough for Ashton, but Moors needed all three points.

For a long time in the game, it looked as if Ashton were going up as they led with a 12th minute goal, but Moors came storming back in the last fifteen minutes. Keith Gorman glanced in the equaliser from a right wing cross, then Snapper Shaw scored another header. And the Brewery Field was rocking right at the end when Keith Gorman fired in the third. Mattie said: "The players did fantastic in the last few weeks of the season. Not only were some physically tired, they were mentally tired too. It has been a magnificent achievement to win two cups and promotion."

Team; Adrian Swan, Richie Watson, Ralph Petitjean, Paul Harnett (Sub Andrew Fletcher), Wes Saunders, Dean Gibb (sub Gordon Ramshaw),

Moors clinch it!

Northern Premier League

THREE goals in a pulsating last 15 minutes earned Spennymoor promotion for the second successive season in front of a four figure crowd at the Brewery Field.

Moors' hopes of going into the Premier Division seemed dead as Ashton United led by a single goal, but the match turned completely in an amazing last quarter of an hour.

Victory means Moors will join former Northern League colleagues Bishop Auckland and Whitley Bay in the top division next season.

But as well as clinching promotion, they have lifted the Durham Challenge Cup and NPL Cup to complete probably their best campaign.

Manager Mattie Pearson said: "The players have done fantastic this season, especially in these last few weeks. At times, not only were some physically tired, they were mentally tired too. It has been a magnificent achievement to win two cups and promotion."

Ashton took the lead after only 12 minutes, when Adrian Swan could only push a shot from Mark Edwards on to the post for Andy Whittaker to put it home.

The tension seemed to be getting to Moors until the 75th minute, when Craig Veart crossed for Keith Gorman to score with a glancing header.

Moors then took control, and nine minutes later Richie Watson broke down the right and crossed for Andy Shaw to head in.

Shaw then hit the post but the celebrations started when Veart split the defence again with a diagonal ball for Gorman to fire

■ GOING UP: Spennymoor's John Cook rise

Moors on the up – confirmed

Non-League Football
By RAY SIMPSON

SPENNYMOOR United have been told that their promotion to the Premier Division of the Northern Premier League is safe.

Moors finished second in the First Division after beating Ashton United on a memorable last day of the season, and have already started planning for the new campaign.

But there were misgivings at the weekend, when it was learned that Leek Town may not be given a GM Vauxhall Conference place because they have failed to meet financial criteria. And with Witton Albion relegated into the NPL, there could be 23 clubs in the Premier Division.

Moors chairman Barrie Hindmarch said: "We have been told that we are a promoted club, and will be treated as such. We will not be denied promotion."

Newspaper cuttings from when Spennymoor United clinched promotion to the Premier Division of the Northern Premier League.

Gary Powell, John Cooke, Keith Gorman, Andrew Shaw, Craig Veart. Together with the League Cup and Durham Challenge Cup, Moors sealed a magnificent season by winning three honours in the space of ten make-or-break days, and scored 159 goals in total for the season.

The Northern Premier League Cup run 1993-94

In the first round on October 23rd 1993, Moors completed a hat trick of early season victories over Bamber Bridge by beating the Lancashire club 3-1, with goals by Gary Cowell (2) and John Cooke.

They pulled off a big shock in the second round, defeating title chasing Marine from the Premier Division by 3-0, with goals by Brian Healy, Jason Ainsley and "Snapper" Shaw. Marine would go on to win the league, but were unable to take promotion to the Conference because their ground wasn't up to standard.

John Cooke

Moors then beat another Premier Division side, Whitley Bay, by 2-1 despite having Wes Saunders dismissed for swearing at the referee when Moors were a goal down. Craig Veart and Keith Gorman, with a penalty, scored in the second half. Wes had served his suspension by the time they played their traditional rivals Bishop Auckland in the quarter final at Kingsway, and he scored a late winner to give Moors a 2-1 win.

Moors were underdogs against Accrington Stanley in the semi final, but they beat them 3-1 in the first leg at the Brewery Field even though Snapper Shaw missed two penalties. Andy Fletcher (2) and Jason Ainsley scored. Moors more than held their own in the second leg, and did even better, winning 4-1 with goals by Brian Healy, Snapper Shaw, Andy Fletcher and Mick Holmes.

Moors were superb in the final, beating Premier Division Hyde United by 3-1 on April 28th 1994, even though Craig Veart was sent off just before the break. Keith Gorman scored from a Wes Saunders pass after three minutes, and after Hyde equalised, Brian Healy beat two men and restored Moors' lead. Snapper Shaw scored from a Craig Veart free kick before half time.

Moors beat five Premier Division clubs on their way to winning the competition, an achievement unsurpassed before or since.

Team; John Hopper, Ritchie Watson, Ralph Petitjean, Micky Holmes (sub Paul Harnett), Wes Saunders, Brian Healy, Gary Powell, John Cooke, Keith Gorman (sub Andy Fletcher), Andrew Shaw, Craig Veart.

The Durham Challenge Cup run 1993-94

Moors started with an easy win in the first round, by 4-0 over Herrington, with Keith Gorman (2), Snapper Shaw and John Cooke scoring, and in the second round they were behind twice at Billingham Synthonia before a late Craig Veart lob won the game for them.

They ran riot in the third round at home to Billingham Town, winning 8-3 with John Cooke and Snapper Shaw both scoring hat tricks – ironically Moors signed Billingham Town keeper Adrian Swann after the game -- and they had another comfortable win, by 4-0, at Northern League Shildon, then managed by former Spennymoor boss Ray Gowan. Former Boro player Billy Askew scored direct from a corner for one of the goals.

The final against Bishop Auckland on May 2nd 1994 in front of 1,100 at Darlington will be remembered for a magnificent overhead kick by Brian Healy from a cross by John Cooke that won the Cup for Moors in extra time by 3-2. Gary Cowell put Moors ahead from a Craig Veart flick, but Bishops hit back. Moors thought they'd won the cup with eight minutes left in normal time when Craig Veart curled in a free kick, but Bishops forced extra time.

Team; Barry Richardson, Richie Watson, Ralph Petitjean, Gary Cowell (sub Kevin Bush), Wes Saunders, Brian Healy, Gary Powell, John Cooke, Keith Gorman, Marty Hewitt (sub Gordon Ramshaw), Craig Veart.

Moors also had a good run in the FA Trophy, beating Northern League Stockton 3-0 and Hyde United 2-1 before going out in the second round by 2-1 to Conference club Halifax Town in front of a crowd of 1,426.

Unfortunately, the team started to break up the following season. Midfielder Jason Ainsley eventually went to Fourth Division Hartlepool United for £5,000, the fee decided by a Football League tribunal. Hartlepool had offered a pre-season friendly, but chairman Barrie Hindmarch said: "The receipts would come nowhere near what we want for a player who has been outstanding for us."

As League Cup winners, Moors lost the pre-season Northern Premier League challenge Shield on August 13th 1994 against champions Marine by 3-0, but three days later they won the briefly-revived Durham Benevolent Bowl 3-1 against Bishop Auckland with goals by Dave Robson, Richie Alderson and Brian Healy. Eight players were booked in the game, so rivalries weren't exactly set aside.

Moors picked up their momentum again in the league, and stayed in the top half of the table, but well behind runaway leaders Marine. They eventually finished sixth, level on points with Boston, but 27 behind Marine. That was the standard they would have to match if they wanted to progress any higher.

The 1994-95 FA Cup run

Moors started in the first qualifying round with a 4-1 home win over Shildon on September 10th 1994, Steve Cuthbert scoring twice.

Graham Kelly, who was secretary of the FA at the time, was an interested spectator at Moors' tie at home to Consett in the second qualifying round. Chairman Barrie Hindmarch said: "He stood on the terraces for most of the game, despite the rain. He enjoyed the banter with the locals." Wonder what some of the characters of the terraces said to him? Keith Gorman, Brian Healy and John Cooke were the scorers.

Moors then needed two attempts to see off Northern League Tow Law. After a 0-0 draw at Ironworks Road, Moors won the replay 2-1 thanks to an extra time goal by Snapper Shaw after Keith Gorman had equalised just four minutes from the end of normal time.

Moors were drawn at Accrington Stanley in the fourth qualifying round, but for the second season running, they beat them, this time with an "audacious" goal by Brian Healy with five minutes left when he ran through and chipped the keeper. "It was an amazing goal, I don't think anybody else would have attempted what he did," said manager Mattie Pearson.

Moors' reward was an away trip to Wigan, who were then in the Fourth Division, on November 12th 1994, but on a heavy pitch, they lost 4-0. Keith Gorman and Kenny Goodrick both had efforts saved in the opening minutes, but Wigan went 3-0 up before half time in front of a crowd of 2,183.

Keith Gorman evades a Wigan challenge on the water sodden pitch.

Team; Gareth McNary, John Tinkler, Ralph Petitjean, Ritchie Watson, Wes Saunders, Phil Mason, Dave Robson, Kenny Goodrick, Andrew Shaw, Keith Gorman, Craig Veart. Subs not used; Gary Cowell, Gary Powell, Adrian Swann.

The 1994-95 Durham Challenge Cup run

Moors started the defence of the Cup with a 4-1 away win at Evenwood, who took a first minute lead, but John Cooke, Dave Robson, Snapper Shaw and Keith Gorman scored for Moors, and then they hit six past West Auckland in the second round, Snapper scoring two of them. Snapper, Kenny Goodrick and Dave Robson all scored in the last fifteen minutes to give Moors a 3-0 win at Eppleton in the quarter final.

Moors left it even later in the semi final against Billingham Synthonia. They trailed 1-0 until the last ten minutes, when Snapper and Keith Gorman scored. Moors included defender Gary Coatsworth, who had won promotion with Leicester City and Darlington, in their squad.

Coatsworth, along with another former Darlington player Mark Sunley, both played in the final on April 17th 1995 for strong favourites Moors against South Shields from the Northern League second division, but the game finished 1-1. Moors missed a hatful of chances before Dave Robson put them in the lead, but former Spennymoor player Steve Pidgeon equalised – hence the Northern Echo headline "Pidgeon's late swoop punishes slack Moors."

Pidgeon's late swoop punishes slack Moors

Team; Adrian Swann, Gary O'Hara, Wes Saunders, Ritchie Watson, Gary Coatsworth, Brian Healy, Kenny Goodrick, John Cooke, Mark Sunley (Sub Dave Robson), Keith Gorman (sub Gary Cowell), Craig Veart.

The crowd for that game was 580, but there was 850 in Filtrona Park for the replay, which Moors won 3-0 on May 1st 1995. Keith Gorman broke through on 55 minutes, then Richie Alderson scored the second from a Dave Robson pass. Snapper Shaw curled in the third.

Moors also reached the semi final of the Presidents Cup against Lancaster

City, but after pulling the aggregate scores level to 3-3 at the Brewery Field, they lost to a second half goal.

Moors had a ground inspection carried out by the Vauxhall Conference officials on 27th November 1994, and were told their biggest job was to increase the seated capacity of the main stand from 296 to at least 400.

Moors played their first ever game on an artificial surface on Boxing Day 1994 at Hyde United, where they drew 1-1. Moors prepared for the game by training on an artificial surface at Coxhoe Sports Centre.

Moors didn't improve on their league position in season 1995-96, and they had to be happy with ninth place. Their cause wasn't helped by a flare up between Jason Ainsley and Wes Saunders in the game at Droylsden, which resulted in Jason being sent off. "I have told them both that their wage packet will be considerably lighter this week," said manager Mattie Pearson.

However, Moors were left kicking themselves in the FA Cup, and they missed an excellent chance of progressing past the first round.

The 1995-96 FA Cup run

Brian Healy scored the only goal at Glasshoughton in the first qualifying round, and then they had a good 4-2 second qualifying round win at Workington, with Brian amongst the goals again. New signing Anthony Skedd also scored one.

Brian maintained his record of scoring every round up to that point by scoring twice against Billingham Town in an easy 6-1 win in the third qualifying round. Keith Gorman, on his return from injury, came on as a sub against Lancaster City in the fourth qualifying round and he scored the winner with just seconds to spare with a shot that went in off the post.

To their initial disappointment, Moors were given a home tie on November 11th 1995 in the first round proper against fellow Northern Premier League side Colwyn Bay, but they saw the tie as a chance to progress into the second round because they had already beaten their opponents previously that season.

But it wasn't to be, as the Welshmen came out on top by a second half goal, after Brian Healy had put a penalty high and wide. "We're disappointed that we didn't win," said Mattie Pearson. "The penalty was a golden opportunity for us." But overall, Moors just couldn't get going on a wet and windy day.

Team; Adrian Swann, Gary O'Hara, Anthony Skedd, Gary Coatsworth, Wes Saunders, Brian Healy, Richie Alderson, Jason Ainsley, Keith Gorman, Lee Ludlow, Craig Veart. 18 members of the newly-formed Spennymoor United Support club travelled from Macroom, near Cork in Ireland for the game.

Jason Ainsley had spent a season at Hartlepool and then had played in Australia before returning to the Brewery Field.

The 1995-96 Durham Challenge Cup run

Moors just scraped past Wearside League club Birtley in the first round on October 31st 1995, beating them 3-2 with goals by Richie Alderson (2) and Gary Cowell, then in the second round they beat South Shields, their opponents in the previous year's final by 3-0, with Lee Ludlow (2) and Brian Healy scoring. New signing Steve Osbourne, who replaced the departed Keith Gorman, scored one of the goals at Tow Law in the 2-0 win in the following round.

Jason Ainsley

Snapper Shaw scored the only goal of the game against Northern League Dunston in the semi final, to set Moors up for a final against Durham City on their opponents' ground on May 6th 1996. Moors missed several good chances, but they broke through just before the end of extra time when Gary Coatsworth nodded down a left wing cross for recent signing Lee Innes to sidefoot in.

Team; Adrian Swann, Gary Coatsworth, Craig Veart, Ralph Petitjean, Wes Saunders, Brian Healy, Jason Ainsley (sub Gary Cowell), Andrew Shaw, Lee Innes, Anthony Skedd (sub Steve Osbourne). Subs not used; Ritchie Watson, Mattie Pearson.

Moors had a good run in the League Cup, beating Bishop Auckland 3-1 in a second round replay and Emley 5-0, but they lost 3-0 at Boston in the quarter final.

Former chairman Jackie "Tiny" Smith passed away at the age of 83 in February 1996. Jackie played in the Football League for Gateshead, Barnsley and Plymouth Argyle before the war, and on his return to the north east, he was a committee man at the Brewery Field from 1946, and chairman from 1963 to 1979. "Jackie was the sort of man who could never have had an enemy," said Barrie Hindmarch.

In comparison to previous seasons, Moors had a poor season in 1996-97, and finished fifth from bottom in the Northern Premier League Premier Division, but were never in any real danger of being sucked into the relegation fight. However, the financial danger signs were looming, as Moors' income had decreased drastically, partly due to the impact of the National Lottery and reduced income from the clubhouse. The Lottery wiped out the club's successful letter draw, which was bringing in £30,000 per year. Barrie Hindmarch said prophetically in the Northern Echo in December 1996; "Unless clubs can get a constant source of income to sustain the level at which they play, then there's no future."

They were hoping for a prize money boost from the last qualifying round of the FA Cup to which they had exemption, but after a 2-2 draw with Southport at the Brewery Field – Lee Innes scored twice -- they lost the replay 2-1.

The team started to break up during the season. Jason Ainsley went to Singapore, Brian Healy put in a transfer request, then Wes Saunders was released for disciplinary reasons after refusing to be a sub at Knowsley.

Bishop Auckland beat Moors 2-0 in the FA Trophy in January 18th 1997 – their first win over the Moors in nine years – and just to prove that the hoodoo was really broken, Moors lost to them in the Durham Challenge Cup final at Durham City.

Bishops end Moors' Durham Cup reign

Durham Challenge Cup run 1996-97

Moors started with a comfortable 5-0 away win at Whickham, with Snapper Shaw scoring two of the goals, then he did the same again in the 3-0 away win at Jarrow Roofing in the second round. Jason Ainsley scored from the edge of the box against Consett in the quarter final – one of his last appearances before leaving for the far east – and in the semi final against Murton, Snapper scored another two in the 3-1 win.

That set up Moors, winners for the previous three years, for a final showdown at Durham City against their old foes Bishop Auckland on March 31st 1997, and for the second time in a cup competition that season, Bishops came out on top, this time by 2-0 with goals by David Bayles and Lee Ellison.

Team; Adrian Swann, Andy Purvis (sub Dion Raitt), Graham Pepper, Kevin Todd, Graham Paxton, Ritchie Watson, Ritchie Alderson, Gary O'Hara, Mark Sunley, Gary Cowell, Craig Veart (sub Andy Elliott). Former Newcastle midfielder Kevin Todd replaced Dave Barton as assistant manager midway through the season.

It was Moors' first defeat in the competition since they'd lost to Chester-le-Street in the second round on January 20th 1993, a run of twenty matches. It was also part of a dismal end of season run that saw them lose their last eleven straight matches in league and cup.

*Spennymoor United 0 Bishop Auckland 2.
Durham Challenge Cup Final, March 31st 1997.
Back: K. Todd, A. Purvis, G. O'Hara, A. Swann, G. Paxton, G. Cowell, M. Sunley.
Front: (Mascot), R. Alderson, R. Watson, C. Veart, G. Pepper.*

Moors had a revival in 1997-98, and they finished in 14th place in the Northern Premier League Premier Division, as well as winning the Durham Challenge Cup. During the season, they signed striker Ali Dia, who only played one game at Chorley and scored in the 2-0 win, and he left the club for Southampton in the Premiership.

The Durham Challenge Cup run 1997-98

Richie Alderson and Paul Richardson helped them to a 2-1 home win over South Shields in the first round on October 28th 1997, and in the second round Paul Richardson, who had turned down a move to a club in Malta, scored a hat trick as they brushed Sunderland Kennek Ryhope aside by 5-0.

There were goals galore against Evenwood in the next round, Steve Preen, playing in his first home game, scored a hat trick in an 8-0 stroll, setting up Moors for a semi final against Bishop Auckland, the latest in a long series of games between the two teams in the Challenge Cup. Subs Gary Cowell and Lee Innes scored for Moors in the 2-2 draw at the Brewery Field, and goals in extra time from Steve Preen and Gary Cowell gave Moors a 3-1 win in the replay at Kingsway.

Moors came up against a good Hartlepool United side in the final at Durham City, just winning 2-1 – the 16th time they had lifted the Cup. Wayne Edgcumbe scored from a Steve Preen pass to give them the lead, and by the half hour they were 2-0 up when Hartlepool defender Glen Davies put through his own goal when he was trying to clear a long ball from Craig Veart.

Team; Adrian Swann, Graham Pepper, Gary Lowes, Simon Bates, Gary O'Hara, Richie Watson, Lee Innes, David Robson, Steve Preen, Wayne Edgcumbe, Craig Veart. Unused subs; Dion Raitt, John Parnaby, Mattie Pearson.

Wayne Edgcumbe was a Spennymoor fan as a youngster, and was also a mascot on several occasions.

Moors finished the season in 14th place, but manager Mattie Pearson decided to quit after nearly seven years in the job, stating that he felt unable to work with some members of the committee. Chairman Barrie Hindmarch tried to persuade him to stay, but to no avail.

During his stay at the club, Mattie guided the team to promotion from the Northern Counties East League and Northern Premier League First Division, four Durham Challenge Cup wins, the Northern Premier League Cup, the Northern Counties East League Cup, and two FA Cup first round appearances. It was to be the last real taste of regular success for Moors – and it truly was the end of a golden era.

Chapter Eleven

"Beggars at football's banquet"

Mattie Pearson's departure saw the club fall into gradual decline, despite the efforts to maintain its position in the Northern Premier League.
Falling attendances, increased running costs and the impact of the National Lottery meant that Moors couldn't attract the same quality of players which they had done during their halcyon years.
Saturation television coverage of the Premiership and players' increasing wage demands didn't help either, which suggested that Spennymoor, like many other non league clubs, were "beggars at football's banquet" as a Northern Echo headline succinctly put it.
It was against this backdrop that Moors appointed their former player Colin Richardson as their new manager during the summer of 1998 but despite having one of the best managerial track records in the north east, "Ricco" found it tough going as the club struggled financially.
Moors had a miserable season in 1998-99, and the lack of attacking success in the 2-0 home defeat by Worksop in October prompted this observation from the club's programme; "There were no shots on goal from a Spennymoor player. The only time the Worksop keeper was called upon was to a save a deflection from his own defender." To the fans' relief, Moors improved after that, and they finished fifth from bottom of the table above the relegation zone.

Moors also suffered embarrassment in the FA Cup, losing heavily by 4-0 at Flixton in the second qualifying round on October 3rd 1998.
They had a big bust up with Durham FA over the arrangement of one of their Durham Challenge Cup ties. Moors easily beat Silksworth 5-2 thanks to a hat trick from Trevor Laidler on November 9th 1998, and were then scheduled to meet the winners of the Evenwood v South Shields tie. Moors wanted to play the game on November 24th, but Durham FA insisted that the game should be played on November 17th, the same night as Moors were due

Micky Nelson went on to play for Bury and Hartlepool

to play Gainsborough in the Northern Premier League Cup. Moors secretary Brian Boughen claimed that they couldn't play their Durham Challenge Cup tie because they had to give Gainsborough five clear working days' notice that the League Cup match was off, and went ahead and played the game. But Durham FA ruled that Moors should have contacted both Evenwood and South Shields on the night they beat Silksworth to arrange their Durham Challenge Cup tie, and kicked them out of the competition.

Moors' finances suffered another severe blow in November 1999 when Rothmans, who had sponsored the club since 1984, announced that they were closing their factory down in Spennymoor and thus ending their sponsorship. The club was already losing £1,000 per week, and chairman Barrie Hindmarch said: "We have had a wonderful relationship with them and I can't see how we can go on without their help. We will be lucky if we make it to the millennium." Moors only just managed to avoid relegation from the NPL Premier Division, finishing third off bottom.

Spennymoor United, 2000-01.
Back row: P. Carey (Physio), R. Foreman, M. Sowden, R. Jones, D. Bellamy, P. Zand, B. Boughen (Sec.). Front: C. Leonard, E. Hebron, C. Makin, J. Jackson, C. Veart, M. Bowes, A. Swalwell, D. Andison.

The misery continued for Moors in 2000-01 as the season unfolded into one of their worst ever. They went six league and cup games without scoring at one point, and they failed to score a league goal at home between October 21st 2000 and March 10th 2001. They were relegated from the NPL Premier

Division, with just four wins and 17 points to their credit. However, there was one positive note for Moors, the signing of centre half Rob Jones, who later went on to play for Stockport, Grimsby and Hibs.
But the club was again facing major financial problems, which ran close to six figures, and subsequently that state of affairs didn't suit a succession of managers who tried valiantly but unsuccessfully to strengthen the team.
However, Sunderland businessman Benny Mottram was introduced to the club in 2001, and after the club members voted to change from a private members' club to a public limited company, Benny became the club's new owner and paid off the debts. "We had a lot of interest in the club, but that didn't materialise into anything concrete," Barrie Hindmarch was quoted as saying at the time. "There were people who were appeared to be keen to get involved but when they saw the situation we were in, their interest soon disappeared. But Benny Mottram was a Victor Kiam type. He liked us so much he bought the company."

Rob Jones

With Moors' finances in much better health, they launched an assault on the NPL First Division promotion places, but after finishing fourth in the table and missing the automatic spots, they lost 3-1 in a play off to Ashton United on May 6th 2002 – revenge for the visitors after their defeat eight years previously in the promotion decider. Former Middlesbrough midfielder Jamie Pollock was appointed manager midway through the season, Moors' fourth in as many years following Colin Richardson, Peter Mulcaster and Peter Quigley.
The play off team was; Jim Provett, Richie Watson, Chris Lynch (sub Carl Beasley), Matt Robson, Leigh Grant, Anthony Lee, Stephen Bell, Lee Ellison, Danny Brunskill, Steve Pickering (sub Andy Banks, who himself was subbed by Jarrod Suddick). Anthony Lee scored Moors' goal, a consolation penalty in the last minute.

Jamie Pollock

They almost equalled their feat as a First Division club of eight years previously, when they nearly reached the league cup final, but they lost 1-0 at home to Worksop in the semi final. However, they suffered a big shock in the Durham Challenge Cup, losing 2-1 at Northern League Evenwood on October 24th 2001.

There were two disputes during the summer of 2002 that caused problems for the club. There were issues over a new lease with the council that were resolved before the start of the new season, then the FA wouldn't allow the club to start the season because they were unhappy with certain aspects of the club's transfer from a members' club to a public limited company. The FA thought that certain creditors hadn't been paid, but eventually they were satisfied after long drawn out negotiations thanks to the help of a solicitor and pressure on the FA. Because of the delay, Moors nearly didn't participate in the FA Cup, but the FA allowed them to play eventually. Moors nearly made it all the way to the first round, beating Consett, Ashington, Atherton and Droylsden, but they lost 2-1 at Northwich Victoria in the last qualifying round.

But there was no faltering in the Northern Premier League (UniBond) First Division, when Moors finished second in the table on goal difference behind Alfreton, just keeping their nerve by beating Witton Albion in their last game of the season to win promotion. "Snapper" Shaw, in his second spell at the club, scored fifteen goals in total.

Moors appointed former Newcastle and Ipswich striker Alex Mathie at the start of the 2003-04 season, but he left within two months, and was replaced by Tony Lee, one of the most successful north east managers.

Moors finished in 18th place in the Premier Division table, but because of the introduction of two new divisions in the Conference, the league above them in the pyramid, they became involved in a play off for a place in the newly created Conference North against Bradford Park Avenue, but they lost 3-1.

"We made two horrendous mistakes in defence for their first two goals, then they caught us just after half time," said manager Tony Lee.

The team; Liam Sutcliffe, Phil Brumwell, Paul Talbot, Steve Hutt, Michael Gough, Christian Hanson, Andy Brown, Jon Cullen, Steve Preen (sub Jonathan Milroy), Danny Brunskill, Simon Colligan (sub Chris I'Anson). Danny Brunskill scored Moors' goal when the score was 3-0.

Jon Cullen was a former Hartlepool player who was once transferred to Sheffield United for a £100,000 fee, and scored a hat trick of penalties against Ossett Town in the League Cup on November 18th 2003, two of them for handball. Phil Brumwell played for Darlington in the 1996 Third Division play off final.

There were hopes of lifting the Durham Challenge Cup, but Moors lost 3-2 on penalties to Northern League club Billingham Town, the eventual winners, in the semi final after a 1-1 draw in extra time.

During the season, long serving former chairman Barrie Hindmarch, who had continued to help the club following Benny Mottram's arrival, decided

Spennymoor United 2003
Back row: B. Hindmarch (Chairman), P. Carey (Physio), S. Bell, M. Robson, D. Goodchild, M. Kearney, J. Pollock (Manager), S. Hutt, A. Shaw, N. Mohan, L. Grant (Assistant Physio), B. Boughan (Secretary). Front: B. Ryan, S. Brightwell, J. Ainsley (Assistant Manager, Captain), C. Lynch, S. Preen, D. Brunskill, N. Bishop, A. Woodhouse.

The last ever team photo of Spennymoor United
Back row: M. Gibbons (Physio), R. Allen, A. Brown, S. Hutt, D. Horrigan, D. Brunskill, S. Niven, P. Talbot, J. Cullen, T. Metcalfe (Secretary), P. Carey (Physio). Front: C. I'Anson, T. Raw, S. Corrigan, P. Brumwell (Captain), M. Summerbell, M. Jack, J. Butler, J. Agbotar.

to sever his connections because of ill health. On Christmas Eve 2003, the clubhouse was destroyed in a fire that was started by a discarded cigarette, a serious blow in many ways.

Nobody realised at the start of the 2004-05 season that the forthcoming campaign in the Northern Premier League Premier Division would sadly be the last ever for Spennymoor United.

There were few indications that trouble was looming at the start of the season, although there seemed to be a revolving door for the manager's post. Tony Lee occupied the seat on three different occasions after patching up his differences with the club's owner, but he left again to be replaced by his assistant, Graeme Clark.

The dark clouds started to gather in January 2005 when Benny Mottram said that he was withdrawing his financial support following what he called "a cumulation of things," but he continued to attend matches. There were suggestions that the players might have to cover their own travel expenses to matches, but then there was huge controversy over Moors' Presidents' Cup semi final at Witton Albion on Sunday March 6th 2005, an issue which would start the ball rolling on the club's demise.

The game had to be switched from the Saturday to the following day because Northwich Victoria, who groundshared with Witton, had a Conference game, and Benny said: "It says in the FA rules that no club or player should be compelled to participate in a game on a Sunday. We are having problems getting a team out, and one of our players is refusing to play on religious grounds. The league didn't even ask us if we wanted to play on a Sunday." Moors were unable to raise a team, didn't travel to Cheshire, and were kicked out of the competition. The league also told the club to carry out 19 ground improvements after a routine inspection, or be fined £250 on each count.

Moors' problems deepened, and they again failed to raise a team for an away game at Leek Town in Staffordshire, which meant another three point deduction. To make matters worse, the FA threatened to suspend the club for failing to pay an invoice from Hartlepool United for the loans of players Jermaine Easter and Mark Robinson. The club was beginning to spiral out of control.

After Moors failed to fulfil three more games, first choice keeper Darren Horrigan moved to Gateshead on transfer deadline day, and the league turned down a request from the club to sign an emergency keeper. The league said that Moors had other keepers registered – Moors argued that they were tied to Northern League clubs and wouldn't play -- so another game, the fifth, was postponed because yet again Moors couldn't raise a team.

The League kept their patience with Moors amidst all the chaos – there were suggestions that Moors would quit the league – and there seemed to be a dim light at the end of the tunnel on April 7th 2005, when Moors managed to find a team to play Blyth at the Brewery Field, but the crowd was only 131. It seemed that most of the pessimistic fans had lost patience and given up hope. Despite taking the lead twice through Danny Brunskill and John Hutton in the first half, Moors conceded two goals in the last 14 minutes and lost 3-2.

Moors then failed to fulfil any more fixtures, and controversially in the eyes of some other league clubs, the Northern Premier League decided not to expunge their record and instead awarded three points to those clubs who hadn't played them – which in turn caused outrage at some clubs, prompting threats of legal action. For their offences, Moors were fined £10,000 and had 24 points deducted – a sad and ignominious end to over a glorious century of history at one of the north east's oldest non league clubs. The fine was never paid.

The last team to play in Spennymoor United's colours was; Phil Naisbitt, Chris Scott, John Hutton, Stephen Capper, David Coulson, Stuart Niven, Andrew Brown, Phil Brumwell, Danny Brunskill, Anthony Skedd, John Toft. Subs; Keith Graydon (for Skedd), John Butler (for Capper), Nick Lyons (unused).

The Northern Echo wrote; "If the temptation is wholly to blame Benny Mottram, it should be resisted. He put his money where others only put their mouths. What would dedicated former officials like Barrie Hindmarch, his late wife Joyce or the late Stan Bradley have made of the awful, apparently irredeemable mess in which they (Spennymoor United) now find themselves?"

"The club never officially folded, it just drifted out of existence," said one depressed fan. All that was left was an empty football stadium, with long grass and weeds growing where some of the greatest Moors players had trod, and dereliction where many generations of fans had stood and watched. What would former greats Johnny Dixon, Duggie Humble and Laurie Wensley have thought? Senior football in Spennymoor, as many knew it, was no more, and saddened and disgruntled Moors supporters were left to reflect on the death of the club. The epitaphs were written and the debate was fierce, but only memories remained.

But then in the summer of 2005 came an unexpected and very welcome twist. Sixty determined fans turned up at a meeting to discuss the formation of a Supporters Trust, and considered the idea of forming a new club to compete in the Wearside League, should the support and finance be forthcoming from the town.

A few days later, a consortium, headed by Alan Murray and Ken Houlahan, announced their plans to move Evenwood Town, whose ground was being repeatedly vandalised, to the Brewery Field. The move had the full support of the Northern League.

The supporters group agreed to stand aside when those plans were made public, and even though there was some opposition to the disappearance of Evenwood Town, a new club was formed with the help of the football authorities. Some fans happily embraced the notion that football would still be played in Spennymoor, although others were less than happy that in their opinion, it wouldn't be a true Spennymoor team.

The new club tried to persuade the FA and Durham FA to accept them as Spennymoor United, but their request was turned down. Instead, the name of Spennymoor Town was agreed to everyone's satisfaction – almost a century after Spennymoor Town had become Spennymoor United.

After a summer of planning and rebuilding, football returned to the Brewery Field on Friday 12th August 2005, and a healthy crowd of 511 was there to welcome it back. The team that played in the first Arngrove Northern League game against fellow newcomers Darlington RA was; Jonathan Collinson, Gary Sivills, Richard Bailes, John Guy, Ian Lowe, Darren Griffiths, Stephen Houlahan, Martin Houlahan, Kristian Dinsley, Lee Mason, Stuart Owen.

Moors won a thrilling game 3-2, with Martin Houlahan – son of manager Ken – with two, and Kristian Dinsley scoring the goals in front of one of the best attendances in the second division that season. Despite having the highest crowds in the division, Moors could only finish eighth in the table. Moors also played for the first time in the FA Vase – the competition for clubs across the country at Northern League level – but they lost in their first game by 4-1 at home to eventual quarter finalists Crook Town on October 1st 2005, Kristian Dinsley scoring the goal.

But just like the old club, controversy was never far away. The relationship between chairman Alan Murray and director of football Ken Houlahan deteriorated during the season, to the point that businessman Murray was replaced as chairman in his absence by a board meeting, and then refused to put any more money into the club.

At one stage, there were two managers in charge of the club. Ken Houlahan appointed Justin Perry as manager, while Alan Murray appointed Jamie Pollock as manager, with former long serving player Jason Ainsley as his assistant, to be effective

Jason Ainsley

at the end of the season.

After more debate and argument, Ken Houlahan and most of the players left during the summer of 2006, with only four staying at the Brewery Field. The "two Js" took over management affairs, recruited some players and guided the club to promotion from the Arngrove Northern League second division at the end of the 2006-07 season, winning the league by ten points, and losing only two games all season. They went unbeaten in the league from November onwards, a run of 25 matches.

"After we lost at South Shields in November, we were very determined not to lose any more games," said Jason, who took over as manager in June 2007 after Jamie Pollock left.

The feelgood factor had returned to the Brewery Field, but not for long because the start of the 2007-08 season was shrouded in more controversy. The Town Council served an eviction notice on the club, but after Northern League chairman Mike Amos intervened and mediated between the club and the council, a new lease was agreed. "We are very grateful for what Mike has done," said Alan Murray. So were the fans – they gave Mike a standing ovation for his efforts at a meeting.

Mike Amos

On the field, the new season started well in the FA Cup, with Moors beating Garforth and Brigg Town, both from the UniBond League, but then they lost embarrassingly to Clitheroe by 8-2. The club also formed a ladies team and a junior team.

Thomas Grant would have been proud of the way that the club rose from the ashes, and the wholehearted backing and encouragement from the fans. He probably didn't think that his vision of a football club for the "young men of Spennymoor" would last as long as it has. Over the last 100 years many long standing clubs, such as Stockton, have fallen by the wayside, but the Moors have, for the most part, managed to bathe in glory and overcome many hurdles.

When the football authorities agree, Spennymoor Town intends to change its name back to Spennymoor United – after all, to many, it will always be United.

Beggars at football's banquet

Spennymoor Town chairman Alan Murray shakes hands with Joan Wood of Spennymoor Town Council after the lease is agreed.

Players, officials and fans pose for a group photo in September 2007

We'll Always Be United

President : F. E. HAMILTON, ESQ.   Chairman : T. SMITH

SPENNYMOOR UNITED A.F.C.

COLOURS : BLACK & WHITE STRIPED SHIRTS, BLACK PANTS.
MEMBERS' FOOTBALL ASSOC.   DURHAM FOOTBALL ASSOC.   NORTHERN LEAGUE

Hon. Sec. : S. BRADLEY
Hon. Treas. : J. MEGGESON

GROUND :
BREWERY GROUND,
SPENNYMOOR.
TEL. 2100

7th June, 1966

R. Bell Esq.

Dear Sir,

   re: Appointment of Coach.

  Further to your application for the above position and your meeting with us on Saturday last, we are pleased to advise you that your application has been successful and you have been appointed Coach to the above Club for the coming season 1966/67.

  Conditions as under:-

  Attendance two nights per week and Saturday afternoon.
Wages: £3. 0. 0d. per week, plus any expenses incurred on the Clubs behalf.
Termination of Employment: 7 days notice to be given for both parties.

  Would you please confirm your acceptance as early as possible.

          Yours faithfully,

          S. BRADLEY
          (Hon. Secretary)

Please reply to Secretary : "OAKLANDS", 27, WEST TERRACE, SPENNYMOOR, CO. DURHAM
     Treasurer : 51, HALF MOON LANE, SPENNYMOOR, CO. DURHAM

The letter from the Club to Bob Bell appointing him as coach in June 1966

Chapter Twelve

Officials' memories

Bob Bell

Bob introduced a revolutionary new tactical system to the Brewery Field which many believe laid a solid foundation for the future.

Bob took over at the Brewery Field following the departure of coach Jackie Newton in May 1966, and immediately put into practice what he'd learned at Lilleshall, the FA's coaching centre. "Previously, training sessions consisted of running round the field six times, and then kicking the ball for half an hour. I was a fully qualified coach, having been on several coaching courses to gain my full badge, and so I was full of ideas straight from the FA.

"One of them was to play 4-4-2, instead of the old system of 2-3-5 (two full backs, three half backs and five forwards). The players took it very seriously at the time, although I got the impression that when I was out of earshot, they were wondering what I was talking about!

"I remember my first away game in charge, I think it was at Whitley Bay. Under the 4-4-2 system, the two central defenders wore the number 4 and 5 shirts, whereas under the 2-3-5 system, the number 4 shirt was worn by a half back.

"When I dished out the shirts, I gave central defender Peter Joyce the number 4 shirt and Billy Lovejoy the number 5. Peter, being a proud central defender, didn't want to wear the number 4 shirt, so he and Billy tossed a coin for the number 5 shirt – and Peter lost!

"The 4-4-2 system worked very well in the second full season we used it, so much so that after we lost to Shildon in an early midweek game, we went through the rest of the league season undefeated and won the title.

"There were some very good and intelligent players in the team, like Graham Defty, Ralph Wright and Stan Summerill. In my first season, John Gatens was excellent. He was very confident in what he did, and could beat people on a sixpence. I didn't have to tell the players all that much, the style of play which we used came so natural to all of them. I used to say to them; "Play like you did last week."

"The 1967-68 season was very satisfying and very exciting. We won the treble, the Northern League, the Durham Challenge Cup and Northern League Cup. But it was disappointing not to do well in the FA Amateur Cup. We lost a game against Prestwich Heys on a very windy day, and they scored with a shot from the halfway line that flew over keeper Dave Crampton's head into the net."

After five years in charge, Bob decided to quit as coach to devote more time to his family, and his FA coaching duties. He still attended Spennymoor matches for many years afterwards and pointed the club in the direction of talent he had spotted, in particular Steve Cuthbert and Brian Healy.

Kenny Banks

Kenny came to the Brewery Field as a 16 year old midfielder and eventually became player-coach in one of the most successful periods in the club's history.

Kenny, who had been an amateur at Middlesbrough and Darlington and was also a former Wolves triallist, was probably one of the greatest players to wear the black and white shirt -- he helped the team to win five Northern League titles between 1968 and 1978, five Durham Challenge Cups, two Northern League Cups and agonisingly came to within 45 minutes of an FA Trophy final appearance at Wembley. During his nineteen years at the club as a player and player-coach, Moors only finished outside the top six on four occasions.

He made his debut just after Moors returned to the Northern League in 1960, after two years travelling long distances in the Midland League. "I'd been playing junior football, and one day near the start of the season when Harry Bell was manager, we were playing at West Auckland. I thought I was just going there as a reserve, but Harry told me that I was playing.

"I was just 16, and very nervous, so the physio, Jack Flanagan, took me into the changing room and introduced me to the players. I think I managed to do ok in the game, because I played a few more games that season.

"Harry Bell left the club in 1964 and after Jackie Newton had a spell in charge, Bob Bell took over, and he built a team that could win things. There were a lot of good players, and the team spirit was excellent. That particular team played together for four years, and eventually won the

Kenny Banks

treble in 1968 – the Northern League, Northern League Cup and Durham Challenge Cup."

Kenny has played with, and coached, several Moors' greats. "There were some really fantastic players during my time at the club. Kevin Reilly was one of the best non league strikers in the country, because he had two very good feet and had loads of pace and bags of skill.

"Defender Peter Joyce was a Spennymoor legend. He was a no-nonsense centre half, who had a habit of tackling people by extending his leg to get the ball at just the right time. He didn't lose many battles in the air or on the ground. Butch Simpson was another who was as tough as nails, and he looked a rough lad as well. He used to strike fear into opponents.

"Albert Hickman read the game very well. He could see danger developing against us, and how we could create danger for the other team. He was one of the voices in the dressing room, and was a good organiser.

"Billy Robson was the club joker. He was a hard man on the pitch, but two of the other hard men in the dressing room turned the tables on him. We used to have a players' pool, which was run by Butch Simpson and John Heaviside. One day, those two decided to fine Billy for something really trivial just to wind him up, and Billy said: "You can't fine me for that!", so they sat either side of him in a gangster kind of way and whispered "You will, Billy, you will." Billy paid up!"

Butch Simpson

Kenny was player-coach when Moors pulled off one of the shocks of the 1975 FA Cup against Football League club Southport, beating them 4-1. "I think that was probably one of our best performances when I was coach," he said.

"We worked very hard on our setpieces, and it was quite satisfying when I scored from two of them. We always believed that we could beat Southport after we'd been to see them play. Southport took the lead early in the game, but once we were level, we got well on top and thoroughly deserved to win.

"I didn't score many goals at that time, and not many of those were with my head. I once scored with a diving header at Blyth. The ball came over from the left, I closed my eyes, launched myself at the ball, and it went into the roof of the net!

"I used to love games against Blyth. They did really well in the league in that era, just like we did. They had a really good run in the 1978 FA Cup when they got to the fifth round, and I used to wonder why we couldn't do that, because we used to believe that they weren't any better than us."
As well as being part of so many triumphs in the seventies – for example Moors won the Durham Challenge Cup four seasons in a row -- there were also disappointments.
"I was really disappointed not to get into the third round of the FA Cup. We missed our chance in 1967 in the season we won the league and two Cups. We beat Goole in a first round replay, but then lost 2-0 at Macclesfield in the second round. Macclesfield weren't in the Football League then, and at the time, we really fancied our chances of going through especially as they were a non league club just like us.
"The other big disappointment was the Trophy semi final against Leatherhead in 1978. We lost 2-0 at their place in the first leg, and to be honest, I thought that was a fair result.
"But in the second leg we played really well, and were 2-0 up at half time, and level on aggregate. The lads came in at half time high as kites, and I remember going into the dressing room wondering what I could say to keep everybody's feet on the ground. I believe that psychologically, some of the players thought they had the game won, and I had to calm them down. Unfortunately, Leatherhead scored early in the second half. We threw everything at them, but we just couldn't score again.
"We also missed out on a place in the Amateur Cup semi final in 1973. We drew at Walton and Hersham in the quarter final, but then we lost the replay 1-0 at our place. Dave "Harry" Bassett, who went to be a manager in the Football League, was in their team, a Billy Bremner type of player, one who gave everything and more in midfield, and broke things up.
"He butchered me at one point from behind, and he got booked for the tackle. It was a surprise that he'd done that to me, because we knew each other so well, but that was the character he was.
"I remember when I went on tour with him with the England Amateur team. We finished the tour at Heathrow, all wearing our England suits. Dave approached us all, and asked if we wanted to sell them to him. One or two of the lads did, so Dave made a few extra quid and so did the lads. I didn't, I kept mine."
Kenny played all over the country with the Moors as they embarked on Northern League, FA Cup, Amateur Cup and FA Trophy campaigns.
"Away games used to take ages, because it was long before the motorway system was developed. Even in the Northern League there were a couple of long trips. When we used to play at Penrith, we used to stop at the

Stainmore café at the top of the moors for a bite to eat, and when we went to Whitby, there was a little café near the ground where we used to have our dinner before we went on for the match. You can do those trips now in half the time it took us.

"It was sometimes an eye-opener playing in the south. We played at Wycombe when they played at their old ground, Loakes Park, which had a slope on it. When we got there, they'd watered the pitch, and we thought they'd done it deliberately just to upset us, but we discovered that they did that before every game.

"The biggest defeat I was ever involved in was an 11-2 defeat at Kingstonian in the FA Amateur Cup. Their ground was a real culture shock to us because it had floodlights and a training ground right beside their pitch. We didn't have lights at the time, in fact not many did in the Northern League, and it was totally different to anything we'd seen.

"Our regular keeper was injured, and so we had to put a young replacement in goal, and he was weak on crosses. I scored the two for us, but every time the ball went down our end, it seemed to go in. I went back to work on the Monday, and people thought there'd been a misprint in the papers, and we'd won 2-1!

"It used to be a nightmare getting people off work if we were involved in midweek replays. We certainly had problems for the away game at Shrewsbury in the FA Cup. We drew with them on the Saturday at our place, and then we had to go to their ground on the Tuesday night. We had problems getting a couple of the lads off work and their employers refused to pay them, so the club had to make it up for them. The players couldn't afford to lose half a day's wages, which was fair comment.

"The club once refused to pay the players' wages when the floodlights failed and a match had to be abandoned. One of our players was a sort of unofficial shop steward, and just before we were due to play the next game, he wouldn't let any of us get stripped unless the club paid up. It was 2.55 when the club relented.

"We used to have plenty of laughs though when we played away. When Billy Bell was coach, we went on a pre-season tour, and played a couple of games at Hayes and Wycombe. Keith Storey decided to play a trick on Billy, so he tied his doorknob to the next one in the corridor and Billy couldn't get out of his room. Billy was absolutely furious, we could hear him swearing through the door!"

Kenny was approached by several clubs to move away from the Brewery Field, but he remained loyal, even though there were some lucrative deals put on the table. "Blyth and Bishop Auckland both wanted me to join them. Bernard Hathaway, who was connected with Bishop, came to visit me and offered me megabucks to move to them.

"But I was happy to stay at Spennymoor, even though the other clubs offered me more than the £4 per game I was earning in Bob Bell's time as coach, for example. I think most of the players had better offers but decided to stay, because we knew we had something going for us and we could see what Bob was trying to achieve.

"It was nice to get what I thought was a few bob for playing for the Moors. After I got paid on Saturday night following a game, my wife and I used the money to do the weekly shopping.

"The players in the south of England were on really big money, and remember this was meant to be amateurism. Some players I met up with on the England get-togethers couldn't afford to turn professional, because when they added the income from the two jobs together, they would have lost out badly.

"I was happy with my full time job as a teacher, although there were one or two awkward moments. When we had a big match coming up, I was always photographed with the kids from my school at Ferryhill Station, but when I used to take the school team to somewhere like Rosa Street in Spennymoor, the little kids from Rosa Street would come up to me and say something like "Great game last Saturday, Kenny!" and my kids would look at each other as if to say "Why can't we call him Kenny?" Maybe they respected me a little!"

Kenny's performances and growing reputation as a skilful midfielder earned him a call up for the England Amateur squad for a tour of Europe.

"I applied for leave of absence from school, at the time I was teaching six and seven year olds. The Education Authority wrote to me and said that I wouldn't be paid at all while I was away, but I could have the time off. That was no good to me, because I had a young family to look after, and with no pay, I was going to pull out of the tour. I just couldn't afford to go. I got the union involved, and in the end, the Authority gave me time off with full pay.

"I nearly didn't go though for another reason, because I went over on my ankle in training just before the tour started, and it came up like a balloon. The England physio said that I would be fit, but I didn't think I had a chance. I flew back home on the Sunday from Bisham Abbey, and back down to Heathrow to fly out again on the Tuesday. However, the physio was true to his word, and he had me fit after the second game, and I played in the last three matches of the tour.

"The worst injury I ever had was in a Sunday game. I was playing for a pub team near St James' Park in Newcastle, and I tore my cartilage. The physio of the Sunday team was also the Evenwood physio. My knee was in a hell

Officials' memories

of a state, and I arranged to go up to Evenwood and meet him the following week. He twisted and pushed my knee in every direction while I howled in pain, and after a few minutes of manipulation he said; "You'll be all right for Saturday."

"Was that a miracle cure? No chance. I didn't feel any better and went to a surgeon. He cringed when I told him the story. I was off work for nine weeks, and when I started playing again, the injury didn't get any better, because there was still a piece of cartilage floating around. So the surgeon had to operate again, and I was off for another nine weeks!

"Billy Bell, who was the coach at the time – Spennymoor didn't have a manager as such then -- didn't speak to me for ages. He was so enthusiastic when I was fit, but it was only when I was ready to come back that he started speaking to me."

Kenny was also a bit of a practical joker in his early days at the club, especially when his close friend Billy Roughley was around.

"We had a pre-season tour somewhere down south, and I roomed with Billy on one occasion. I left the room one evening, and when I came back, every pair of football boots along with five balls had been stuffed in my bed. So the next night, after Billy had had a few drinks and was fast asleep, a few of us picked him up and tossed him in a bath of cold water. Billy splurted; "What's on here, like?" as he lay in the bath."

Kenny once tried to confuse Moors' opponents before a big match by switching the team's numbers around. "We had a big Trophy game coming up, so I knew that the other team would send spies to watch us play. I couldn't leave players out, because I didn't have a big enough squad. So I handed the players different-numbered shirts – for example, I gave Kevin Reilly the number five shirt, but of course I still played him up front. When the players ran out on to the field, one of our supporters shouted; "What the hell's Kenny doing? Kevin Reilly's playing at centre half!"

The end of Kenny's reign as coach came unexpectedly in the 1978-79 season, a decision that came as a big shock to Kenny as well as the fans, especially after the success he'd helped bring to the club.

"There had been suggestions that I should bring in some new blood because some of the players were in their thirties, but I wouldn't do so unless I could find somebody better. I thought Alan Shoulder was going to sign for us at one point, but instead he decided to turn pro at Newcastle.

"We lost three games in a row, and I was called into a committee meeting one night, and was told that they had decided to replace me as manager. I couldn't believe it, and I must admit, I wasn't happy with the way it was done. When my dad heard what had happened, he went ballistic. I was asked to stay on as a player, but I didn't want to.

"But the team that was supposed to be too old still won the league that season, so I must have done something right. I went to Ferryhill as manager after that, and I must admit that I had huge pleasure when I came back with Ferryhill, and we won 4-1 at the Brewery Field."

A satisfying victory perhaps on that occasion – but there were many, many more in Spennymoor's colours at the Brewery Field.

Peter Mulcaster

Peter had two spells at the Brewery Field, his first as assistant manager to Ray Gowan in the club's first season in the Northern Counties East League in 1990, and his second as manager in the UniBond League a decade later.

"My first spell at Spennymoor was one of my best times in football. It was a very happy club when I first went there near the end of the 1989-90 season, to be assistant to Ray Gowan. One Saturday I was manager of South Bank in the Northern League, and the next Saturday I was sat on the bench alongside Ray for Spennymoor's last game in the Northern League against Billingham Synthonia.

"It was a big, refreshing change to the Northern League. We went to completely new places, faced different challenges, and we brought in some very good players, like Derek Ord, Gary Boagey and Ged Hartley, who was a one-off in terms of commitment and attitude. Our away trips really opened my eyes, and they were really good for team spirit. Every other Saturday we were on a coach together, and it was great being a part of the banter."

The highlight of that first season was the FA Cup run, which ended in a narrow 3-2 defeat at Fourth Division Chesterfield in the first round. "There was a really big crowd in the Brewery Field for the fourth qualifying round replay against Northwich Victoria, who were in the Conference at the time. It was a cracking night, we played some great football, and we beat them 2-1 with a goal late in extra time. I think we were one of the first teams from the Northern Counties East League to reach the first round proper of the FA Cup.

"We played Chesterfield away in the first round, and even though we lost the whole of that day was brilliant. We gave them a huge shock when Gary Boagey scored to pull the score back to 3-2 in the second half, and we nearly equalised late on. At the end of the game we were given a standing ovation by their fans as well as ours. I popped into their dressing room after the game to congratulate them, and their manager, Paul Hart, was blasting his players. I tried to say something, but they all just glared at me!

"Trouble was, everybody wanted to beat us in the league after that. We lost three matches soon after, and I think I sulked all the way home. Opposing teams raised their games to beat us, but that's a part of football. We finished third that season, and then I left midway through the next."

Peter's next spell was as manager, when the club was going through a lean spell in 2001.

"I came back when the club was struggling in the UniBond Premier Division. While the organisation off the field was excellent just like the first time, the team on the field was different. Some of the players were poor, and the club didn't have the money to attract good new players.

"But the players we had still battled hard, and we just managed to avoid relegation when we beat Marine on the last game of the season. I brought in players I knew from Northallerton, such as Mark Forster and Rob Jones. Rob was magnificent, and he made it into the professional game."

Barrie Hindmarch

Barrie was a fan who became club chairman and made the club his life – and one thing's for sure, nobody could doubt his whole-hearted commitment and love of the club.

He started his Moors "career" as an avid fan in the club's North Eastern League days in 1950s, hardly missing a game either home or away. His first hero was Duggie Humble, a lethal forward who scored nearly 200 goals, regularly scoring hat tricks. "Duggie was the hero of a lot of kids," said Barrie. "When we played football in the back street – I lived just 400 yards away from the ground -- everybody wanted to pretend he was Duggie Humble, and not one of the players from the big clubs. The games against Bishop Auckland were always one of the highlights of the season, because you would dare bet that Duggie would try to put Bishops' keeper Harry Sharratt over the goalline with the ball. It was legal to challenge a keeper like that in those days and score.

Barrie Hindmarch

"Duggie had another great game in an FA Cup tie against Bishop Auckland when they were going well in the Amateur Cup. Our ground was absolutely packed, with around 8,000 people inside, and because I was small at the time, I managed to squeeze through to the front of the crowd, and lie down against one of the concrete posts with my feet on the grass. Duggie scored twice in the second half that day to put us in the first round.

"One day, we thought he was going to be sent off for fouling one of the opposition. Just as the referee was about to do send him to the dressing rooms, Duggie pulled up his shirt, pointed at some stud marks, and said to

the ref; "What do you think these are, love bites?" The ref let him off!
"When I went to work at Smart and Browns, I used to work as an apprentice in the tool room near Norman Field, another one of the best Spennymoor players, and he later became coach. Norman used to tell me all sorts of stories about life as a pro with Portsmouth and Mansfield Town."

The North Eastern League fell apart in 1958 when the Football League clubs pulled their reserve teams out, so Moors joined the Midland League, which meant much more travelling and some brand new adventures to new places. "As a youngster, I used to go to matches with my brother Dennis on buses organised by Alice Armstrong. She ran them from King William Street, and there used to be as many as four buses, either from OK or Jewitts, going to away games.

"We went all over the place, even to towns like Peterborough and Grantham for midweek games. Peterborough weren't in the Football League then, and they used to pay overnight bills for some clubs. But in the end, it got too expensive for Spennymoor to play in that league, because there was hardly what you would call a motorway network in those days and there were a lot of overnight stops because of the long journey times.

"I can remember a cup tie against Goole away from home in 1952. It was easier to get there by train, and I can remember there were so many carriages full of supporters that two engines were needed to pull them all from Spennymoor railway station. We lost the game 4-3, but their winner should never have been allowed. Wilf Chisholm, our keeper, dropped the ball over his shoulder, and the ref said that he'd dropped it over the line, but he didn't, we could tell from behind the goal."

There was another memorable trip to Goole a decade or so later. "There was a good crowd of Spennymoor fans down that night, and one of them played a bugle all the way through the game. One of our fans once piddled on an opposing keeper in a home game from behind the goal, but Goole's ground was oval shaped then, and somebody said; "You'll have a job piddling on him tonight, lad."

"There was some really good banter amongst the fans. I can remember an FA Cup

Wilf Chisholm

tie at Brandon, when some of our fans were getting on the players' backs a little because they hadn't been playing well in the previous games, so they started to slow handclap. I think it was Jimmy Soakell who shouted; "Slow down, they'll think you're applauding them!"

"There were times when the club needed money, and the supporters would rally round. Nellie Downs was typical – she used to take a suitcase full of cigarettes and sell them around Smart and Browns, and give the profits to the club. The supporters used to carry a flag around that was named after her, they called it "Nellie's Flag".

"There was another chap called Harry Blair, who we used to nickname the "Spennymoor foghorn". He used to work at Raines Coachworks, and when he shouted, I could hear him inside our house 400 yards away! He used to work in the town, and during his lunch hour, he used to go down the ground and do odd jobs. Roy Heales was another bloke who used to spend his lunchtimes doing odd jobs for us.

Nellie Downs

"A group of supporters always used to sing during matches, and we nicknamed them the "Choir". They used to stand behind the goal, and really get behind the team. One of my favourite songs, to the tune of "Aye, aye, aye, aye," was "Aye, aye, aye, aye, Crampton is better than Yashin. Banksy is better than Eusebio and Goole Town are in for a thrashing." Some opponents used to say that the "Choir" was worth a goal start."

After Moors beat Goole in an FA cup tie in 1967, they were drawn away to Macclesfield Town in Cheshire. "I think Macclesfield's ground was unique. There was a pub on the corner of the ground -- it's gone now -- called the Moss Rose, and you had to walk through the pub to get into the ground! Unfortunately, we lost that game 2-0, and we missed out on a trip to one of the really big clubs in the third round."

Barrie's favourite player in the seventies heyday was striker Kevin Reilly, a player who was a real crowd hero, and probably one of the best players at non league level in the country, let alone the north east.

"When Kevin got married, the ceremony was just before dinner time, and it didn't look as if he could play at home for us in the afternoon in the FA Cup.

"But one of the committee men, Bob Hunter, came to the ground one night and said that Kevin was going to play, and sure enough he did. We managed to arrange transport for him – we even went with two cars to pick him up in case one broke down! Kevin had an absolute blinder, and the player who was supposed to be marking him just couldn't get near him.

"Kevin was watched by a lot of Football League clubs, but he didn't want to leave home. Nottingham Forest, who were flying high at the top of the First Division and in Europe at the time wanted to sign him, but he actually said "no" to Brian Clough – not many people dared do that!

"Kevin had a great understanding with Kenny Banks in midfield, and the pair of them worked together really well. Kenny was one of the quickest thinkers I've ever seen on a field, and he could think two or three passes ahead. He used to get a load of stick from supporters for misplaced passes, but that was because some players weren't thinking along the same lines as Kevin, or weren't even thinking at all. Kenny could see a pass, and they couldn't. Maybe if Kenny had a yard more pace, he might have played a bit higher if he wanted to, but he was happy doing what he was doing.

"Kevin had loads of flair, which is what the supporters loved about him. He scored some tremendous goals, and he played up front with Geoff Hart and John Davies -- the three of them would score 100 goals between them a season. What a great return that was.

"Everyone has a favourite goal by Kevin. Against Bishop Auckland at our place, he cut in from the right, opposite the 18 yard line, looked as if he was going to pass across the field, but instead checked, wrong footed the centre half, and put a left foot shot into the top corner. That was top quality.

"Some of the defenders we've had at the club have been really tough and physical characters on the field, but by and large they played the game fair. Peter Joyce was a magnificent centre half, and should have been capped by England at amateur level. He had an uncanny ability to climb and hang in the air in order to win the ball, and he seemed to have a hook on the end of his foot. He used to slide for the ball against an opponent and somehow hook it away from him.

"But he wouldn't take any nonsense either. An opponent – I won't say who – clattered into the back of Peter's leg, and Peter stayed down injured, which was very unusual for him. Somebody said that it might be best to take Peter off because he knew what would happen next – and sure enough the same opponent had to be carted off a few minutes later.

"Butch Simpson was another great defender, and also wouldn't let opponents get the better of him. He was once clattered from behind by an opponent, and Butch grabbed the lad by his ears and lifted him up. The referee and the linesmen both looked the other way!

"Butch once tried to take a free kick against Tow Law, but one of their players stood over the ball. Butch shouted "If you don't move away from the ball, I'll kick you." The lad didn't move, so Butch kicked him!

"He got some stick at Blyth one day from the part of the ground known as the Shed. Butch made to climb over the barrier, and you should have seen the crowd scatter! He visited our ground one day when he came back from Australia, and he shouted at our full back, "Have a word with him" and then turned round to me and said; "I would be sent off if I did that nowadays."

"I remember when we took David "Kid" Curry to Holland with Middlesex Wanderers, and he played against a little Dutch winger who was really tricky. David stopped him making one run with a really crunching tackle which won him the ball, but flattened the player. The Dagenham boss, Laurie Wilkinson, was in charge of the team, and when he saw that the referee was making a fuss of the challenge, he said: "That was a good old Northern League tackle. I hope the ref isn't going to send him off. I'd have been proud of a tackle like that." The ref didn't book him or send him off on that occasion, but after another tough tackling game with the Wanderers, Sir Stanley Rous, who was the FA secretary at the time and had been at the game, came to see Kid in the changing room and said, quite sincerely, "I hope you continue to prosper in your football career."

"Those players were part of the team that reached the semi final of the Trophy in 1978 and would have done well in today's Conference. They won the League, League Cup and Durham Challenge Cup regularly."

Moors peaked at the same time as another Northern League team, Blyth Spartans. When Moors reached the semi finals of the Trophy, in the same season Blyth had their legendary run to the fifth round of the FA Cup. "There were some titanic matches between the two teams when they played. No quarter was asked or given, but there were some very strong friendships formed also after the game. The relationship was a bit like Manchester United and Liverpool are today.

"You knew that the games between the two clubs would have a bearing on the league title. The winner would always have an advantage in the league until the next time they met. Between 1971 and 1984, the league title went to either Blyth or Spennymoor -- those two teams would dominate the Northern League even now."

There were some physical battles as well, Northwich at home in particular in the FA Trophy. "Northwich had knocked three Football League clubs out of the FA Cup that season, and one of their players, John King, had established a reputation for himself as a tough midfielder.

"One of our defenders, Butch Simpson, always looked after his team mates, and this lad King clattered into young David Curry. At the end of the game, which we won, King went over to Butch to shake hands, but instead Butch flattened him.

"The ref saw what happened, and tried to follow Butch into the changing room. Butch quickly took his strip off, jumped in the bath, and when the ref came in looking for him, couldn't see him for all the steam! The ref gave up in the end, especially when the other players got in the bath as well.

"I sat with their chairman before the game in our clubhouse, and he asked me how much we were paying, and I told him £8 per man. He couldn't believe it, he nearly spluttered out his beer. "I owe each of my team £600 in bonuses from the FA Cup," he said. It just goes to show how well we did with our resources."

The 1978 FA Trophy run was nearly washed out before it really got going. Moors won at Gainsborough, but then they had an away tie at fellow Northern League club Whitby, who themselves fancied a run in the competition. Whitby were emerging as one of the challengers to the big two.

"It was absolutely chucking it down with rain in Spennymoor, and my late wife Joyce, who was secretary, rang the Whitby secretary Ken Graham, to ask if the game was still going ahead. Ken said that the weather was beautiful, but when we got there, the pitch was absolutely waterlogged. But despite the conditions, we won 5-3, and Kevin Reilly scored a cracking goal from outside the box, the keeper didn't know what went past him."

After beating Atherstone and Dagenham, Moors were drawn with Leatherhead in the semi final. Leatherhead had been giant killers in the FA Cup in previous seasons, and inspired by Chris Kelly, nicknamed the Leatherhead Lip, had beaten Football League clubs Brighton, Colchester, Cambridge and Northampton, and were actually 2-0 up against First Division Leicester on one occasion before losing 3-2.

Moors lost the first leg by 2-0 in Surrey, but in the second leg at the Brewery Field came back with some great football to level 2-2 on aggregate, only to concede a crucial goal in the second half.

"At half time, some friends of mine from Hayes said that we had played so well, that it looked as if we were going to Wembley. But in the second half, we were flat, when the match was there for the taking. The goal that won it for them must have bounced nine times before it went over the line, it was agony for everybody. The referee, Colin Seel, couldn't believe the final result as well. "What happened?" he asked me. I just didn't know. It was probably my greatest disappointment as a Spennymoor fan, and that would be the same for a lot of other people in the ground that day as well."

Barrie used to go on scouting trips with late secretary Stan Bradley, and when Moors drew Southport in the first round of the FA Cup in 1975, they travelled to watch Southport, then bottom of the Fourth Division, in action at Northampton.

"Southport wore yellow shirts, and believe it or not, the number nine on the centre forward's shirt was written in felt tip pen. We couldn't believe that a Football League club was doing that because it looked so sloppy and unprofessional.

"So the next day in Spennymoor, the women's section -- who had some pretty good fundraising ideas and were a big help to the club -- bought us a brand new Admiral strip and brand new tracksuits. The players really looked the part in them, and they gained an important psychological advantage over Southport before the game even kicked off. I never thought we would lose that match beforehand, and we didn't, we won 4-1. Kenny Banks was magnificent that day."

The following round Moors were drawn away to Bury, and Barrie's son Adie was mascot. "Adie thoroughly enjoyed himself, waving at the crowd and joining in the warm up. After the referee tossed the coin to decide kick off, he gave Adie the coin and told him "If the team is as good as you, then you'll win." Unfortunately, Moors weren't.

Committee early 70s. B. Hindmarch, W. Dixon, T. Smith, A. Dixon, I. Ferguson, R. Heale, M. Robinson (Vice Chairman), R. Hutchinson, J. Meggeson (Treasurer), J. Smith (Chairman), S. Bradley (Secretary), N. Robinson.

Barrie's closer involvement with Moors began one day after a game in 1970, when he was sat in the clubhouse with one of his friends, and as secretary

Stan Bradley walked past, he complained about something. "It was just one of the typical moans from a fan in the clubhouse after a game, I can't even remember what it was. So Stan turned round to me and said; "If you can do better, put up for the committee." So I did, and I was elected by one vote! Stan was a very good organiser, and I got to know him quite well. He certainly did a great job for the club.

"He was a staunch Arsenal fan, and knew people everywhere. When we played in London, he always managed to arrange to use the training facilities at either Arsenal or Spurs. We once trained at Chelsea for a game, and the players left their boots behind, but Stan arranged for somebody from Chelsea to bring them to us.

"Stan was the number one poacher of players, he could find out all sorts, and he gained quite a reputation. One day, my wife Joyce and I were having a break in the Lake District, and we decided to pop up to Penrith and watch them play Evenwood in a league game. Gordon Coe of Evenwood saw us, walked across to Walter Brogden, the Penrith secretary, and said; "You want to watch your players, Walter, Stan Bradley's apprentices are here!"

"One day, Stan and I decided to visit Stuart Leeming, who lived near the Peregrine pub in Chapel House in Newcastle, to try and persuade him to join us. We sat in the car outside his house waiting for him, and after a while, the woman next door knocked on the car window and said that he had gone to the hospital.

"So we decided to go back up the following night, and we'd only been there a few minutes when a police car pulled up and asked what we were doing. One of the neighbours must have thought we were up to no good – I suppose in a football sense we weren't!"

Jackie Smith was the chairman for several years until 1980. "Jackie came from Littletown, and he had an accent just like Bob Paisley, who came from that area. He used to call everybody "hinny".

"We went to Runcorn to watch some future opponents in action, and we were invited into their boardroom for a half time drink. Jack was asked if he would like some scotch, and he was given just a mere drop. He said to me in a theatrical whisper; "By hinny, they don't give much away here." You could have heard a pin drop!"

Jackie Smith

Barrie became vice chairman in the mid

160

seventies, but then nearly left the club in 1980. "Ferryhill asked me if I wanted to go there as chairman, but I didn't fancy it because Spennymoor was the only club for me. I wanted to be chairman of Spennymoor one day, but only when Jackie was prepared to stand down. I didn't want to stand against him or anything like that, and I told him so.

"Jack got to know about Ferryhill's approach, and he asked me if it was true. I said that it was, but I had turned them down. The next thing, he told me that he was standing down, and I could take over. I didn't ask him to step aside or anything like that, it was his own decision."

Barrie stayed in the job for over twenty years, as Moors continued to be a force in the Northern League and beyond, as the newly formed pyramid spread its influence.

"If the seventies were remembered for glory, then the eighties were remembered for hard work. We had some very good committees, all of them working hard for the club. We tried to move forward in the town from a commercial point of view. We wrote to lots of businesses and got a poor response, until I was invited to meet a chap called Ken Newell, who had an office above a bike shop in the town. The club took off again thanks to his support and backing.

"Ken went with me to talk to a bank manager about expanding the clubhouse and building a new stand, and the bloke, who was well into football, asked: "What happens if you win the Northern League, which league would you go into?" "None," I replied. His response was "Bit stupid, isn't it?"

Ken Newell

"Even though the bank manager didn't realise it, he had sown the seed. We went to see an accountant, who asked; "If you're going to build a new stand, how are you going to pay for it? Why are you spending this amount of money to stay in the Northern League?"

"Bishop Auckland and Whitley Bay left for the Northern Premier League in 1988. When Bishops left that season, I went to a funeral in London, and showed some people the press clippings from the Northern Echo afterwards. Someone asked; "When are Spennymoor going, Barrie?", but when we wanted to follow a year later, there were no vacancies in the Northern Premier League.

"So we applied for the Northern Counties East League, which was an alternative route to the NPL. We quit the Northern League in the summer of 1990, the AGM was actually in our own clubhouse. I was scared stiff of being in limbo, because the Northern Counties East League clubs might not have allowed us in, because they might have thought Spennymoor was too far a distance, and we wanted to go straight into their Premier Division. Cliff Morris, the league chairman, assured us that we would get in, and I suspect the Northern Premier League might have had a word with him as well. Sure enough we got in, but we had a very nervous evening at Worsbrough Bridge while the issue was debated.

"It took us three years to get out of that league, it was tough going, and expensive. In our second season, I asked the Winterton chairman how much he was paying -- I was simply looking at one of his players at the time and not admiring him -- and he told me £75. I thought it was for the player I was looking at, but he said; "No, £75 is for the whole team!" I pointed at our subs' bench, and told him that there was two months wages for him just sat there. We were spending a fortune.

"I went for a drink one night in the Ferryhill FC clubhouse, and I chatted to their secretary David James. Ferryhill were going well in the Northern League with Mattie Pearson as player-manager, and when I came home, I decided to ring Mattie and within a few minutes I offered him the job.

"Mattie turned our fortunes around. He got us promotion to the Northern Premier League, through their First Division and into the Premier Division with a couple of cup runs as well. I always remember going to Whitley Bay, and Tommy Moody, one of their officials at the time, came up to me and said: "I'm pleased you've done so well.""

However, the club hit tough financial times. "We had a really successful letter draw going until the National Lottery came along. It absolutely crucified the letter draw, and we had to look for other means of bringing in money. Fortunately, we were successful to a degree with the clubhouse, but we were relying heavily on sportsmen's dinners. That was the beginning of the end, really. More televised football, and then the Rothmans' closure didn't help at all."

Barrie quit as chairman, partly due to ill health, in 2003 – and still trying to win the lottery.

Ray Gowan

Ray was the club's manager when Moors left the Northern League in 1990 and joined the Northern Counties East League.

Ray was appointed following the departure of Tony Monkhouse on March 11th 1989, and was in charge for nearly three years.

"I took over when Spennymoor were halfway up the Northern League First Division. I inherited a very professional outfit from Tony, and there were some very good players there, such as Stephen Storey, Paul Ross, Jackie

Sheekey and Colin McLeod. I built a team around them, and there was some good young talent coming through from the under 19 and under 18 teams.

"We had one full season in the Northern League, 1989-90, and we finished eighth, which was a bit disappointing, because I had wanted to go out with a bang. We also brought in another youngster, Jason Ainsley from Guisborough, who was outstanding at the age of 17. For a young kid, he scored lots of goals. The club then decided to go for the Weekly Wynner League – the Northern Counties East League.

"In that first season, counting all the cup ties, we played 47 games, and Ged Hartley, who had come with my assistant, Peter Mulcaster, at the end of the last Northern League season, played in all of them. Stephen Storey and the keeper, Steve Toth, also played in all but one of them. We built a team together that summer, brought in a few more Northern League players, and made Ged the captain – he seemed the natural choice.

"We got off to a great start, winning our first game at Guiseley, who would be pushing for the title that season. But near the end of that season, we got caught out with fixtures because of our run in the FA Cup. We were left with a lot of games to catch up with in the closing weeks of the season, especially away from home. Our finish was quite difficult, against Denaby, Winterton, Maltby, North Ferriby and Brigg, and we slipped down to third place.

"I thought that the top six or seven teams in the NCEL were better than the Northern League, certainly us, North Shields and Guiseley were handpicked with the aim of winning promotion.

"One of the most memorable games for me was the win over Northwich Victoria in the fourth qualifying round of the FA Cup, when there were around a thousand people in the ground.

"Considering that they were in the Conference, and we were in the Northern Counties East League, way below them, it wasn't a bad result at all. We drew with them at their place, and brought them back to ours for the replay. They didn't have a bad side at all, for example, they had Peter Barnes, who had played for England, in their team, and Roy Sproson, who had played hundreds of games for Port Vale.

"They took the lead though, and we absolutely bombarded them after that. Eventually, Paul Ross equalised with a header, and then one of their defenders scored an own goal in the last minute to put us through. I think that achievement was understated, but nevertheless, the celebrations went on long and late into the night, even Northwich didn't go home until after midnight.

"And then we gave Chesterfield a great game. Coincidentally the referee,

David Allison, was the same one that refereed Doncaster v Brandon two seasons earlier when I was manager at Brandon. Chris McMenemy was assistant at Chesterfield and when we handed in the team sheets I said to Allison; "Are we playing penalties today ref?" He didn't tumble until I reminded him of the previous time we met. Chris thought that the crack was great.

"The only player to give us a problem that day was the centre forward. He had been around a bit, put himself about and was causing Ged Hartley and John Elliott problems. Although Don Peattie equalised at 1-1 we were 3-1 down at half time all due to him. A quiet word with Ged at half time put that right and there was only one team in it in the second half. Boagey's goal with half an hour left was a purler and we murdered them. The crowd of 4000 plus also turned against their own team and there was a great atmosphere. We changed from 3-5-1 to 4-4-2 and tore them to pieces and should have at least equalised. David Allison refereed it fairly, which was most unusual in a David v Goliath encounter.

'The whole crowd gave our players a standing ovation at the end and the Chesterfield manager Paul Hart blanked me although to be fair he telephoned me on the Monday to congratulate us and apologise for his actions. There were no luxuries then - we stopped in a lay-by on the A1 for a packed lunch in Ray Fairley's luxury double decker coach!"

The failure to win promotion, however, increased the pressure, and after four months of the 1991-92 season, Ray was replaced by Mattie Pearson.

"I resigned as manager on November 30th. We were in sixth place, and I really thought that we were on course to win promotion. The problem was, that there was only one promotion place available, and North Shields had a good lead."

Ray was heavily involved in bringing Manchester United to formally open the new stand in 1991. "I had a relationship with Manchester United at the time, which went back to when I transferred Paul Dalton to them from Brandon a couple of years earlier.

"They sent us a good team, which included Gary Pallister, who was recovering from injury, Mark Robins, Ryan Giggs, and Scottish international keeper Jim Leighton.

"I said hello to all the players when they got off the bus, and about 45 minutes before kick off, Jim Leighton came up to me and said; "Ray, can you get me a ball to warm up with?" I said, "Just have a word with Les near the changing room," to which Jim said; "I have, but he won't let me have one until 30 minutes before kick off." He said, "I know you're Jim Leighton, but I don't care if you're Jesus Christ, you're still not getting any balls until thirty minutes before kick off!"

Action from the Spennymoor v Manchester United game at the Brewery Field, United winning 3-1.

Mattie Pearson

Mattie was very successful at the club both as a player and a manager, and has got the medals to prove it. He played in the team that carried all before them in the late seventies, and was manager when Moors blasted their way up the pyramid in the nineties.

"I signed for Spennymoor in 1975, and played for them in midweek games, and for Leeholme Juniors on Saturdays. After I'd played a few games in midweek for Spennymoor, I had a real taste for it, and started playing every week. I worked as an apprentice stonemason in a place at Kirk Merrington, and then as a fork lift truck driver at Courtaulds.

"I'd never been paid to play football before, I thought it was great. I was very hungry and very strong, and when David Curry came along a year after me, I don't think there were two more scruffy so and sos than us two!

"I made my debut aged 16 in some controversy away to Crook. We didn't have a phone at home, and when I came in from work, there was a message from the club to get myself over to Crook for a game that night. I didn't expect to be playing, I thought I was just going over there to make the squad up. I walked into the dressing room, and there were seventeen players in there – I couldn't really understand why I was there.

"Anyway, Kenny Banks named the team, and he announced that he was dropping Tony Rosethorn, whom the club had paid big money for from Dagenham, and was putting me in the team instead. Tony didn't take it well at all. He kicked his bag, and stormed out of the changing room. That didn't bother me, I was ruthless, I wanted to play in the team, and I think I did well, I crossed the ball for Albert Hickman to score.

"I never looked back after that until 1979. We won the league, had a few cup runs and reached the semi final of the FA Trophy. Seven or eight of us in the team were turning out as well for Sunday team Langley Park Rams Head, who were paying ridiculous money.

"The club weren't too happy about that, so they asked the players to sign a contract, but I refused. I got a torrid time from Jack Meggeson the treasurer, and secretary Stan Bradley, because they thought I'd been tapped by Blyth. I hadn't been. The club said that I owed it to them to sign a contract, but I'd given them three or four very good years. I took offence and dug my heels in, and in turn, they left me out of the team for a few games. This went on for nearly four months, and I was getting sick of it, because I just wanted to play for Spennymoor.

"Then one day at the end of a game, somebody ran on the pitch, put his arm around me, and shoved a piece of paper in my hand. On it, was the name of an agent and I contacted him.

"He wanted to take two players to Australia, and he already had one signed up – Kevin Elliott from Ferryhill, who was a quality striker. I was single at the time, and I decided to sign a two year contract out there."

Mattie stayed in Australia for only a year, in which time he won a couple of best player awards and also caught chickens for a part time living. When he came back to Ferryhill, he discovered his family had moved house without telling him!

"I'd been back three days when Stan Bradley and Albert Hickman came to see me, and asked me if I wanted to sign again, and I said only if they would get me a job.

"So Stan set me on at Smart and Browns on a metal press – I didn't want to do that – so he found me a job in the stores. But the glory days were coming to an end then. Bobby Elwell took over as manager, but he didn't gel with some of the strong characters that were in the changing room.

"Right back Butch Simpson was the hardest man in the changing room. Once, he shoved me, and I shouted at him, lashed out and caught him. There were looks of disbelief and shock on the faces of the lads, as if to say; "How dare he speak to Butch like that?" as they waited for the reaction. But

I think we respected each other more after that.
"I had nothing but admiration for another defender, John Heaviside, who later became manager of the club. He was one of the best motivators I ever played under, and he used to get me so wound up before the game, that he had to pull me back and calm me down just before the kick off.
"One mistake we made around that time was when we played John's previous team, Brandon, away in the FA Cup. Brandon were in the Northern Alliance then, but we dropped a clanger by getting changed in the dressing room at Spennymoor, and then going to Brandon by bus! Brandon made good use of that. My mate, Dave Tolson, played for Brandon and he tortured me. I learned a lot that day."
Australia called again in early 1982, and Mattie decided to travel to the other side of the world again. "I wasn't enjoying it as much at Spennymoor the second time around, and I went to play for a Yugoslavian club over there."
Mattie was there for four seasons this time, playing for the State side and also winning several honours in Dubai and Asia before he returned in November 1985.
"Spennymoor had a new manager, Billy Bell, and I was invited to training at Houghton-le-Spring. But Billy and I didn't hit it off, and even though Spennymoor tried several times to get me to sign, I went to Bishop Auckland instead. They sorted out a job for me as a tyre salesman, but I refused to play for them until I started the job, and on the night I refused, they were beaten by Peterlee in a league game. There was hell on.
"I played for them in the Durham Challenge Cup at Ferryhill John Dee, who played on the Dean and Chapter ground near where I lived. We comfortably won 11-0. I got clean through once, and instead of scoring, I squared the ball to Phil Linacre – I didn't dare score because I knew I would have to face some of the Ferryhill lads in the town that night!"
A third spell in Australia followed, this time along with defender Paul Gibbon from Spennymoor, and up and coming midfielder Kenny Lowe, later to play professional for several Football League clubs. Mattie returned for good in 1987. "When I came back, I was offered a job at Vaux Breweries, who also had a team in the Wearside League at the time. They had a real chance of reaching the FA Vase final, and after I played one league game for them, I played for them in the Vase. The pitch must have been ankle deep in mud, which was no good to me, because I was used to hard pitches from my time in Australia. We got beat, and I had an absolute nightmare.
"Kenny Banks then asked me if I fancied managing Ferryhill. Vaux agreed to release me because they were out of the Vase, so I took over at Ferryhill. There wasn't much money there at all. I signed several players for kegs of

beer -- for example, I bought Paul Harnett for two kegs of beer and Keith Gorman cost about four kegs from Brandon! I built a decent team at Ferryhill, and we pushed our way up the league. We also had a great team spirit. For example, for one game I told the players that they had to come in stockings and suspenders and for another to bring a dog!"

Ferryhill's improvement under Mattie didn't go unnoticed just a few miles away at the Brewery Field, where Moors were now in the Northern Counties East League, and trying to battle their way up the pyramid. "Barrie Hindmarch rang me one night, and asked if he could come and meet me. I agreed, and he arrived with John Norman, the vice chairman. But I told him that I wouldn't be interviewed, so he said; "Can we ask some hypothetical questions?" to which I replied; "You'll get hypothetical answers." So we had a long chat, and I said; "If I get the job and I don't get you out of the Northern Counties East League, then you can sack me."

"The same night, Barrie said that I'd got the job, and I quit Ferryhill, replacing Ray Gowan at Spennymoor. I couldn't wait to take over. Barrie thought that I shouldn't play, but I said that I would add something to the team if I played. I made the club mine, I changed the squad around, and only kept a few of the previous players. I brought in John Parnaby, Lee Redhead and Keith Gorman from Ferryhill, and I went after Andrew "Snapper" Shaw from Whitley Bay.

"They were interested in signing Gary Boagey, who wasn't part of my plans, so before I went to talk to them, Barrie gave me £500 to cover the cost of it all. We expected to pay quite a bit for Snapper. Anyway, Whitley Bay said they weren't prepared to pay more than £300 for Gary, taking Snapper into account. I couldn't believe it – I shook hands on the deal straight away. I went back to Spennymoor with £800 in my pocket."

Spennymoor United Northern Counties East League Champions 1992/93

Under Mattie, Moors built a strong, hard-working team that won the Northern Counties League which earned them promotion to the Northern Premier League, or the HFS Loans League as it was then.

"I didn't think the Northern Counties East was as good as the Northern League. They were all very fit sides, and all of them were intent on beating us, but our team wouldn't roll over. But there was a time when my assistant, Dave Barton and I, thought that we might not make it. We were fourteen points clear at one point, but then we started to lose games, and one day we lost at Denaby to give the teams behind us a real chance to catch up.

"The players had left the changing room, and Dave and I were just sat in there, very despondent, thinking what we had to do to put things right. Trevor Beaumont, the club president, then came in, and said; "Come on lads, it can't get any worse."

Dave Barton

"Dave piped up; "Yes, it can, we can play loads worse than that!" I laughed so much at what Dave had said, and in doing so I realised that I had to relax myself, and not to drive the players too hard. I switched off, the players responded, and we got to the last game of the season needing at least a draw against Winterton to beat Pickering to the title.

"I played in that game, and I've got a video of it. About eight or nine minutes from the end with the score 0-0, one of their lads ran towards our penalty area, and I took him out on the edge of our box. The referee gave a free kick against me, and when I checked the video, my tackle is clearly inside. The referee did us a favour. We got the draw we wanted, and we were promoted."

If one nail biter wasn't enough, then another was to come. Moors took the

Trevor Beaumont

Northern Premier League Runners-up 1993/94. Spennymoor Utd 3 Ashton Utd 1

Northern Premier League by storm and on the last day of the 1993-94 season they needed to win to claim the second promotion place, but their opponents Ashton needed only a draw to win promotion themselves.

"They went 1-0 up, and at half time, I told the lads that Ashton would get more nervous the longer the game went on. With fifteen minutes left, it was still 1-0 and we hadn't had a sniff. Suddenly, Keith Gorman scored and that changed the mood and the game completely.

"We scored a second goal, and the kick off had to be delayed because Brian Healy, who wasn't even playing, was still celebrating in the middle of the field. We then ran up the other end and scored a third while two of their players were still on their knees. It was pandemonium. There were loads of celebrations at the final whistle, but I was emotionally drained and I didn't go into the clubhouse for ages afterwards.

Wes Saunders

"Dave Barton and I went to the bar, and we arranged to open some tabs. My brother, David, came in with four of his mates, and I stood on the other side of the clubhouse chatting to Barrie

Officials' memories

Hindmarch.

"Our David said to the bloke behind the bar; "I'm Mattie's brother, and I'm on his tab." "Are you sure?"

"David waved at me, and I waved back, not realising. The barman agreed. Much later in the evening, Barrie pulled me to one side, and said; "How much beer did you drink?" and I said, "Dave and I just had a few pints". Barrie let me off, obviously thinking there had been some sort of mistake. It was only a day or two later that I realised it was our David and his mates buying drinks for everybody!"

Moors established themselves as an exciting attacking side. "We had Jason Ainsley, Brian Healy and Craig Veart in midfield, and to be honest, I don't think there was a better middle three in the country. When those three played, we were phenomenal. Not only did we win promotion that season, but we also won the Durham Challenge Cup, and we won the Northern Premier League Cup – the first team from the First Division to do so. Craig had a tremendous left foot and could score from anywhere. Jason was a very skilful player and could open up defences, and Brian was the backbone of the team. He never looked graceful, but he had it all. He left for Morecambe, and eventually he ended up at Torquay, thanks to Wes Saunders. Having said that, we had quality players right the way through the team, but the midfield was key. Snapper was an excellent player with his back to goal, and Keith Gorman was the fastest player I knew over ten yards."

John Cooke

But the team started to break up over the following seasons. "If we had the strength in depth, then we could have won the UniBond. Jason went to Hartlepool, Brian Healy went to Morecambe, and Snapper eventually left for Bishop Auckland. Wes Saunders, who had been magnificent for us, refused to be sub one day and he had to go. John Cooke moved to Sunderland as physio. In the space of a season, we lost the backbone of the squad and didn't have good enough quality players to replace them. With what I had available financially, I couldn't rebuild a squad that was good enough to keep us in the top three or four of the Premier Division. I brought in some players, but I was outbid by Northern League clubs for others. For example, I went for striker John Milner when he was at his peak, but he decided to stay at Bedlington.

"When I'd been at the club nearly seven years, I decided that I'd been there long enough. The club had progressed nicely for a few years, but had then stood still. However, some of the committee weren't happy with things, and I explained to them that they would have to be patient, and let the players gain experience. I think some of the committee expected me to find players of the same calibre as Brian Healy and Wes Saunders, but it couldn't be done.

"The friction between me and the committee grew, and in the end, I'd had enough, and went round to Barrie's house and resigned. Barrie had supported me throughout and did his best to change my mind, but it was obvious that I didn't see eye to eye with the club. Midtable in the UniBond wasn't good enough for them, even though during my time at the club as a player and a manager, I'd won 17 trophies.

"In the meantime, Gateshead had dropped down from the Conference. They tapped me once at the UniBond presentation night, which was outrageous because their approach was blatant in front of Barrie, but they came along again in the summer of 1998, and I agreed to go there."

Cool-headed Mattie wasn't nervous before games, with just one exception – the home leg of the FA Trophy semi final against Leatherhead in 1978. "The whole area was talking about the second leg, and about our chances of getting to Wembley.

"My own family talked about it and I suddenly realised how big the game was, which made me nervous. When we got to the ground that day, there were a lot of people around the ground, there were press men, a television crew, and the adrenalin was pumping. But if nerves got hold of you, you're in trouble. We played so well in the first half, that we tore them apart. At half time, we were level on aggregate. We pummelled them, we were physically on top of them and nobody thought there was a way back.

"People have suggested that half time in our dressing room was a joke, suggesting that there were committee members and sponsors in there, and we never really had a team talk. Well, I can't remember anybody in there apart from the players. We just didn't get going in the second half."

Mattie gambled on going ahead with the game at Wigan in the first round of the FA Cup in 1994. "When we got to their ground, the match was clearly in doubt because there were a few wet patches on the pitch. The referee was Uriah Rennie, and to give him his due, he came over to me and said; "Look, you're the underdogs, what do you want to do?"

"I said;" We want to play, because on an even keel, they'll beat us." So the referee gave the game the go-ahead. Meanwhile, in the dressing room, Wes

Officials' memories

Mattie Pearson and Bishop Auckland manager Tony Lee place bets before the FA Cup first round in 1994. Neither of them won.

Wes Saunders

Saunders was trying to keep everybody relaxed, and when the ref walked in, all of our players were sat on the floor, playing chase the ace! By the time the game started, their nerves had gone, and for the first 25 minutes we were brilliant until we conceded a goal.

"Wes was one of the strong characters of the dressing room. I had to play in an away game once because we had a few players out injured, and Wes pestered me and pestered me. "Because you're playing, can I be manager?" I said; "Go on then" so he ordered himself a whisky!

"We played Bishops in the Durham Challenge Cup final at Darlington, and my dad, who was a keen Newcastle fan, came to the match. My brother David said; "Keep an eye on Wes Saunders." Dad was excited, because he could remember seeing Wes play for Newcastle. "Point

173

Spennymoor Utd 3 Bishop Auckland 0 (AET) Durham Challenge Cup Final, May 2nd 1994, Feethams.

him out," he said. But our David couldn't see him warming up with the rest of the lads. All of a sudden, Wes walked on to the pitch, in his strip, ten minutes before kick off, smoking a cigarette.
"My dad said: "He's smoking."
"Well, he is a bit unorthodox, dad."
"Wes stubbed out his cigarette, and my dad said pointedly; "He doesn't give a sh*t".
"But what happened? Wes was magnificent that day, and we won in extra time. But what people don't know is, that we didn't want a replay. The game was on the Bank Holiday Monday, and the following Saturday, we were playing Ashton United in the promotion decider. Halfway through extra time, I learned that if we drew that day, then the replay would have been on either the Thursday or the Friday following, which would have been no good to us at all, because winning promotion was the top priority. The Saturday game meant absolutely everything to the club.
"I went down the side of the pitch, and checked with Barrie Hindmarch in the stand, and he confirmed that the game would be replayed the following Thursday. So I had a quick word with Wes and Brian Healy, told them of the problem, and said that we would have to score an own goal to make sure there wasn't a replay.

Officials' memories

"Barry "Bart" Richardson was in goal for us that day. About halfway through the second period of extra time, Wes decided to score the own goal, because he didn't dare leave it too late in case we didn't have possession later in the game. He put the ball towards his own net, and Barry pulled off a cracking save and cleared the ball upfield.
"I went ballistic on the sideline. I screamed; "Why didn't somebody tell Barry?" Meanwhile, the ball had gone up our right hand side, went into the middle, and Brian Healy scored the winner with a cracking overhead kick! We pulled everybody back into defence after that, we didn't dare concede an equaliser otherwise Wes would have had to try again!"

Barry "Bart" Richardson

Mattie was a fitness fanatic from his first day as a player at the Brewery Field, and when he became manager, he was a more than capable replacement in the team when necessary.
"I always tried to keep myself fit, even when I wasn't playing regularly. When I first joined Spennymoor, I always used to be first back on the training runs, and the older players, like Albert Hickman and Butch Simpson, were a little embarrassed. They used to shout at me to stay with them up to the Cock of the North, and then on the way back I used to speed up through Croxdale and leave them behind.
"When I became manager, I took the players on a training run one night, and I led them back through Ferryhill. I went past our house in Ferryhill well ahead of them, and my wife Linda came out and asked; "Where's the players at?" "About half an hour behind," I replied.
Mattie played with many great players at Spennymoor, and reckons Kevin Reilly was the best of the lot. "I can remember when we played away at Durham City, and the ball was driven in from the right. Kevin sprinted down the middle, and while he was on the move, pulled off an amazing overhead kick which flew into the top corner of the net. It was a magnificent goal. I don't think even he knew what his best foot was at times. He once took two penalties in a game, one with his left foot, and the other with his right, and scored them both!
"When Peter Taylor, the Forest assistant manager, came along to try and sign him, Kevin wasn't interested. He went to the clubhouse instead for a

pint. When somebody said that Kevin wasn't going to Forest, I raised my hand, and said; "Can I go instead?"
Just like Kevin Reilly, Mattie remained at the Brewery Field to become one of the club's greatest ever servants.

Alan Murray

Alan was one of the key figures in the rebirth of football at the Brewery Field, and was deeply involved in the negotiations to move Evenwood Town to Spennymoor and start the new Spennymoor Town club – and one of his ambitions is to see the club revert to its old name of Spennymoor United.

"Ken Houlahan asked me if I wanted to get involved at Evenwood when he was manager. My sponsorship, if you like, started with a bottle of champagne for the man of the match, and I would also pay match expenses. I think everybody deep down wants to be involved in football, so if you've never played, then helping to run a club is something you want to do.

"I then became chairman of the club, but it became obvious that if wanted to achieve our ambitions then we would have to leave Evenwood, because there were problems with the parish council and vandalism.

Alan Murray

"A number of clubs approached me and asked me if I would like to join them, and I was asked if I wanted to put money into Spennymoor in 2004, but I refused because I didn't think the circumstances were right at the time. The situation at Spennymoor changed in early 2005. I'd been told about the history and support at Spennymoor, and how unbelievable and passionate the supporters were. So Ken went and checked a few things out.

"When Spennymoor United went out of existence, we knew with the Wimbledon situation that it was possible to move Evenwood Town across without there being too many problems. There was hardly any support at Evenwood, a lot of money had been spent, and the ground was literally being destroyed by vandals.

"I was, and still am, very ambitious, and I wanted to be successful. The FA, Durham FA and the Northern League agreed the switch to Spennymoor, and we put a business plan together for the council. We heard about the

group that the fans had put together, so we contacted them, and they came on board with us. It was obvious that the supporters didn't want the club to die, and it was better that there was only one proposal rather than two. "We had a meeting with the supporters at the Penny Gill pub, and then another one in the Catholic Club. Everybody was very keen and enthusiastic to get the club going again. Alan Courtney, who knew the people of Spennymoor, agreed to come on board as vice chairman. As an outsider not coming from the town, going into the club didn't bother me, because I knew that if we asked for help and had an open door policy, the supporters would rally round."
And the supporters certainly got behind the club, with over 500 at the first game of the season against Darlington RA. "It was a real boost to see that many people in the ground, and I knew that we were on the right lines. But the relationship between Ken and me deteriorated, unfortunately, and we didn't see eye to eye on a few things. It got to the point where the board gave me a vote of no confidence while I was away on holiday, and I wondered whether I should pack in and move on. Four supporters then came to see me, and after a lengthy meeting, it was quite clear that they wanted me to stay. They were as keen as I was to see the club climb out of the Northern League second division. But there was no way I was going to continue putting money into the club while Ken was there, so I pulled it out.
"I spoke with Jamie Pollock and Jason Ainsley about taking over as manager and assistant manager at the end of the season, and they agreed. The club actually had two managers, because Ken had appointed Justin Perry as manager. He had already spoken to Jamie and Jason, but they weren't too keen at the time. I actually stopped them from taking over at another club and persuaded them to come to Spennymoor.
"I didn't have an axe to grind with Justin Perry at all. The fact was that I wanted success, and in my view the way forward was with Jamie and Jason.
"Mike Amos, the Northern League chairman, offered to act as mediator. I was prepared to go to court to be re-instated as chairman, and I suggested that if the board didn't want confrontation, they should resign instead. After some discussions, that's what they did, without any conditions."
After that row, the dust started to settle in the summer of 2006. "Jamie and Jason did very well to put a strong side together because they only had four players left over from the previous season, so they had to start from scratch. I liked what I heard from them.
"We had a great season. I think one of the highlights for me was when the police turned out in force for some reason when we played at Goole for

some reason, and the chief inspector came up to me during the game and told us that we would be leaving straight after the match, and I replied that we weren't, and we were staying instead!

"The season went to plan on the field, and I was absolutely delighted when we won the league. When we were given the Second Division championship trophy, I did some research and discovered that it was the Oxo cup – the same cup that had been presented to the club when it won the North Eastern League at the turn of the last century! We achieved what we set out to achieve, which was winning the second division, and it was fantastic to win it by ten points.

"At the end of the season, Jamie said that he wanted to leave in order to take his coaching badges, and I wanted Jason to take over – but he seemed frightened to take the job until he spoke with me and a few other people." But then just before the start of the season, the club was threatened with eviction by their town council landlords over several issues that were happily resolved later with the help of Northern League chairman Mike Amos.

"Maybe there should have been more meetings between us and the council, but I was taken ill during the season. I hope that the club can work closer with the council in the future, after all, there's been a good partnership between us in the past.

"What I would love to do now is to persuade the football authorities to let us call ourselves Spennymoor United again. I've tried a couple of times, but each time they've said no. After all, I've always said "United we stand.""

Ken Houlahan

Ken was the other half of the double act which saw Evenwood move across to the Brewery Field and renamed Spennymoor Town in the summer of 2005.

Ken had watched Spennymoor United in action in the UniBond League earlier in the year. "I went to see Spennymoor play in what turned out to be its penultimate home game, and I'd had the idea of moving Evenwood about a month before that.

"I sold the idea confidentially to the board at Evenwood, and their agreement to it was crucial. After Spennymoor played Blyth in their last home game and then failed to fulfil any more fixtures, I spoke to Mike Amos, the Northern League chairman about the idea, and he was all for it. "The whole ethos was about creating a club that was rooted in the community and wasn't relying entirely on one man's money. Everybody was in favour of the idea, and I had the job of changing the name to the approval of the full members' committee at the FA and Durham FA.

Officials' memories

"I became stuck in the middle of tripartite negotiations with the FA and Durham FA. I suggested Spennymoor United, but the FA told me that there would be no way that particular name would be accepted. I got sick of trying to find an agreeable name, and in the end, I had one on my mobile, and the other on my landline at the same time – a sort of conference call, if you like – and we all agreed on the name Spennymoor Town. Legally, it was Evenwood Town trading as Spennymoor Town.

"We were delighted with the response of the fans at the time, and what appealed to the Town Council was having a club from the community that could afford to play at any level. We developed a football partnership with the councils, and discussed setting up a women's team and a youth team.

"The new club got off to a great start in the Northern League and I must admit I was a proud man when our Martin scored a beauty, a curler into the top corner in the 3-2 win against Darlington RA in the first game.

"But it was obvious that if we were going to mount a promotion challenge, we were going to need some defenders, but we couldn't afford them.

"Later in the season, Alan Murray and I fell out over the plans for a privately owned clubhouse and the terms of the ground lease. We both had very different viewpoints over them, and in the end, I felt it best to resign because we were at odds with each other all the time. To me, it was all about having a sustainable club that could pay its way in the community."

Chapter 13

Fan memories

Garry Nunn

I first started following the Moors in 1976, my first game was an away match at Ashington. I don't know why I decided to travel away instead of going to a home game first, I think I just fancied it. We drew 3-3, and I was hooked after that.

During the FA Trophy run in 1977 and 1978, I was serving in the Navy, and when we were at sea, I used the ship-to-shore telephone to keep in touch with results. We were allowed to use the phone at a subsidised rate, but it must have cost the Navy a fortune.

There's a Spennymoor scarf somewhere on the Falkland Islands. I helped to build the new runway after the 1982 conflict, and I managed to lose it – I think it's underneath the concrete somewhere!

I became involved with the club after I did an IT course. I had an interview at the Job Centre and the bloke who was interviewing me said that he had "heard" that the club was looking for a voluntary programme editor, but even though there was no money involved, it would give me the chance to learn and use my skills. I contacted Barrie Hindmarch and began at the start of the 1996-97 season. I didn't have a car at the time, so on a couple of occasions I walked through to Chilton to Barrie's office so then I could put the programme together!

Three games stick in my memory. The 2001 FA Trophy tie at Atherstone when Wayne Edgcumbe was sent off after an argument with their chairman, who had come storming furiously on to the field to insist that he was dismissed for some reason. Jason Ainsley scored a cracking winner for us. Another game was when we beat Ashton United at home to win promotion to the NPL Premier Division at the end of season 1993-94.

Ashton only needed a point for promotion and led 1-0 with fifteen minutes left, we needed to win. Snapper scored from a right wing cross to make it 1-1 and Keith Gorman scored another one. The atmosphere was terrific inside the ground that day. It was a great season, because we also won the League Cup and we beat Bishop Auckland in the final of the Durham Challenge Cup.

180

Fan memories

I went to Wigan in the FA Cup, and when I got to the ground, their programme editor was very apologetic because they didn't have a proper programme because their machine had broken down, and all they had was an A5 leaflet. He bought me a pint as an apology. The highlight of the game was Gummer (Keith Gorman) being one on one with their keeper, not a defender in sight. It had been raining heavily all day, and there was lots of surface water. With five yards to go to the box, it looked a definite goal, until the ball got stuck in a puddle. Gummer reached the box, but the ball didn't.

Keith Gorman

Roy Heales

I joined the committee in 1967, and I used to help do lots of jobs around the ground in my spare time. I used to be a tipper driver, and chuck timber and bricks over the wall to use on the ground.

There used to be about two dozen people all going for the 19 places on the committee – you had to be a season ticket holder before you could stand -- and so it used to go to a vote. One year, I came second in the vote, which I was really chuffed about, there was only Mattie Robinson who beat me.

Roy Needham

I can remember when there used to be entertainment on the ground before and during the match at half time. There used to be military bands, tug o wars and once we had the Durham Light Infantry Band. We even had a big firework display.

The game against Goole at their place was a unique occasion. My dad was on the committee at Goole, and I was on the committee at Spennymoor! My dad didn't come to the replay at Spennymoor, which we won.

Russell Ferguson

One of my heroes in particular was Kenny Banks (whose daughter Joanne became a close friend of mine through the Joanne Banks dance group and as such I became good friends with Kenny and his wife) together with the likes of Kenny Heslop, Albert Hickman, Geoff Hart, Paul Main and of course the legendary Geoff "Butch" Simpson.

During an away game at Bishop Auckland when they played at the

Kingsway ground, the Spennymoor supporters were at the Kingsway end of the ground and a group of Bishop youths were in the old wooden stand, they were hurling abuse at our supporters in an attempt to possibly cause trouble. Some police officers came into the ground where the Spennymoor supporters were, heard the abuse that we were taking from the "youths" and then went back out of the ground. They returned with two police dogs and immediately walked to the "youths".
They were frogmarched up to the top end of the ground towards the Spennymoor supporters by the police, once they got these youths at the top end, right at the front of the supporters the police officers totally humiliated these youths by saying "come on children it's time for you to go home to your mummy". We absolutely howled with laughter at their embarrassment.

When Gary O'Hara played for Spennymoor United, he used to play bingo in the clubhouse on Saturday nights. When the number 33 was called he used to shout it out in his Irish accent which was very amusing, as a result I had my shirt printed with "OHara 33" on the back to show my support for this great lad, which I still have to this day.
We made plenty of noise when we followed the team away from home, in fact we made so much noise at an away game at Emley, that the referee threatened to report us all for inciting a riot. He went to the sidelines, and told Emley to broadcast a warning over the PA system about all the noise we were making. We didn't take any notice of it!

Graham Smith
The FA Cup tie at Chesterfield in 1990 was probably one of the best away trips we had. We went a goal down after about 15 minutes and I couldn't really see us getting back into it. Their supporters were singing all sorts of songs but when we equalised after about 20 minutes you could have heard a pin drop on their side of the ground. We all erupted into "you're not singing any more". They got two late goals at the end of the first half so it looked like damage limitation but halfway through the second half Gary Boagey got one back with a volley from outside the box and in truth it could have gone either way, both sides created chances. Chesterfield hung on and their supporters were mightily relieved to hear the final whistle. In truth they were a more skilful side and made the better play and probably deservedly won but we just doggedly battled and contested every ball.
We played Radcliffe Borough at home in the UniBond League First Division in season 1993-94. We won 4-1, and one particular incident got the biggest cheer of the day. A Radcliffe defender cleared the ball from the edge

of his box, and the ball went clean through one of the open bedroom windows on Tyne Crescent. A few minutes later, the occupant came to the window, and you should have seen the angry look on his face. Chairman Barrie Hindmarch said to one of the committee men, "You'd better get yourself around there, and take this cheque book with you."

I couldn't watch much of the promotion game against Ashton United in 1994 when we needed to win, and Ashton needed to win or draw for promotion. I was really worried that we would go an early goal down, and they would put eleven men behind the ball to make it difficult for us. There was a long queue to get in the ground that day, the crowd was probably over a thousand, and I had to run over to Tees Crescent to get into the ground because there was a long queue outside the main gates.

My worst fears were realised when they went 1-0 up after about ten minutes. I couldn't watch any more, so I went into the clubhouse, drank half a coke and hoped to hear the roar of the crowd if we equalised. But it never came. I couldn't go out for the second half either, and when there was about ten minutes left, I decided to go in the ground and see the game through to the bitter end.

We were attacking the top end, and the ball came into the middle, where Snapper stuck out a foot and the ball went in. Five minutes after that, another goal went in, and instead of people moaning and groaning, suddenly they were leaping all over the place. And people were still jumping around when Gummer got the third one. The ground just turned from despair to euphoria in the space of a few minutes. There was a hell of a celebration at the end, everybody ran on the field, shouting and singing. And when we went in the clubhouse later, Barrie Hindmarch bought everyone a drink. It was our second successive promotion, but I felt sorry for the Ashton supporters, because their team had missed out for the second year running.

Funnily enough, we lost the first three games of that season against Warrington, Goole and Netherfield, and some of the fans thought there was a danger of us ending up in the Northern Counties East League again. But then Mattie (Pearson) signed Wes Saunders, and we never looked back. I remember when Wes and the Guiseley centre half got involved in some argy-bargy off the ball, and Wes lamped him one. The lad had to be carried off with concussion.

I went to a game at Alfreton once, and thought we'd won, when we hadn't. I went with a friend of mine, John Plummer, and we had a couple of beers before the game. We missed the first goal because we were still in the clubhouse, and we missed our equaliser just before half time because we were in the clubhouse again. We didn't know that Alfreton scored just after half time to go 2-1 up because we were finishing off our drinks, so when we went outside, we thought it was 1-1 still. So when we scored, we thought we were winning 2-1. It was only when the final whistle went then we heard from the other Moors fans that the game had ended in a draw. So we'd only seen one goal out of four in the match!

Sometime in the early 90's we were drawn against Billingham Town in the Durham Challenge Cup. They were in the Northern League Div 2 at the time. This game is the only game I've seen Spennymoor score eight goals and after the end of the match we signed the opposing team's keeper, non other than Adrian Swann, who was to become a permanent fixture in our most successful seasons in the Unibond Premier. The first half was dominated by Spennymoor and we had built up a 5-0 lead by half time, the game looked over and we appeared untouchable, it could have been more had it not been for Swanny saving a penalty and numerous other efforts, from what I recall you couldn't have blamed him for any of the goals. The game was totally different after the restart. Billingham came at us and scored straight from the kick off, a consolation goal we thought? Then five minutes of sustained pressure gave them a second. Still they pressed and after another five minutes or so they got a third. We were panicking – surely we can't throw away a five goal lead. They continued to press (and reduce our supporters' life expectancies) but eventually we were able to get the sixth which really killed them off. We then regained our dominance, added another two goals and Swanny saved another penalty, final score 8-3. We must be the only team in the country to have put eight past a side and then signed their keeper. To be fair, despite the scoreline Swanny actually had a hell of game and it would have been a lot worse for them without him!!

When the club was struggling and the wage bill had been slashed, we had a lad called Paul English on the books. He was a great lad, but not the best dresser, shall we say. Darlington had agreed to loan us two players, who turned up looking very smart – you could tell that they were from a professional club – and waited near the players' tunnel. Paul English then turned up, wearing some knackered old jeans and carrying an Asda carrier bag with some muddy boots ticking out the top. The looks on the Darlo lads' faces said; "what the hell are we doing here?" Paul turned round and said; "Don't worry lads, I'm sponsored by Asda!"

John Gibbons

One of my first memories of following Spennymoor was when I was allowed to travel on the team bus to an away game in 1964. I was nine at the time. My gran went to an over 60s club, and one day she got chatting

Fan memories

to Spennymoor secretary Bob Hutchinson, who arranged the trip for me as a treat. I was king of the world for a day, I was chuffed to bits to be on the same bus as the players. I sat in the middle of the bus, on my own, but all the players were quite chatty. Alan Iceton asked me to carry his bandages in to the ground for him, so then I didn't have to pay to get in! My favourite player at the time was forward Keith Walklate, mainly because he had longer hair than all the other players, he played with his sleeves rolled up, and he reminded me of Denis Law, the famous Manchester United player. It was another forty years before I travelled on the team bus again, to Eastwood Town.

I travelled regularly on the supporters' bus, and one day we had to stop at Sacriston so then full back Brian Berryman could get on. He'd missed the team bus for some reason. But maybe Derek Fawell should have caught the supporters' bus one day to Stanley. Derek, who didn't come from this area, went to the wrong Stanley – he went to the Stanley near Chester-le-Street and not the one near Crook, and he didn't arrive until the second half.

I went all the way down to Kingstonian for the FA Amateur Cup tie in 1964. I think I was wearing the black and white shirt I bought from the Co-op for five shillings, it was meant to be a Newcastle shirt, but to me it was always the black and white of Spennymoor. We got beat 11-2 that day, and by the time we got behind the goal which we were attacking, we were 2-0 down. Every corner we got that day, they seemed to score from at the other end! The occasion was too much for our keeper, George Carney, who was a bag of nerves.

When we played Wycombe at home in an Amateur Cup replay, quite a few of their fans came up, and one of them was dressed like Merlin the Magician. There was a big blue ball on the centre circle, and he waved his magic wand at it.

We'd been to Wycombe before, and the supporters' buses got lost on the way to the ground. We didn't get there until twenty minutes before kick off, and when we popped into the snobbish local pub, they wouldn't serve us pints, so we asked for 18 half pints instead.

I think the best Spennymoor performance I ever saw was at Skelmersdale in the Amateur Cup. They were a very good team, and the previous year they'd lost in the final at Wembley. But we played magnificently, and John Tobin scored our winner.

We also celebrated one day at Emley in the UniBond League. We played really well, and when Keith Gorman scored, Joe Curry (David's dad) was that pleased we had scored, he threw his cap up in the air – and it got stuck on the top of the fence! We all had a good laugh as he tried to clamber up in order to retrieve it.

Jimmy Soakell was also a character. He also used to give opposing players some stick, and one day at Evenwood, the ball went out of play at the top end. Jimmy started to shout something at Evenwood player Bob Tookey, who winked at the rest of us, and said to Jimmy "You and me, outside after the game." Jimmy was on the supporters' bus by 4.30.

When we beat Bishop in the Durham Challenge Cup final at Darlington in 1994, the Bishops' players were distraught as we waited for the cup to be presented. Jimmy walked amongst them, saying "Not good enough today, lads."

Frank Smith

I can remember when Craig Veart scored straight from the kick off at Whitby in September 2000. Whitby had just gone 3-1 up, Craig scored from the kick off and we ended up with an unlikely 3-3 draw. That was one of the very few highlights in the nightmare season of 2000-01. Towards the end of April, we still only had eight points in the league, and had only scored one home league goal since October. And when we finally did score again after waiting so long, I was in the old tea hut buying a pie and missed it! The same match (April 26th v Leek) was our first game after Peter Mulcaster's resignation. Craig Veart took charge as temporary player-manager and went on a four game unbeaten run, ending the season with the mighty total of 14 points. Apart from being one of the best Spennymoor players I've seen in the last forty years, I reckon Craig's unbeaten managerial record is second to none!

Jon Le Poidevin

I was only ten when I went to Chesterfield for the first round FA Cup tie there. Gary Boagey scored one of the best goals I've seen from the just outside the box, the ball flew into the net. In the second half, we won a corner in front of the Spennymoor fans, and Percy Armstrong, one of the fans, ran on to the pitch and took it!

I also went to Wigan for our first round tie there. We fancied our chances because they weren't doing too well in the Fourth Division. We had masses of fans in Wigan but some never got to the game because of public order offences. My mate told me that they had to go back to Wigan a fortnight later to face the Magistrates Court. After they all had pleaded guilty and been fined, the three magistrates asked if they had anything to say and Tog (my mate) said; "Yes, I'd like to wish you, you and you a merry Christmas and Happy New Year."

My dad once did a streak at Whitby. We were losing 3-0 in the closing minutes, and he decided to strip off on the spur of the moment. He handed me his clothes, and ran on to the field where the ref blew a halt to the game and three stewards chased him and tried to wrestle him to the ground. Both sets of players were laughing, and Jason Ainsley shouted; "Stop laughing lads, that's my dad!"

Afterwards, when he'd got his clothes back on, we made a dash out of the ground before the police came, and after the great escape was complete, we decided later to go back to the clubhouse while all the players were there, and you'll never believe what my dad decided to wear so he wouldn't be noticed? A Mexican sombrero style hat. As soon as he walked in the clubhouse there was a massive cheer.

The Whitby streaker

My most memorable game was beating Bishop Auckland in the final of the Durham Challenge Cup at Durham City's ground. After the game we all went back to the clubhouse where Barrie Hindmarch filled the cup with lager, and officials, players and fans passed it around taking it in turns to have a drink.

Another funny moment was when we lost 1-0 to Colwyn Bay in the FA Cup first round. Brian Healy missed a penalty at 0-0, he put it over the bar. In the clubhouse afterwards the fans were booing the ref, Uriah Rennie, and he turned round and said; "I gave you a penalty and you blew it, what more do you want?"

Ron Graves

I was ten years old when I went to the Amateur Cup game at Kingstonian. My dad, Cliff Graves, was a cutter man at Mainsforth Colliery and had been working through the night before. He arrived home to find me waiting, dressed and wearing a black and white bobble hat, scarf and rosette, ready for him to take me to the match. We had to catch the supporters' bus early, because the trip to Kingston-on-Thames was very long and the furthest from Spennymoor that most of us had ever been. Everyone was full of optimistic anticipation and expecting a good run in the cup.

When we arrived at Kingstonian's Richmond Road ground and got off the bus some wags starting shouting, "Lock up your daughters" and "The Spenny lads are here" and (I think as a satire on southern ignorance about where Spennymoor was) "The Vikings are here". Actually, being so far south (further than Darlington!) did feel a bit like being in a different country and I was particularly intrigued to see Afro-Caribbean people in the streets, something that in those days you didn't exactly encounter in County Durham.

Once inside the ground and standing behind the goal a rumour began to circulate that there was a problem with some of the players: there'd been an accident, possibly a car crash, someone was injured and wouldn't be able to play. I don't remember the full details, but we definitely didn't field the expected team that day and almost from the beginning it was obvious that we were under the cosh. I kept hearing the same voice slowly intoning, almost in a drone, "Come on you K's" and Kingstonian just kept scoring, netting five (I think) by half time. When the referee blew to end the first half, the poor Moors keeper (he was a replacement for the usual custodian) seemed shell-shocked and stood immobile in his goalmouth until one of the trainers, either ours or theirs, walked him off the field.

The second half was no better. Although we supporters never stopped shouting the players on, and my hands ached from rattling the black and white crake I had with me, Kingstonian remained dominant. The goals kept coming and, despite at least one breathtaking save from our keeper - when he parried the ball and then twisted through the air like a corkscrew to push the returning shot around the post – Spennymoor United went down to a crushing 11 – 2 defeat. But it didn't end there.

Kingstonian showed us all great hospitality and the evening was spent in what seemed to us to be an opulent clubhouse. Of course, my ten-year-old heart was broken and I remember a Kingstonian club official coming to talk to my dad. He appeared to be a very pleasant man and complimented Spennymoor United on how well we had taken defeat.

My dad just replied, "It'd be difficult to cry foul when you get beat 11-2." Then, the man put his hand on my shoulder and said, "Would you like a glass of Coca Cola?"

"We won't forget you," was the only reply I could make, choking back the tears, but the man seemed to understand and got me the Coke anyway.

Later, two groups of eleven supporters stood behind lines that had been chalked on the floor. Each man had a glass of beer at his feet and the idea was to see which group could be first to drink eleven pints. When a "referee" blew his whistle the first man would pick up his pint, drink and as soon as his empty glass was back on the floor the next man would take

over. There really was no competition. The devastation of the result on the pitch was matched by the hammering our Spennymoor lads visited upon the Kingstonian supporters - but it was only fleeting compensation.
I seem to recall that travelling home through the night dad and I sat behind the legendary Moors supporter Ellen ('Nellie') Downs, who sobbed a lot and pored over an autograph book holding the signatures of everyone from Kenny Banks, who had played that day, to Duggie Humble from years before. She told me we'd recover from this defeat and that it would be better next week, but her tear-stained face simply seemed to confirm that loving your hometown club meant having to bear heartbreak.
Almost home, early on Sunday morning, dad and I walked from the Brewery Field to our house at 28 Dean Road, Low Spennymoor. As we came down Weardale Street a lad was delivering papers on the opposite side and, seeing me wearing the Moors' colours, called out, "Did we win?"
"No, we got beat."
"Well in the 'Pink' it said eleven two, so everybody thought it was a mistake. Did we not win two one?"
"No, we didn't," dad shook his head sorrowfully, "The 'Pink' was right."
I also went to the Chesterfield game in 1990. I recall the police made a bit of an issue about some Moors fans who, they claimed, had thrown a pool ball onto the pitch. This was before the game kicked off and absolutely nobody but the policeman who produced the pool ball saw any sign of it being thrown. I was quite close, too.
During the game, the local constables had another go - this time about Moors fans standing too close to where a Chesterfield player was taking a corner!
At the end of the game the Spennymoor players were applauded all around the ground by the Chesterfield fans and the local media said we were the best opposition seen there so far that season.

Peter Bennett

I was eleven (nearly twelve!) at the time of the Leatherhead game in 1978 and would say that Spennymoor were one of the best non-league teams in the country at the time. I had little doubt that we would overturn the 2-0 first leg deficit.
We had beaten many good sides already, including Dagenham (before they merged with half of East London). At half time it seemed we were going to Wembley. I had no doubt that we would score more in the second half, we had played them off the pitch in the first half.
Somehow that goal didn't come and then disaster when Alan Porter dropped the ball from a corner after I think colliding with Geoff "Butch"

Simpson and Leatherhead scored. The horror of realising that Wembley was no longer beckoning was awful.

I do remember seeing Geoff Hart crying. I can't recall if I did run on the pitch or say anything to the players. I suspect I probably did as I know I watched the second half from near the old wooden stand by the toilets and I left the ground numb and crying via the Durham road exit, despite needing to head back into the town centre.

Since then, I graduated to following Newcastle home and away from the mid-late 80s, and have seen Newcastle lose two FA Cup Finals and two cup semis. Nothing watching Newcastle - even relegation, humiliations etc -- has ever hurt as much as that Leatherhead defeat.

I was nine years old for the Southport game in 1975. I knew it was a big result only because of the media coverage and the size of the crowd that day. To think my parents let me travel down from Kirk Merrington to the game unaccompanied by an adult. It wouldn't happen today.

I remember Southport scoring early on and then Spennymoor fighting back, led by Kenny Banks. He was a class player and a great servant of the club – Spennymoor's own Roy of the Rovers. However, my favourite player of that era was Kevin Reilly, he always reminded me of Arsenal midfielder Liam Brady, a very skilful player who could have played at a much higher level. The whole team of the seventies was full of good players though. No nonsense defenders like Butch Simpson, Albert Hickman, who always seemed ancient even then on account of his grey hair. Geoff Hart up front, and in the eighties, Dennis Foster was one of my heroes.

I can remember one goal that Kevin Reilly scored against Evenwood, when he picked the ball up on the halfway line, ran to the edge of their box and curled the ball into the top corner – unstoppable.

It was around 1982 we played Consett in a cup semi-final at home in a night match. The game ended 1-1 but by the end of the first period of extra time it was 3-1 to us. Before the fans had swapped ends for the second period of extra time Consett had pulled the two goals back and it went to penalties. The number of penalties was high. I remember it well as I had cycled down from Kirk Merrington for the game and my parents were worried as I didn't get home till well after 11pm- remember it was long before mobile phones!

Andrew Robinson

I can remember the Manchester United game vividly. It was the year after Italia 90 and Jim Leighton was in goal for the Reds that night.

We gave him a load of grief from behind the goal with regards his antics

Fan memories

and bloopers against such teams like Costa Rica the previous year when he was in goal for Scotland in the World Cup. I also seem to remember that he had daubed a thick wad of Vaseline on his eyebrows to stop the sweat from rolling into his eyes – it was a warm, balmy evening in Spennymoor. Mark Robins was cracking for United that evening and they had a strong side with them.

My dad, Norman, ran the supporters buses for years and years and a lot of memories probably wouldn't have happened if it wasn't for my dad organising coaches week after week – my childhood was interrupted on an almost daily basis by people phoning or knocking on our door to arrange their seat on the coach for the next away game! He even stumped up cash from his own pocket on several occasions in order that folk could get to the game.

Stockton v Spennymoor August 27th 1949

We'll Always Be United

CARTOONIST DUDLEY HALLWOOD on Saturday watched the Durham County Challenge Cup-tie at Blaydon between Blaydon and Spennymoor United, with the above result.

A cartoonists view of the 1953 Durham Challenge Cup tie between Blaydon and Spennymoor United.

Chapter 14

Player memories

Alan Kell

Alan Kell

Inside forward Alan was a real Spennymoor lad, who was born within a stone's throw of the ground, and gave over a decade's service when the club was at its peak in the seventies.

"My dad was a butcher, and because he couldn't play football on Saturdays, he used to play for a team called Spennymoor Wednesdays, because that was the afternoon off for all of the shop workers during the week.

"I had hoped to be a professional footballer with Darlington, but I wasn't good enough, I just played a couple of first team games, and I was one of the regular amateurs in their reserve team. There were a few apprentices, a couple of first team players who were coming back from injury and out of favour, and a couple of amateurs, like me.

"I was approached by two Spennymoor committee members who came round to our house. I made my mind up that I wasn't going to play for Darlington reserves in the Wearside League, I wanted to play for Spennymoor. I'd played for Darlington against Spennymoor in a friendly on the Brewery Field, and I ran my socks off – but I couldn't get anywhere near the Spennymoor players.

"My first game was in the Northern League against West Auckland, who at that time were a middle of the table team. Keith Hopper, who had been my coach at Darlington, was playing for them, so you can imagine that there was some banter between us. We were losing 2-0, and we won a corner. The ball came over and was cleared out to the edge of the box, I came running in and volleyed it into the roof of the net. It was a good job the net was in

193

the way because the ball would have cleared the pond behind the bottom end!

"Secretary Stan Bradley and coach Bob Bell must have thought that I was a goalscoring machine, because in the next game away to South Bank, I was moved further forward to support John Tobin, but I didn't score again for another ten years. I think it was a header from a Geoff Hart cross."

When Alan started playing, the Moors' team was always chosen by the committee, and not the manager or coach. "At away games, Stan Bradley, Jack Meggeson and Jack Smith would pick the team whilst they were standing in the middle of the field. We always knew that there were problems when somebody took their hat off! Bob Bell would stand nearby and only speak if he was spoken to, and then he would come back into the dressing room and say; "Right lads, this is what they've given me" – it was his way of saying "Don't blame me if it goes wrong!" There was many a time when we said that we wanted the coach to have the responsibility of choosing the team, and eventually the committee, to their credit, accepted that.

"My game was placed on a lot of energy and effort, of taking the ball and giving it. I rarely did a defence-splitting pass, my job was simply to find one of our forwards or midfielders. Whenever we played Blyth, their midfielder Eddie Alder was always on the losing side against us, because I nullified him, got the ball and gave it to one of our players. Even though part of my job entailed winning the ball, I was never booked in thirteen years.

"The team hardly changed during the time I was there. If you look at a picture of the team when I started, and then compare it with a picture of the team when I left, eight or nine players would be on both.

"The biggest reason why we did so well together wasn't because we were the best eleven players in the league, but because we were the eleven who played as the best unit in the league. We were a real core of players that blended together well. Only very rarely did we make a mistake against a lesser team. Teams used to think that they could beat us, and say that they could sometimes, but we always used to shake hands and say hard lines to them at the end of matches!

"When Kenny Banks became manager, for some reason he would have a dilemma every now and again about whether to play himself. He had a huge amount of skill and could create goals from nothing, and maybe sometimes he talked himself out of playing when he shouldn't have.

"I have never come across anybody as dedicated as Billy Bell when he was manager. If ever a guy was fanatical, it was Billy, because he must have spent ages working out his coaching techniques. He taught us how to do

crossovers and setpiece routines, simple basic stuff that we did very well.
"We used to train at Spennymoor Grammar School under the floodlights. One night, they weren't working, so we thought training would be abandoned, or we would just go for a run. But Billy had other ideas – he told us to park our cars, facing the training area, and switch the headlights on! He managed to hold a full training session like that."

One of Alan's early tastes of FA Cup action was against Shrewsbury in the first round proper in 1972. "I was left out of the home game at the Brewery Field, but I came back into the team for the replay the following Wednesday. We played very well, but it didn't help us when we picked up a couple of injuries, one of them to our keeper Dickie Adamson.

"I remember at 0-0 in the first half that Geoff Parker hit a real screamer which the keeper just managed to keep out, and I still don't know how he managed it.

"We played very well in the first thirty minutes, and I think Shrewsbury didn't enjoy being outplayed. They had more nous than us, maybe we were a little naïve, and a couple of challenges by their players were arguable and were intended to upset us, which they did. We lost our cool a little bit because we weren't wise enough to handle it. I can also remember that we played in yellow that night – I think we only played in that colour once."

But despite that FA Cup setback, Moors dominated the Durham Challenge Cup in the following years. "We won the Durham Challenge Cup four years in a row, and we were given a little personal cup on a black stand every time, which seemed to get a quarter inch smaller every year we won it, almost as if the price had gone up!

"People say that we played a lot of games in those days in a short space of time, but we didn't mind. We thought nothing of playing three games in four days, maybe a league game on Good Friday and Easter Monday, and the Durham Challenge Cup final in between. We were very keen to play. We always seemed to play Ferryhill on Good Friday and Easter Monday, and there was one season when we lost to them and didn't win the title. Blyth pipped us.

"I can think of only one occasion when we let ourselves down, away to Rotherham in an FA Cup tie when we lost 6-0. There were some very poor individual performances that night, people doing things they shouldn't. We were very bad, probably the worst we played in my time there.

"There were some fantastic games. I can remember when we played Whitley Bay, and we were 5-0 up by half time, and just ended up winning 6-5. All but one of the goals came downhill, because there was a strong wind blowing down the pitch! We attacked them straight from the kick off at the start of the second half, and by the 50th minute we were 6-0 up. We attacked them more in those five minutes than what they had done in the whole of the first 45. But then Billy Wright, their big centre forward, tortured us, and we couldn't do a thing with him, but we managed to hang on. Our goalkeeper, Dickie Adamson, took a goal kick, and the wind was so strong, that the wind caught the ball before it left the penalty area, and blew it straight back over his head.

"We used to enjoy kicking uphill best of all at home, because we were playing towards our fans. There seemed to be a better atmosphere behind the top goal. When we lost to Leatherhead in the Trophy semi final, we kicked towards the top end in the first half, and led 2-0 at half time. They bundled in a corner in the second half to give them the goal they wanted to go through. At the final whistle, one of their lads came over to me to shake hands, and said: "You don't like kicking downhill as much as you do uphill, do you?" I agreed. "We thought so. When we watched you play in the Northern League, we made a note of that." So they'd done their homework – they made sure they kicked downhill first half."

Alan left the club for Whitby, who themselves were becoming a force in the Northern League. But he didn't score a blinding goal on his debut!.

Geoff Hart

Centre forward Geoff set a Northern League record that is unlikely to be surpassed or equalled – he is the only player to have won seven Northern League championship winners' medals at two clubs, four with Spennymoor and three with Blyth Spartans.

Geoff joined Moors in 1973 after playing for Durham City, who were then managed by former Spennymoor player Ray Wilkie, and he actually started his career as a centre half before moving up front.

"I played centre half in junior football, and then one night I played up front for Durham against Gateshead in the Vaux Floodlit League. I scored a couple of goals in that position, but when Ray left, things changed at the club and I wasn't very happy.

"Stan Bradley, the Spennymoor secretary, came to see me, and said that he wanted me to come to Spennymoor. But it wasn't easy getting away from Durham, and it all got a bit nasty. I had to pretend that I was injured, so then I didn't play after February 1st, which meant I wasn't registered. Stan was a lovely bloke, he was 100 per cent committed, and he sold the club to me."

Geoff took his place in a Spennymoor side that was starting to elevate itself above the other clubs in the Northern League.

"There were some very good teams in the league at that time. North Shields had just won the Amateur Cup, and at one time you couldn't hold a candle to them. Willington were strong, and had players like Tommy Holden, Jackie Foster and Howard Murray. Evenwood had Bob Tookey, Tony Monkhouse and Colin Hallimond, and had won the league a couple of years previously. Blyth would challenge Spennymoor all the way through the seventies, and there were other clubs in the league who would give you a tough game."

One of Moors' best performances when Geoff was there, came against Football League side Southport in the 1975 FA Cup, when Moors produced a giantkilling act, winning 4-1. "We were magnificent against Southport. I can remember Billy Robson did a crunching tackle on one of their lads early on, and there was going to be a scuffle until one of their lads stepped in and broke it up.

"We tortured them from start to finish, and Kenny Banks was magnificent in midfield. Southport took the lead, but we just shrugged it off and took control of the game. We could have won by more. Kenny was that good, he could have played in any position on the field, and he stood head and shoulders above everybody else.

"We used to say that Albert Hickman had the best job in the world playing in defence. Butch Simpson would scare opponents to death at right back, Peter Joyce was a centre half who should have been capped by England at amateur level and John Heaviside, who was very hard and very quick at left back. And if anything got past those three, Albert would be sweeping up behind. With the team we had, we always went into games believing that we were going to win."

Geoff scored the goal that put Northwich, who had just had a good FA Cup run, out of the FA Trophy in 1977. "Apart from the goal, what I can remember about that game was the performance of the referee, Keith Hackett, who was a Football League referee. His control of the game was excellent, we never noticed him. If something went on, he would just come over and have a chat."

The defeat by Leatherhead in the 1978 FA Trophy was by far the most upsetting defeat for Geoff in his Spennymoor career. "Leatherhead really tore into us in the first half hour at their place, and we chased shadows. We went 2-0 down, but we sorted ourselves out and stayed in the tie. John Davies missed a chance near the end to pull a goal back for the second leg. "As everyone knows, we went out in the second leg. One report said that I left the pitch in tears – and that was absolutely correct. I have never been more upset over a game of football than that. At half time, we were very confident of going through, but a place at Wembley was snatched away from us."

Geoff had a very good relationship with the fans, especially one in particular. "The fans were very passionate and noisy, especially when we were playing towards them at the top end. One fan was very persistent with me, always saying "Come to my house for tea". After he'd asked me several times, I said that I would, just out of curiosity, and I had a very nice evening. I think the lad was delighted that he could say to his mates that "Geoff Hart had been round our house for tea!"

Geoff's career at the Brewery Field came to an end in the early eighties, when John Heaviside was manager. "John pulled me to one side, and said that I could get another club. Bishop Auckland came in, and I went to see Bernard Hathaway from Bishop Auckland at one of his factories – Brian Newton was manager there at the time. But the move was blocked by Spennymoor, who said that a different club was in for me, but wouldn't say who.

"I found out one night at Whitley Bay. John left me out of the starting eleven, and put me on the bench. I didn't even get on the field. But when I walked up the tunnel at half time, here was Jackie Marks from Blyth waving at me, saying "Come here, I want a word with you." Jackie persuaded me to sign for Blyth – and I won another three Northern League championship medals, to make seven in all. Tommy Dixon of Blyth also won seven, all of them with Blyth.

"I was at Spennymoor for seven years, won the league four times and the Durham Challenge Cup five times. The crack was magnificent, everybody got on well together, there were no cliques in the changing room. There was a really good team spirit.

"Maybe Spennymoor thought that the team was starting to age, and needed refreshing, but I'd like to think I proved people wrong."

Paul Bryson

Paul was one of several players who made the move from Tow Law to the Brewery Field in 1985 when Tony Monkhouse was manager.

Paul was a big money purchase for Moors. "I'd been at Tow Law for four years, and then Paul Haley, Tommy Mason and Stephen Storey all went to Spennymoor. Tony Monkhouse, who was manager at the time, paid £1,250 for me from Tow Law, which was quite a bit of money. Tony had bought me for taking setpieces, to put good crosses into the middle for Barrie Fowler and Micky Heathcote, who scored loads of goals from centre back."

Paul was part of the Spennymoor team that finished third in the Northern League in 1987, and narrowly lost to Tranmere earlier that same season. "Playing in the FA Cup first round, to a player on a day to day basis, is a very big thing. I'd been at Tow Law when they reached the first round against Bradford City, and I really thought that we had a chance of beating

Tranmere at our place.

"We gave them a really good game, but they beat us 3-2. Ian Muir scored a hat trick for them, two of them were penalties. Micky Heathcote pushed the ball over the bar with his hand for one penalty, it was pretty blatant. He would be sent off these days, but he stayed on the field.

"The best midfielder I ever played with was Ian Mohan. He would do all the donkey work, win the tackles, and then give it nice and easy. He would do all my work for me!

"We had two very good forwards in Barrie Fowler and Dennis Foster. They were awesome at times. Dennis was very good at holding the ball up and hitting the ball from long range, while Barrie was excellent in the air."

Paul didn't score many goals in his time at the club, but he has a special fondness for one. "We played at Whitley Bay, and I played a one-two with somebody and hit a rising shot perfectly into the top corner of the net. It was easily the best goal I ever scored.

"On my wedding day, when my wife walked down the aisle, I jokingly told her that she was the most beautiful thing I'd ever seen – apart from the goal I'd just scored at Whitley Bay!"

Paul also has an association with a cartoon character. "We all went to Blackpool on an end of season trip, and after we'd all had a few drinks, one of the lads, I think it was Marc Irwin, suggested that we should have our backsides tattooed. One of the lads had Laurel and Hardy done, and I had Fred Flintstone. It's still there to this day!"

Paul admits it was his own fault that he left the Brewery Field. "I signed a contract when I came to Spennymoor, which didn't allow me to play Sunday football. But one Sunday in Newcastle, I went to watch my mates play, and they persuaded me to turn out as well. I thought I would get away with it because I thought Newcastle was a good distance from Spennymoor, but I should have known that word would get back. I was heavily fined by the FA and the club for breaching my contract, and after three years at the club, I ended up leaving to play for Eppleton in the Wearside League. It was a crazy thing for me to do."

Ian Mohan

"Mo" was one of Billy Bell's signings in his second spell in charge.

"Billy had football in his blood, and his knowledge was extensive, but the club felt that some of the young players weren't responding to him, and he moved upstairs to become general manager. But Billy wasn't the sort of man who could take that role, because he wanted to be involved all the time. He couldn't take a back seat, he wasn't that sort of man.

"In my first year at the club, I didn't drive, but when I signed, Billy and his assistant, Tony Monkhouse, said that I would be picked up and dropped off for training. At the time, we trained at Houghton-le-Spring, so I used to get the bus from Newton Aycliffe to Croxdale, where Robin Gill, who lived in Bishop Auckland, picked me up on his way to training. I did that twice a week and never missed a training session, until one day, my wife, who was expecting, was rushed to hospital.

"Spennymoor were a very well organised club, and at the end of the week, there was a proper pay packet. Billy had a rule that if anyone missed training, they were fined £3, and when I opened my packet, I'd been deducted £3, which I thought was a bit harsh considering the circumstances. So I went to see Billy after our next game.

""Billy, it's about my wages, I've been deducted £3." I said. Billy flicked through his file, and replied; "Yes, you missed training last week."

""But my wife was in hospital."

"You know the rules. The fine stands. How would you think it would look if somebody else had missed training that night, and he'd been fined and you hadn't?"

"I couldn't believe it, but the chairman, Barrie Hindmarch came over, and said that he would reimburse me.

"Billy's book went back years, and had so much detail in it, even to the extent of which way the wind was blowing during a game. I'm sure some of it was written in Latin. I bumped into him once in a betting shop in Newton Aycliffe, and he was carrying another thick book, this time about horse racing form.

"One thing I'm sure he wrote down was the song we came out with one day before a game, just for a laugh. Jackie Sheekey started it, and we sang; "Here we go, here we go, here we go!" which was doing the rounds at the time. We went out and won the game 5-0, but I don't think it had anything to do with the song, just that we hit form.

"Anyway, Billy made a note of it, and for every game that season, he insisted that we sung it, saying that it was good for team spirit. We were sick of singing it by midway through the season.

"I loved Billy's dedication, but Tony Monkhouse had a more modern approach to his players, and could communicate with them better than Billy. I didn't have a phone in those days, so I used to go the payphone at the local shop and ring Tony for the arrangements for the game on the Saturday. Tony would talk for ages, and it would cost me a fortune to ring him.

"We had a really good team when we finished third in the table and won the league cup. Jackie Sheekey and Micky Heathcote got about fifteen/twenty goals between them from the back, Paul Bryson was our dead ball specialist and the two lads up front were outstanding. Barrie Fowler finished top scorer, and Dennis Foster was a goal behind him.

"Micky Heathcote was a young lad who improved all the time and eventually signed for Sunderland, but he was as daft as a brush.

"When we went to Blackpool at the end of one season, we went to the disco at the Tower Lounge. Micky had left us, had gone to the local sex shop and come back with a blow up doll. He blew it up, and went on to the dance floor with it. People rolled about with laughter. It was on the same trip that after a few drinks, we decided to have our backsides tattooed. So we all went to see this tattoo artist, and I had a Union Jack with "Mo" inscribed on mine. Some of the others had the Pink Panther or Donald Duck."

"Mo" was a popular player at the Brewery Field, but not with everybody. "Going to Spennymoor was a step up for me. In the first few games, I could hear two or three people clearly shouting out at me. I was taken aback, because that hadn't happened to me before, and I didn't dare make a mistake. I suppose it was because the club was in transition, and had paid £1,600 to Ferryhill for me. But as the season wore on, the criticism eased off, and I was happy with the way things had gone. At the end of my first season, I won three player of the year awards – from the club, the other players and the supporters.

"In the very first game of the following season, I hit a bad ball, and immediately one of the supporters shouted; "Will you get him off – he's useless!"

Just like the rest of the town, "Mo" was buzzing when Frank Worthington came to town with Tranmere in the 1986 FA Cup first round. "There was so much resting on the fourth qualifying round game against Gretna that we didn't dare lose, and when we heard that we'd drawn Tranmere, everybody got a huge lift.

"On the day, Tony took us to a restaurant, Whitewings, for our pre match meal. Most of the players ordered poached egg on toast, I ordered fish and chips. Having such a big meal never used to affect me. Tony said: "You must have seen my team sheet!" – but he was only joking.

"When we got to the ground, we could really sense the atmosphere, because we were in the little changing rooms in the corner of the ground – the old stand had just been pulled down.

"We went 1-0 up through Barrie Fowler, but then they scored with two penalties to go 2-1 up at half time. We thought the game hadn't gone too badly, and Tony said to keep doing what we were doing. Just after half time, Marc Irwin picked the ball up the left, and all of a sudden I was in the box, I stuck my toe out more in hope than with intent when the ball came over, and it went in. The goal looked much better on television later.

"It was a brilliant feeling. My wife, who was in the crowd, hugged a complete stranger and shouted; "That's my husband who's just scored." "Tranmere got back in front, and we had the chances to force a replay, but couldn't score. The main thing was, we didn't disgrace ourselves, and the defeat felt like a victory. Frank Worthington himself came on as sub with fifteen minutes left, maybe to showboat a little bit and to make the occasion, because he wasn't exactly known as a defensive midfielder, was he?

"I never thought that I would get that far in the FA Cup. We came down to earth pretty quick, because the next game was Hartlepool Reserves away at the Victoria Ground, and going into the dressing rooms was like going into the dressing rooms at our local park pitch. There were six inch nails in the walls to do for pegs. We really came back down to earth – there were only about thirty people watching as well."

There was some consolation that season, with victory in the League Cup final against Easington. "I was offered a job down south, which meant that I couldn't play in midweek games. I didn't want to miss the game which was on a Monday, so I arranged to have the day off. After the game, which we won in extra time, I caught a National Express bus from Darlington, and got to my hotel at about five in the morning."

"Mo" thinks that one of the best individual performances he's seen was from Moors striker Dennis Foster. "Dennis was a big lad, but Jackie Marks of Blyth slipped up one day. At the time, there was an American footballer, William Perry, who was a huge strong lad and nicknamed "the Fridge."

"Dennis would agree that he was carrying a bit of weight at the time, and Jackie Marks, who was manager, nicknamed Dennis "the Fridge." It didn't go down well at all, and it was the perfect motivation for Dennis, who then scored a hat trick as we thumped Blyth 6-1."

Marc Irwin

Marc was one of the youngest members of the Spennymoor team in the mid eighties.

He took the news of the FA Cup home draw against Tranmere in his stride. "It didn't really bother me, whereas everybody else was getting excited. I told my dad that I'd gone training one Monday night, and when he saw a team photo in the paper later in the week, I wasn't on it. "Where were you at?" he asked. "I was getting treatment from the physio at the time," I replied. It was nothing of the sort – I'd skipped training and gone to a local club to watch my mates play in a group.

"When the game came around, Stephen Storey failed a late fitness test, which meant that manager Tony Monkhouse had to reshuffle the side, and

I had to play at left back.

"We went 1-0 up with Barrie Fowler's header from Paul Bryson's free kick, and they got level from a penalty when Micky Heathcote handled.

"A couple of minutes later in our penalty area, their lad rolled across my body, and went down in a heap. The ref fell for the three card trick because their lad definitely dived. I got booked for protesting, and they scored from the penalty. Maybe on the day, they had a little more knowledge than us.

"We didn't give up, and we pulled one back when Tommy Mason and I swopped passes, and I crossed for Ian Mohan to tuck the ball into the bottom corner. In the last minute, Artie Graham had a header but he put it over the bar. We deserved a draw out of the game. Their manager, Frank Worthington, was fantastic afterwards. He came in the clubhouse, had a beer or two with us, and commented on how well we'd played."

Marc says that the camaraderie amongst the players at the time was "unbelievable."

"We were a very strong group, and we had some great nights out. We had a great weekend in Blackpool once. We had our backsides tattooed, and Micky Heathcote brought a blow up doll to a disco one night – and then somebody put a cigarette out on the doll's backside.

"We all looked after each other. When we went for nights out in Durham, if somebody was falling behind, then we'd all chip in together and put him in a taxi.

"We all helped each other to pick up win bonuses. The club said that whoever had been on the pitch would get a bonus if we won games, so people would fake injuries so then their mate could come on as sub and share the win bonus! Everybody took their turn to get their mate an extra fiver or tenner.

"There were some characters in the dressing room. At half time in one game, Paul Bryson, who was a midfielder, turned to defender Jackie Sheekey and said; "The back four isn't doing its job," which really was like a red rag to a bull. Jackie grabbed Brysa by the throat and the rest of us had to break them up. Brysa never blamed a defender again, and he never said a word at half time for ages after that.

"Brysa was our setpiece expert, and Ian Mohan alongside him was like a little terrier. Brysa used to walk him on to the pitch on a lead, and let him loose to get the ball. Mo covered every blade of grass, because Brysa couldn't tackle a Sunday dinner!

"Jackie Sheekey was a no-nonsense defender. I remember when we played Brandon in an away game. We had just kicked off, and after only about two minutes, Jackie was sent off for lamping one of their lads, the ball was nowhere near. "I just don't like him," he said.

"Against Chester-le-Street once, he hit one of their lads on the left ankle, it was obviously somebody else he didn't like. "I just need to do the right one now!" he said.

"Micky Heathcote had a very good partnership with Jackie. When we played Bishops and won 2-1 at their place, Jackie had to go off injured, his hamstring had gone. We had to reshuffle, and Micky was outstanding in defence. At the end of the game, he went in the dressing room, and said to Jackie; "There, I've done your job for you!"

Marc hasn't always played in defence, he once had a spell in goal. "When Billy Bell was manager, we had a friendly at Morecambe, but we didn't have a keeper for some reason.

"Billy said in the dressing room,"Who's going in goal?", and I said I would because I'd played in goal for a Sunday morning team. Really, it was because I'd had a skinful the night before!

"For a one-off game, I thought I did ok. I pulled off a couple of good saves, pushed one or two over the bar, dived all over the place and entertained the crowd. The defence made sure I was well protected.

"One game at Consett when it was heaving with rain, I played up front. Barrie Fowler went off injured and I came on as sub to replace him. We were 1-0 down, and I scored twice as we came back to win. I was over the moon, but in the dressing room, someone said; "You were crap!"

I replied, "I scored two and we won the game."

"Yes, but you missed an easy chance for a third." That brought me down to earth – but I still had to buy the drinks afterwards. Barrie, who used to wear a duffel coat like Paddington Bear, said; "I'll be back in the team next week when it's sunny.""

Marc was an eye witness to a famous practical joke on manager Billy Bell. "On the way back from a midweek away game, Billy fell asleep on the bus, so Paul Gibbon put black boot polish all over Billy's face. Billy didn't notice when he got off.

"Billy worked at a leisure centre in Wallsend at the time, and the following morning he got some strange looks from people. He didn't think any more of it, until his wife phoned him at work. "Billy, your side of the bed is all black, what's been happening?" she asked. It was then that Billy twigged, went to find a mirror, and saw that his face was covered in boot polish.

"Billy took it all in good spirits. He would help the lads as much as possible, if you wanted to borrow a tenner, he would let you borrow it even if it was his last one. He even loaned one of the lads his car.

"Before an away game at Tow Law, where it was always important for Billy to win, he ripped his finger open before the game, and he had to go to hospital, leaving his assistant Tony Monkhouse in charge.

"It was very quiet with Billy not there, and out of habit we looked over to the dugout for loud words of wisdom from Billy. Tony obviously had his own way of doing things and didn't say anything much at all. But then, all of a sudden, there was a huge shout "What are you doing!?" – it was Billy, with six stitches in his finger. Nothing was going to stop him being at the match, and we went on to win.

"Billy was a great coach, who was probably ahead of his time. For example, he asked Tony Monkhouse to count the number of shots we had, and work out how far people had run. Some of it sank in with us, some of it didn't!

"In my first game under Billy against Whitley Bay, he pulled me to one side at half time, and told me how to defend at corners. I wanted to mark the nearest man, but Billy insisted that I should put arms out wide, and mark the space. There was once when I was injured, he phoned me up at home, and said; "If you come and clear the snow off the pitch, I'll make sure you get your wages." That's how dedicated and professional he was."

Marc left just after the club decided to put players on contracts.

"Striker Dennis Foster and keeper Aidan Davison were both offered contracts by the club. Dennis said to Aidan, "Be like me, tell them that unless they give you £1,000, you won't sign." Aidan agreed that it was a good idea.

"Dennis went to see the committee, demanded £1,000, the committee offered £250, so he snapped their hands off straight away and signed!

"Aidan, not knowing what had happened to Dennis, went in next, demanded £1000, the committee offered £250, he refused, and got transferred to Billingham Synthonia – from there he ended up playing professionally in the Football League for twenty years.

"Dennis was a great goalscorer. When I played in midfield, we combined well down the left once, and instead of playing me in on goal, he dropped his right shoulder and scored with a well placed shot. "You should still have played me in," I said. "I get paid for scoring goals," he replied. I never did get a pint out of him."

Marc's stay at the club ended after an away game. "I travelled back in my underpants on the bus, because I didn't want beer all over my trousers. I got off at a service area without my trousers, and got told off by one of the committee. I think there was only one way for me to go after that, and I ended up at Gretna – once I found it on the map!"

Micky Heathcote

Micky made his name for Spennymoor as a central defender, but he started his career at the Brewery Field as a striker.

"I played in two positions in my junior career at Trimdon," he said. "Rocky

Hudson, who looked after the juniors, invited me over to Spennymoor, and I played a few games as a striker. But Middlesbrough had also seen me play for Trimdon as a defender, and I had a trial at Ayresome Park.

"I came back, and Rocky persuaded me to return to Spennymoor and I started playing for the juniors again. John Heaviside was the manager at the time, and he decided to put me on the bench one night against Blyth, of all clubs. I came on for the last ten minutes up front, and then I had a fearful moment for a young player. I knocked the ball past Blyth defender Tommy Dixon, ran past him and created a goalscoring opportunity. I jogged back into position, and as I went past him, he said: "Knock the ball past me again, and I'll snap you in half!"

"Looking at him, I thought I'd better take note of what he said. Having said that, if I'd been in the same situation again, then I would have tried to beat him again.

"Boro then stepped in, and offered me a year's contract as a pro, on £80 per week. There were fifteen of us there, playing for the youth team in the Northern Intermediate League. I was released after a year, and by then Billy Bell had been appointed as Spennymoor manager, and he'd heard that I was capable of scoring goals.

"I was willing to try my luck up front, because I wanted a bit of glory, but I was nowhere near good enough. Billy then put me in midfield, and after a few more games I ended up at the back, where I'd always felt comfortable.

"The Spennymoor team made a man of me. There was plenty of quality in the changing room, and the Northern League was a really hard league, in which two thirds of the teams could beat each other. It was very much an even keel.

"Jackie Sheekey was a role model to me. He was a bread and butter centre half, who won headers and cleared his lines, and you couldn't question his commitment at all. He had a wealth of experience, and he brought me on very quickly. We formed a very good partnership, and when we had gone quite a few games unbeaten, we played at Tow Law, Jackie's old club. They had a lad up front who wound me and Jackie up, to the point that Jackie saw the red mist, and got himself sent off. But as he walked off, he pointed his finger and said to the lad; "I know where you live. I'll be round your house."

"We had some very good players in the team. Robin Gill and Tommy Mason were the two full backs, and keeper Aidan Davison came through the juniors like me.

"In midfield, Ian Mohan was so wholehearted that he would have kicked his granny. Stephen Storey could win games on his own because of his pace, and his ability to glide past people.

"Alongside him, Paul Bryson was one of the best at that level because of his vision and his ability, and a lot of goals I scored came from Paul's setpieces. He couldn't tackle though!

"Paul Gibbon decided to take me under his wing, which might have been a mistake on my part on one occasion. We went on a club tour to Jersey, and we had to meet at the club at 11.30 one night. Gibbo said to me; "I'll meet you at 7 at the club."

"So I did along with two committee men, and we went into the town for a drink. I was only a young pup, and I tried to do my best to keep up. When we were in the Kingfisher, he went to the bar and bought two fat cigars, which we were smoking as we arrived back at the clubhouse. We went to Barrie Hindmarch's house, and by then the drink and the cigar were having an effect on me. By the time we got to East Midlands Airport for the flight, I was in a right state.

"On the plane, the stewardess gave me a barley sugar, but I fell asleep with it in my mouth, and it melted all the way down my cheek on to my Spennymoor shirt, which in turn had stuck to my club jacket. When we landed, Barrie Fowler said "Get some breakfast down you!" It took me ages to recover, and I learned never to try to keep with up Paul Gibbon.

"On the field, Gibbo was one of the hardest players I'd ever come across. He once went in for a crunching 50-50 against somebody from Blyth, and both ended up flat out. The lad from Blyth was stretchered off, and Gibbo just ran around in a circle, and shook his injury off."

Micky was annoyed with himself after finishing on the losing Moors side against Tranmere in the FA Cup in 1986. "I was angry with the referee on the final whistle, because I didn't think we'd played forty five minutes in the second half. I was so involved in the game, and it felt as if we'd just kicked off! And I was annoyed with myself because I didn't do myself justice on the day. I gave away a penalty for deliberate handball, but I don't think there was any argument at all about it – in fact I thought it was a good save!

"Marc Irwin gave away a second penalty, but I was more annoyed because I should have dealt with the ball long before Marc had to. It was a harsh decision by the referee, but Tranmere were a bit cuter than us. The ref also disallowed a goal by Barrie Fowler, and I'm sure he didn't know why he disallowed it."

Micky is also a part of a particular Spennymoor legend, the blow up doll affair in Blackpool. "I used to go with the Hare and Greyhound Sunday team to Blackpool every Whit weekend. There was a joke shop on the seafront, run by two old ladies, so I bought a blow up doll and I took it into the Tower Lounge, one of the best places for old time dancing in the town. I taped its feet to mine, and danced around the ballroom, not in a silly sort of way, but dignified.

"When I went to Blackpool with the Spennymoor lads, I went back to the joke shop, and bought another blow up doll. The rest of the lads thought it was hilarious to see me dancing around, and I got a completely different reaction."

After some very good displays in the heart of the Spennymoor defence, there became ever increasing talk of Sunderland, who had just been relegated to the old Third Division, signing him.

"I think as an individual, Spennymoor saw me in my heyday because I couldn't have been any fitter or played any better. I only picked up niggling injuries when I was at Spennymoor, whereas I picked up more serious ones when I went into the pro game, and they slowed my development.

"I was as fit as a fiddle, I had youth and an able body on my side. I worked for Barrie Hindmarch all day, and then I'd go training and play a game.

"There were several clubs watching me, Sunderland, Hartlepool, Darlington and Sheffield United were all sniffing around me, and Lawrie McMenemy, who was at Sunderland at the time, put seven days' notice in for me, but he wasn't too happy when Spennymoor asked him for a fee. McMenemy didn't appreciate that clubs like Spennymoor survive on transfer fees, and the deal fell through.

"A few months later, my dad went out for a meal and bumped into Jim Morrow, the Sunderland chief scout. Denis Smith had become Sunderland manager, and Jimmy said he would have a word with him. Denis agreed to have me in for a week's training, and at the end of it, he offered me a two year contract. I must admit, I'd have signed for nothing, because I was in so much awe of the place, and I didn't listen to the money he was offering. Football was the be-all and end-all for me, and my aspirations were to make a career out of football.

"I nearly came back to Spennymoor, though, because of a back injury. At one point I thought about packing the pro game in altogether, and I applied to be a prison officer, but Sunderland gave me another year's contract. I had an operation, which was a foolish thing to do, and really I should have rested. I went to Stuart McDermott, the Spennymoor physio at the time – sadly he is no longer with us -- and he said not to have a back operation because I was too young for a footballer, and should rest instead. But I was so intent on getting my back right again, I went ahead and had the operation, and never felt 100 per cent again. Stuart wasn't a magic sponge man, he brought a new philosophy to local players when he arrived at the club."

Micky continued in the pro game until 2003, playing for Shrewsbury, Cambridge and Plymouth, and then he played in the FA Trophy final for Hucknall against Grays in 2004.
But none of the dressing rooms he went into saw Micky doing the tango with a blow up doll!

Gary O'Hara
Irish lad Gary was pitched straight into the deep end when he signed for Moors in 1994, with a much anticipated local derby against Bishop Auckland .
Gary started his career at Leeds United, and when he was released, played in the Far East for four years for the Sultan of Brunei's team.
"I was in digs with another lad who used to play for Leeds, Rob Bowman, and he suggested to Mattie Pearson that he should come and watch me. Mattie made a few enquiries about me, and decided to sign me straight away.
"I didn't expect to play for a few weeks, but Mattie told me that there were a couple of players out injured – Wes Saunders was one of them – and I would be making my debut against Bishop Auckland the following day.
"I must admit, because I'm from outside the north east, at the time I didn't appreciate the rivalry that existed between Spennymoor and Bishop Auckland – I didn't even know where Bishop Auckland was! The pitch was rock hard, and so I managed to get hold of a pair of pimples which helped me enormously – and after the game I was presented with the man of the match award. We won the game 1-0, Keith Gorman scored, I think.
"The team spirit was unbelievable. Mattie was an early influence on me because he was a disciplinarian, and he was always on to me about my weight, especially when I put on a pound or two. Mattie wanted a fit side, and that's what he got.
"He took us for a training run one night. We ran down to the roundabout at Croxdale, turned right and ran back up towards Thinford. We all thought that we would turn right again at the roundabout at Thinford, but instead Mattie had us running up the hill to Ferryhill, across to Kirk Merrington and down to the daisy field – about nine miles in total – and then he expected us to put in a full training session afterwards!
"But you have to hand it to Mattie, he took part in the run, and was the first one back. He would always muck in. But it was embarrassing at times for some of the lads, who considered themselves very fit, and then Mattie would easily beat them.
"I was surprised at the standard of the Unibond League, because there were quite a few ex-pros, and also a few youngsters who didn't quite make

it in the pro game. I used to bump into several people I knew from my days at Leeds.

"When I was a young pro, I used to get space to play the ball from the back, but at UniBond level, I didn't. Opponents were in my face for most of the game. But I think I must have done well, because the fans behind the goal chanted my name pretty often.

"I can remember when my team mate, John Parnaby, went to see Tow Law play in the Vase final at Wembley, and walking around Trafalgar Square, he bumped into a Spennymoor fan with my name and number 33 on the back of his shirt!"

Gary's big regret is not advancing in the FA Cup in season 1995-96. "We got through to the first round, and instead of drawing one of the Football League clubs, we were given Colwyn Bay. We didn't mind that much, because we'd already beaten them twice previously in the Unibond League season, quite comfortably as well.

"The conditions didn't help, though, because the rain was lashing down before the game, and there was a risk that the match would be called off. It was only at 2pm that the referee decided that the match would be on, probably because Colwyn Bay had travelled so far.

"It beggared belief that we lost. We got a penalty that Brian Healy put over the bar, and they scored nearly straight away. That day, the draw was made on television straight after the game, and I can remember seeing Colwyn Bay celebrating because they got Blackpool away in the next round. So they enjoyed a weekend in Blackpool, and we didn't!

"Brian Healy was by far our best player, and stood out a mile. Most of us were gutted when he left, because as well as being a big stocky lad, he definitely could play. He always wanted to win, and always had a good opinion in the dressing room and in training."

In an earlier round of that 1995-96 competition, Gary also got some good natured stick from his team mates for a tackle he made that cost Moors a penalty.

"In the second qualifying round, we played at Workington, who were being sponsored by the TV programme "Big Breakfast". They always showed highlights from Workington games on the Monday after.

"We went across there and beat them 4-2, but one of their goals was from a penalty after I slid in and took their lad out. I protested strongly that I played the ball, but yes, I admit now it was a penalty!"

Gary was at the heart of the Spennymoor team which lifted the Durham Challenge Cup on three occasions when he was there.

"We always had a good record in the Challenge Cup. We drew 0-0 with South Shields in the final at Darlington one season, but I missed a good

chance near the end when I was one on one with their keeper. We also beat Durham and Hartlepool Reserves, but Bishops beat us one year. There were always good celebrations in our clubhouse afterwards."
There were also some celebrations on the bus coming back from away games, win, lose or draw.
"We always had a couple of crates of beer on the bus for an away trip, and when we got back to Billingham to drop some of the lads off, we would top up at a nearby off licence. Mattie never minded, because he knew it was good for team spirit. There was always a card school as well.
"Mind, there was one occasion when we got back really late from a midweek away game. We played at Hyde on a Monday night, but the bus was held up because of an accident on the M62, and the game didn't kick off until 8.55, which meant it didn't finish until 10.45. We didn't get back until 3 in the morning."

John Davies

John realised a dream when he signed for Spennymoor, because he was a big fan before he signed.
"I'm born and bred in Spennymoor and started to follow the club when I was twelve years old, and I went on the long trips to places like Peterborough and Grantham in the Midland League, and even further to Kingstonian for an FA Amateur Cup tie.
"I had three trials at Coventry when Willie Carr and Jeff Blockley were both there and they wanted me to sign amateur forms, but I said no. I started playing in the Northern League for Willington, and at that time I was a midfielder under Brian Newton. I was approached by Spennymoor when Stan Bradley came to see me one night, and he changed me into a striker when John Tobin left the club. There were nine local players in the Spennymoor side then, and the others weren't too far away either. I think the fans respected that, although I would still get stick from one particular place in the ground.
"Albert Hickman and Brian Mulligan always got stick from the shed, and I got it from behind the goal. I once scored six in a Durham Challenge Cup tie against Houghton, and one fan still complained that I should have scored more because of the chances I missed. On the other hand, I scored a hat trick once, and I received a card from an old bloke congratulating me, which was really nice – he watched games from the shed, not behind the goal! While the players really appreciated the support they were given, we always said wait until Spennymoor had a bad side, then the fans would know what they've missed."
John was part of two forward lines that helped Moors dominate the

seventies. His first was with Geoff Parker and Tommy Cochrane. "We all helped each other as much as we could, because each of us knew that not only were we there to score goals, we were there to create them as well. I was once told that I'd been brought to the club to score goals, but I didn't see it that way."

The second forward line was himself, Kevin Reilly and Geoff Hart. "The three of us always felt that between us, we could get something like 100 goals per season, which wasn't bad going. I once scored 39 in a Northern League season – Kenny Banks scored the same number once, but some of his were penalties! Kevin should have played in the Football League, he was a very good all round player with loads of skill. Overall though we were a really good team, that played well together. For example, if anything got past Peter Joyce at the back – and nothing much did – then somebody, usually Albert Hickman, would sweep up behind him.

"One night when Kenny was coach, we couldn't train on the field, so Kenny suggested that we should go for a road run – to the Cock of the North and back! It was about ten miles there and back. Kevin Reilly was probably the fittest of us all, so when we were going up one carriageway to the Cock of the North, he was coming back down the other.

"I got back absolutely shattered, and said to Kenny; "That's the last time I'll do a road run, I'd rather do shuttles. You can transfer me if you like, but I was bought to score goals and not run roads!"

"I had two really hard games against Scottish centre half Jim Holton in the FA Cup against Shrewsbury. In the first game at our place, they didn't want to know because they didn't like the conditions, but in the replay they were different.

"I nutmegged Holton once, and he turned round and slapped me in the face! But that didn't stop me taking him on again, and I managed to score late in the game at their place. After that, he was transferred to Manchester United and was capped by Scotland, so I must have made him look good!

"John Heaviside and I nearly couldn't play in the replay. We both worked in the building trade, and neither of us could get the time off work. So the committee had a meeting, put their hands in their pockets and decided that they would pay us our lost wages. I bet Jim Holton didn't have the same problem.

"We felt that we could beat anybody at our place, because of the slope on our pitch. Teams coming to Spennymoor for the first time would take one look at the field, and not fancy it. And the fans played their part as well, the atmosphere around the top goal was fantastic, especially for a night match."

John was labelled a "diver" during his career, but he strongly denies that he was.

"Believe it or not, I'm still called a diver thirty years on at my local cricket club, but I can tell you that I wasn't, certainly nothing like you see on the television these days. I was involved a lot in the opposition penalty area, and if I was touched, I couldn't help but go down. I once went down against Southall in the Amateur Cup, and the referee didn't give a penalty, but when their full back got up, he smacked me in the face, so the ref gave a penalty for that instead!"

It was on his first overnight trip to London with the Moors that John learned more about hotel food. "I roomed with Eric Shaw at the time, and we had a lie in one morning. We decided to go for some breakfast, and on the way, we bumped into John Heaviside, who said: "Try the continental breakfast, it's great." We didn't know what a continental breakfast was but it sounded good, so we ordered it. The waiter brought some rolls and butter which we ate, and ten minutes later he came back. "Can we have our breakfast," I asked. "That was your breakfast, sir!" We realised then that "Heavi" had wound us up."

As well playing in midfield and in the forward line in his career, John also played in goal. "When we played at North Shields with Dickie Adamson in goal. Dickie was about to kick the ball out, when a North Shields player put his foot up, and caught Dickie on his knee. I had to go in goal, because I was always the reserve keeper. Unfortunately, the injury finished Dickie."

John was barred from the league for two years because he wanted to leave the Moors. "At the time, Newcastle Blue Star were the up and coming team – they were in the Wearside League -- and I was approached by their manager, Peter Feenan, to go and play there.

"There was a rule in the Northern League that instructed players to tell their clubs by February 1st if they weren't going to stay the following season, which I did, but Peter Joyce and John Heaviside didn't. Spennymoor reported me to the league for failing to appear for training and matches, and I was banned for two seasons, while the other two were banned for life. I played at Blue Star for a season, and then I went to play for Barrow in the Northern Premier League, who were managed by a friend of mine, Alan Cooke.

"When Kenny Banks took over as player-coach, I came back to Spennymoor and stayed for another five years – and thoroughly enjoyed it until I packed in to concentrate on my business." Which naturally, is in the town.

Brian Mulligan

Brian was one of the longest serving Spennymoor players in the seventies, and part of the team which carried nearly all before them.

Brian arrived at the club following a season at Billingham Synthonia, where his Moors team mate Albert Hickman had briefly played.

"Albert had a season at Billingham, and then moved back to Spennymoor. One night, there was a knock on my front door, and here was Albert with Spennymoor secretary Stan Bradley wanting to speak to me. Albert and I had become firm friends during his stay, and Billingham let me move on to Spennymoor. Bob Bell was coach then, and his methods were a big change to what I was used to.

"Billy Bell took over from Bob in 1972, and in one pre-season friendly – I wasn't playing for some reason – Billy gave me a job to do in the stand. He gave me a clipboard and pen, with instructions to mark the players every time they misplaced a pass.

"Billy sat next to me in the stand. One of the players, Eric Shaw, picked up a knock, and suddenly Bill produced a megaphone from nowhere, and shouted through the megaphone "Shaw, the match is going on, get your arse into gear!"

Brian thought at one point during Billy's reign that he would be leaving the club because he wasn't part of the plans.

"Billy pulled me to one side at the start of pre-season, and told me that he didn't think I was tough enough, and that he didn't want me. Naturally, I was disappointed, and I asked him if it was all right to come along and train with Spennymoor until I could fix myself up. Billy said that there would be no problem.

"A couple of weeks went by during which I spoke to Durham City and Shildon, but I didn't know whether to go or to wait and see if any other clubs were interested. After training one night, I picked up my bags, and Billy pulled me to one side again. "Brian, we've got a friendly coming up, we're short of numbers, can you help us out?"

"Maybe I should have said no because he'd told me I wasn't part of his plans, but I was that taken aback, I said yes. The next game I missed was in November!

"I was injured in a game at Tow Law, and our one and only substitute was already on the field. We were playing a 4-3-3 system, and so Billy moved me, with my knee heavily padded, from my usual position of left midfield, to an even busier position at right back! "

Brian thoroughly enjoyed the big matches in the FA Cup and FA Trophy.

"My first taste of the FA Cup first round was against Shrewsbury at the Brewery Field, when we drew 1-1. I thought that the atmosphere was exciting and wonderful, and I wanted to test myself against the Football League clubs. I'd flirted with professional clubs before when I'd been on trial at Middlesbrough and Blackburn, and I'd played for Hartlepool Reserves without breaking through.

"In every big game we played when Kenny Banks was coach, I always felt that we matched our opponents in terms of skill and ability. When we beat Southport in the FA Cup, Southport got a little bit cocky when they went in the lead. Kenny scored a couple of piledrivers, and I managed to get another. I'd taken an inswinging corner from the right and the Southport defence headed the ball away. I was on my way back across to left midfield, when I spotted a gap between the two centre halves, got put through and dinked the ball over the keeper.

"We gave as good as we got at Bury in the next round. We got a corner when the score was 0-0 just before half time, I whipped the ball across, and Albert Hickman flicked it just inches wide.

"They went straight down the other end, won a corner themselves, and their full back scored a 30 yarder through a crowd of players. The game turned against us in the space of a minute, and we lost 3-1.

"I played out of position in the FA Trophy quarter final against Dagenham, I had to play up front because Geoff Hart was injured. We were playing down the bank when I headed across goal, and their centre half put the ball into his own net, although I think John Davies would have got there anyway to put the ball in.

"That put us in the semi final against Leatherhead. In the first game down there, Albert Hickman, who was out of the side because of injury, stood in the dressing room wearing a brand new sheepskin-type coat. Alan Porter, our keeper, deliberately brushed past Albert with Vaseline on his hands, and we could see the marks Alan had made. So the rest of us followed Alan, and when Albert realised what we'd done, he went berserk!

"We were well on top in the replay. We scored from a training ground setpiece move in which everybody came to the near post, but then Billy Robson sneaked up unmarked into the penalty area to head my corner into the net. That was 1-0.

"John Davies scored a second, and at that stage, there was only one team going to Wembley. Geoff Hart hit the keeper's legs which would have made it 3-0, but after that, the game died down a bit, and we all know what happened.

"I used to love playing against Blyth when they were going strong as well, because you knew that there was always going to be a tough game. In one game, I picked the ball up in midfield, and Tommy Dixon came across and he didn't half whack me. "Bit slow there weren't you?" he said as I lay flat out on the ground.

"We played in front of big crowds in those days, much bigger for league games than they are now, unfortunately. When the 1976 Olympics were on, Alan Kell was getting constant abuse from one of the fans, every time he kicked the ball he got some flak. After about half an hour, there was a hold up in play, and the fan gave him some stick. So Alan went across to the barrier, up to the fan, and said: "If you don't like what you're watching, go and watch the Olympics!"

"We played for just £5 per game, if we had a big Cup tie then we might have got £10 out of it. Other clubs offered more, and two of my teammates went to play in the Wearside League for £7.50. But I wasn't interested, I was happy enough to stay at Spennymoor because there was a real appeal about the club."

Billy Robson

Billy Robson

Billy was a legendary tough tackling defender who didn't let much past him as Moors won four Northern League titles during his time at the Brewery Field.

It was because of disenchantment with Darlington that Billy moved to Spennymoor. "At Darlington, I played in the youth team and reserves, who were then in the Wearside League. I played in every round of the Shipowners Cup and reached the final against Hartlepool Reserves, who said that they were going to play their first team. So Darlo decided to play theirs, and I was left out, which didn't go down too well."

Darlington's loss was Spennymoor's gain, and Billy became part of the backbone of the defence. "I joined in 1968, just after Spennymoor had won the treble. Stan Bradley came in for me and persuaded me to play. My first full season was 1969-70 alongside Peter Joyce, Graham Defty and John Heaviside, and I won the player of the year award at the end of that season. It was a closely guarded secret beforehand, of course, and I wasn't even planning on going to the presentation night, until Stan phoned me up and persuaded me to go. I wondered why he was so pushy on the phone!"

Billy had a great partnership with "Butch" Simpson in the centre of defence.

"Butch and I used to kick lumps out of each other in training. He only had a few teeth, and he used to say that if he had a pink tooth, he would have a snooker set! Butch knew how to look after himself, and the pair of us always gave as good as we got. I can remember an away game – I won't say where at – when Butch grabbed hold of an opponent by the throat and nearly bit him because of a tackle the other lad had put in. I never pulled out of a tackle. People say that I was a hard man and as tough as nails, but looking back, I don't think I was. I always tried to get in an early hard tackle just to put my opponent off a bit. I was always taught that if I went in hard, I wouldn't get hurt.

"I always gave 100 per cent and never pulled out of a tackle, because I knew that if I didn't give 100 per cent, that would be when I would get caught. I alternated between left back and centre half, because I didn't have the height of a centre half, and I didn't have a lot of pace – but I still managed to get my tackles in.

"I remember when we played Wrexham in the FA Cup, and I went for a challenge on one of their lads, and laid him out. I thought it was a clean tackle, but their lad rolled around on the ground a bit. Their centre half ran towards me and said: "I've never seen a tackle like that," but I never got booked or sent off by the referee.

"We played in a Trophy tie at Nuneaton, and I cleanly tackled a lad called Kirk Stephens and put him over the dugout. He later went on to play in the pro game for Luton. But there were players in the Northern League whom I always found to be a handful. There was a flying winger at Whitby, Peter Hampton, whom I didn't like to play against, and I always had a tough game against Alan Shoulder when he was at Bishop Auckland.

"I played a lot of games for the club in two spells, but I also had a couple of breaks through suspension! I used to get into trouble for dissent. But I must have made a good impression on somebody, because Birmingham and Cambridge both came in for me and asked me if I wanted to turn pro, but I didn't fancy it.

"I had nine fantastic years at Spennymoor, although I had a brief spell at Willington at one point. We had some ups, like the Northern League title wins and the cup wins. I think my proudest moment was when we played Blyth in the title play off in their own backyard at Ashington, which wasn't the best of pitches. I was the captain at the time – maybe Stan tried to calm me down a bit because I got in trouble every now and again for dissent – and we won 2-1 to win the league. There were about two or three busloads of our supporters there, and it was a great night.

"We had our downs as well. We always seemed to have a tough game at

Penrith. We once beat them 9-3, but their centre forward gave us the run around and scored a hat trick, which I wasn't best pleased about. One day at Whitby they had a man sent off, but we still lost 3-0.

"Leatherhead, of course, was the worst. I scored in the second leg with a beautiful header, which I admit, I wasn't trying to score with. All I was doing was trying to get it back over for someone to turn in, but instead the ball dropped into the net.

"At 2-0, they hadn't caused us any problems. Going down the bank in the second half, we had everything to play for. Maybe we sat back a little, let them back into it and they scored.

"We were all as sick as parrots later. I went for a Pink afterwards to check the score because I couldn't believe what had happened. All the time, I kept thinking that we'd come so close to playing at Wembley. I didn't think that Leatherhead were all that good a side, and so it proved when they lost in the final."

Billy says that he played with some great players. "Even though he'd been a pro, there were no frills with Bill Gates, and he was a real down to earth bloke. He once invited us all to a party at his house in Middlesbrough – we all went on a bus – and none of us could get over the fish tank he had in a wall, and the photos with players like George Best.

"We had three forwards who could score goals for fun, and one season they scored 87 goals between them, which certainly took the pressure off us lads in defence! Kevin Reilly could ping the ball in from 25, 30 yards without any backlift, and should have been a pro, Geoff Hart was a great target man, and John Davies really covered some ground.

Bill Gates

"Albert Hickman read the game very well and tidied up, while Kenny Banks was another, like Kevin, who should have gone pro. He was a classy player, and at times didn't pick himself because he wanted to keep things right on the field. I can't remember him missing many penalties, he was that accurate. I don't think people realised at the time, how good a team that really was."

Player memories

Billy Roughley

England Amateur international Billy came to the Brewery Field in Bobby Bell's last season as manager in 1970.

"Stan Bradley came to my house regularly to see me, in fact he came that often, that my kids used to call him Uncle Stan. He badgered me and badgered me, and eventually I told him that if I was going to sign for Spennymoor, I would do so on the condition that I had a verbal agreement from him that I could leave at any time. Stan agreed.

"There was a great feeling of togetherness amongst the players and the club officials then, and it was a great place to be at.

"When Billy Bell succeeded Bob, he brought some new ideas to the club. I'd just come back from injury one night, and Billy ordered all the players to run around the pitch six times, the equivalent to a five minute mile. While Billy stood at the back of the stand, Keith Storey and I did the six laps between us – I started, went round once and jumped into the dugout, then Keith would pop out and do a lap. Billy didn't twig what was going on.

Billy Roughley

"Billy had been to a couple of the big clubs to see how they trained. He introduced weights, but when I used them, I tore a muscle behind my knee."

Unsuspecting manager Billy was the target of a couple of practical jokes. "Keith, Kenny Banks and I had all been out injured, and because the team had been doing well, we couldn't get back in the side. We went all the way to Wycombe, and none of us was in the starting line up, only Kenny was on the bench.

"Billy and Keith were rooming together at the time, and one night, after we'd had a few drinks, Keith went back into the room while Billy was asleep, and found Billy's thick file which contained all his notes. Keith then found Billy's team talk for the following day, so he put on an accent like Billy's, and read it out in the hotel corridor to me and Tom Smith, a committee man. And after he finished it, he threw a jug of water over Billy while he was asleep! Fortunately, Billy took it in good humour.

"We stayed in the same hotel after the game. I was rooming with Kenny, who waited until I'd fallen asleep and then with some of the other lads,

219

lifted me out of bed and dropped me into a cold bath. I got the fright of my life!

"The week after the Wycombe game, Billy brought the three of us back into the team, but then we got beat in the following match, and Billy put me on the bench, which I thought wasn't justified. I decided to go and see Stan, and reminded him of our verbal agreement. He said that he would let me go after I'd played one more game the following Saturday against Consett – and I scored a hat trick! Billy came to my house the following day and tried to get me to change my mind, he even had his dinner at our house, but I said no, I was going to Shildon.

"We didn't fall out or anything like that. When he passed away, I went to his funeral, and I was disappointed that there weren't as many people there as I expected because Billy was a great ambassador for local football."

Graham Defty

Graham signed for Moors when they turned amateur after quitting the Midlands League, at the age of 19.

"I'd been at Cardiff City as an apprentice and they offered me terms as a part time professional, but I was serving my time then, and needed to concentrate on my job. Spennymoor manager Harry Bell came through to see me, and persuaded me to sign for them."

Graham was part of the team which won the treble of Northern League, Northern League Cup and Durham Challenge Cup under manager Bob Bell in 1968.

"We had a really good team then. Players like Alan West and Peter Joyce were both around my age, and we had a keeper, Dave Crampton, who was very confident and commanded his box. Dave used to tell the same joke every week in the dressing room, just for a laugh. It wasn't because he was superstitious or anything like that.

"Bob Bell changed the style of football when he arrived in 1966, and everybody adapted to it very well, I think because we enjoyed playing it.

"There were some great games. We beat Goole in the FA Cup on the same day that Tow Law beat Mansfield and we played Sunderland at Roker Park in the Durham Benevolent Bowl. Charlie Hurley was in the Sunderland side that night on his return from injury, and our forward, John Tobin, roasted him.

"Our supporters were magnificent. There was one game at Evenwood when we were losing 2-1 with five minutes left, and they stood behind the goal we were attacking, really lifted us, and we went on to win the game."

"There was another time when we played Skelmersdale in the FA Amateur Cup, the year after they'd won it, and we went to their place and won 1-0."

Graham was only 27 when he had to retire from playing through illness on doctor's orders.

Jason Ainsley

Jason decided to join Spennymoor after he sang at a presentation night.
He started his non league career at Guisborough juniors in the Banks Group Northern Youth League – the Under 19 league that was set up by the Northern League in the mid eighties – and with his Guisborough team mates attended the league's presentation night at Brandon.
"Guisborough wanted me to stay, but Spennymoor were one of our main rivals at the time. After the presentation was over, I jumped on the stage, grabbed the microphone, and started to sing. I didn't do it to impress anybody, it was one of those daft things you do as a teenager. Rocky Hudson, Eddie Sharp and Peter Storey were all there, and they pulled me quietly to one side, and asked me to come to Spennymoor.
"Ray Gowan was the manager at the time, and he fixed me up with a job on a building site at Owton Manor in Hartlepool. I'd never done a day's labouring in my life! The lads on the building site used to call me "Jason One Brick" because I would only carry two bricks, one in each hand. I was quickly moved from there on to another part of the site, building a wall, but I made a mess of that and four or five days later my P45 came in the post!
"I started quite well at the Brewery Field, and it got to the point when Trevor Beaumont, one of the sponsors, wanted me to sign a contract. I didn't want to sign it because I knew that a lot of Football League clubs were looking at me, so Trevor offered me a car, an Orion Injection Ghia, with all the insurance paid for. It had Spennymoor United on a banner on the side just like all sponsored cars do – so I snapped Trevor's hands off and drove around Middlesbrough showing it off to my mates."
Jason was the kingpin of Moors' rise through the Northern Counties East League and into the Northern Premier League.
"We had some great matches. The support we got away at Chesterfield in the first round of the FA Cup was really special. There were loads of Spennymoor fans there, and just as I was about to take a corner, a Spennymoor fan jumped over the barrier, on to the pitch, and kicked the ball into the penalty area.
"I was injured when we beat Ashton United 3-1 at home after being a goal down, but after the game, all the fans went on to the pitch and celebrated. It was a very tense game, because Ashton needed a draw to go up, and we needed a win.
"Night matches were always special at home. In the season we played Chesterfield in the FA Cup, we played Northwich Victoria at home in the

last qualifying round. The place was packed, and the crowd really got behind us. When we won, there was a huge celebration in the clubhouse." Jason has been fiercely proud of playing for the Moors throughout his career. "When I first joined the club, I was given a navy blue tie, which I wore with pride. It was a quite a pull playing for Spennymoor, and still is, and people looked up to you.

"There were players in the dressing room when I started who were just as proud, like Wes Saunders. He was always hard on me when I did something daft.

"I remember before one away game, he produced a bottle of whisky, and he put a dram in everybody's cup of tea before we went out of the dressing room.

"About midway through the first half, I gave the ball away, and he had a right go at me. I saw red, ran up to him and started throwing punches at him. A couple of the lads had to pull me off him, and the referee sent me off.

"I sat disconsolately in the dressing room at half time, and Wes came up to me and innocently asked; " Jason, why did you get sent off for?"

"He'd had too much whisky before the game – I don't know who was the more drunk, me or him!"

Former Newcastle and Darlington midfielder Kevin Todd was another big influence on Jason. "Kevin was a really fit player. Before a game, whether it was at home or away, he used to go through a really impressive warm up routine of press ups and star jumps – we used to call him the Green Goddess after the fitness woman who was on the television at the time."

Jason almost joined the club he supported, Middlesbrough, but he joined Fourth Division club Hartlepool instead. "I wanted to join the Boro, and the manager at the time, Lennie Lawrence, was keen on taking me. But then Lennie got the sack, and was replaced by Bryan Robson, who offered me a three month deal. Hartlepool came in and offered me a year, and I signed.

"I didn't see much first team football at Hartlepool, maybe my best experience was playing against Arsenal in the Coca Cola Cup just after they'd signed Denis Bergkamp.

"After I left Hartlepool, I played in Australia for a year, and came back to Spennymoor when Mattie Pearson was manager, to play for a few months during the Australian close season -- so I was going backwards and forwards quite a bit."

As well as the whisky incident earlier, Jason has also been involved in other embarrassing incidents. "When we played at Trafford on the other side of Manchester, we only had the bare eleven. I wasn't feeling too well at all, and was struggling with bellyache.

"I had to play, and then midway through the first half, I needed to go to the toilet urgently, in fact quicker than that! I dashed up the tunnel towards our dressing room, but the door was locked, and I couldn't find the bloke who had the key. So I had to squat behind the dugout – and at the end of season presentation night, the supporters presented me with a toilet roll!"
Jason fondly remembers goalkeeper Steve Tierney, who had a short spell at Moors before he suddenly passed away in 2005.
"Despite being a really big lad Steve was very agile and agreed to turn out for us at home one Saturday. He must have phoned me at least four times on the morning of the game, just to check where the ground was, and where to park his car. He was really nervous.
"He was due to arrive at 1.30 with everybody else, but didn't. It was five minutes past two when manager Tony Lee turned round to me, looking a bit worried, and said; "Where the hell's Steve?" I didn't have a clue, because I'd spoken to him enough on the morning.
"Then suddenly, the door burst open, and Steve trooped in. Leo looked at him, and Steve said: "Sorry I'm late, but there was a queue at the pie shop!"
As well as playing in three different leagues for Moors, Jason was caretaker manager on several occasions and in the summer of 2007 was appointed manager following the departure of Jamie Pollock. Fortunately, singing wasn't a requirement of the job.

Andrew (Snapper) Shaw

"Snapper" arrived at Spennymoor when they were in the Northern Counties East League, following a spell at Whitley Bay.
"I left Bishop when they were in the Northern Premier League for Whitley Bay, who were in the same division, but I wasn't there for a full year. I was tired of the travelling up to Whitley Bay, and every home game seemed like an away game. I didn't dare have a drink, and part of being in a team is the socialising afterwards. I wanted to play for somebody nearer home.
"When Mattie Pearson became Spennymoor manager, at the time, he approached me to come to Spennymoor. I didn't need a lot of persuading, after all, Spennymoor was on the doorstep for me.
"In effect, I dropped down two divisions,

Andrew "Snapper" Shaw

but the standard of the Northern Counties East League wasn't all that bad compared to the Northern Premier League. The travelling was fine, it was just that sometimes the midweek games got a little bit tedious. Sometimes we didn't arrive home until 2 am, and I had to be up at work for 6.30.

"The team we had in 1992-93 when we won promotion to the Northern Premier League was a really good one, with players like Steve Cuthbert and Keith Gorman up front with me, and other very good players like Gary Cowell and Ralph Petitjean also in the team. The team between 1993 and 1995 was also excellent. All the lads got on well together, and we had some proper good banter. We had a real winning mentality those seasons, plus we always felt relaxed in and around the club. "

Snapper once had a big argument with Mattie when Moors played Ferryhill in a cup tie. "Mattie always let you know when he thought you weren't doing it for him on the pitch. He was very keen that we should do well when we played his old club Ferryhill one Saturday afternoon. Problem was, that I'd been out at a party on the Friday night until about three in the morning. Somehow, Mattie knew that I'd been out late, and he told me; "You'd better be all right."

"He must not have thought so, because he subbed me at half time, and after everybody had left the dressing room for the second half, we had a massive stand-up argument.

"We were both furious, and the argument got so heated, that Mattie slapped me! And just as he slapped me, one of the Ferryhill committee men opened the door to collect the half time tea cups, and he quickly shut it again when he saw what was happening. You should have seen his face, he was so shocked that we were having a right go at each other.

"But after the game, which we won, Mattie took me into the bar, we had a drink together, and nothing more was said.

"Mattie was a winner, even in training. He always wanted to win, and he put 100 per cent into the job. He kept himself fit as well – when there was some running to be done, Mattie was always back first, even though he was a lot older than us."

Snapper can remember one big cliffhanger in 1994. "There was a lot depending on the last game of the season against Ashton United in more ways than one. If Ashton drew or won they were promoted, if we won, we were promoted. But also, the club had promised us a big bonus if we went up, and to be honest, mine was spent well beforehand on a holiday.

"At half time, we were losing 1-0, but we hadn't played that badly. We really went for it in the second half, but the goal just wouldn't come. But then Keith Gorman equalised, I scored with a diving header, and Keith got another late on. The whole place went berserk. It was brilliant for the club

in more ways than one because we spent all night in the bar celebrating!
"We were unlucky not to go up again the following season, when we finished sixth in the Premier Division, but we fell away a little towards the end of the season."
Moors also reached the first round of the FA Cup in 1994, when they played Wigan Athletic, who were then in the Fourth Division, at their old ground, Springfield Park.
"There was very heavy rain on the day of the game, and there were doubts over whether the game would go ahead or not. Both teams decided to play, and we were very unlucky in the conditions. Keith Gorman got clean through a couple of times but couldn't score, and then for one of their goals, the ball was played back to our keeper, got stuck in the water, and their player lifted it over him."
There was always some good banter in the changing room and on the bus coming back from away matches. "Wes Saunders used to like a drink of whisky before the game. As well as the escapade with Jason Ainsley at Droylsden, Wes once got the whisky out before a home game and he passed it around everyone. One of the lads wanted to go to the toilet, but then he noticed that there was smoke coming from the bottom of the toilet door. We thought there was a fire, but it turned out to be Wes drinking his whisky and having a smoke! Wes was great to have around, and he commanded a hell of a lot of respect.
"On the way back from an away game at Lancaster, we stopped at an off licence to get something to eat and drink on the way home. Craig Veart decided to stay on the bus, so he gave me a tenner and asked me to get him something to eat. So I got him a cabbage, a cauliflower and a pound of bacon, put it in a bag, and went back on the bus. "Tell me you've got me something to eat," he said. So I handed the bag over – his face was a picture. To make matters worse, somebody pinched the bacon as well. It was the last time he asked me to do him a favour."

Kevin Reilly

Kevin is regarded by many fans who watched him during his era as the best player ever to wear a Spennymoor shirt.
Kevin was one of the stars of the seventies, when Moors had their run to the semi final of the FA Trophy, reached the first round of the FA Cup, and won the Northern League championship and Durham Challenge Cup.
"Stan Bradley saw me playing for Byers Green, and asked me to go training with Spennymoor the following night," recalls Kevin.
"I wasn't keen on going, but I went along anyway, didn't like it, and returned to Byers Green! Maybe the Byers Green lads knew I could play at

that level, and eventually they persuaded me to go to Spennymoor and train with them a few more nights.

"Bob Bell was the manager then, and there were some very good players in that dressing room. Albert Hickman was the big noise in the changing room, and there were some big characters like Butch Simpson, Peter Joyce and John Heaviside who looked after me on the field. We were one of the best teams in the league, and possibly even the country, for around ten years. Everybody was dedicated to the club. The majority of those players in the dressing room could have played in the Third or Fourth Divisions no bother at all.

"The team spirit was magnificent. After games, if there was anything going on in the clubhouse, we would go home, get changed, and come back and enjoy ourselves. It was a real family atmosphere, which I thoroughly enjoyed.

"I think my main strength was that I could kick the ball well with both feet, and I could strike a ball from outside the penalty area. I didn't score many goals from a few yards out."

Kevin made the national papers on his wedding day when he left the reception and his new wife Ann, to play for Moors in the FA Cup against Goole in the afternoon.

"We got married at 11 in the morning, and when the speeches were finished at the reception, the club sent a car to pick me up and take me straight to the ground. A few days before, some papers said that Ann put her foot down and wouldn't let me play, but that wasn't correct. We weren't going anywhere for our honeymoon that day." Kevin then had a blinder, some said his best ever game for Moors, as they beat Goole 3-1 to put them into the second round of the FA Cup.

Kevin also played a starring role in another FA Cup tie, against Fourth Division Southport in 1975. "Southport were bottom of the Fourth Division, and hadn't won for a long time, so we really fancied our chances at home. They scored first, but then Kenny (Banks) scored from two setpieces, and I slotted one in from the edge of the box."

Kevin caused a real scare for Moors one morning before the 1977 Northern League play off against Consett at Willington.

"At the time, I was playing on a Sunday for Langley Park Rams Head, and we played in the final of the All England Cup and won it. But I cut my head open during the game, and the following day I turned up for the Spennymoor game with a huge gash across my forehead, and Stan Bradley yelled; "What the hell have you been doing?" Kenny Banks nearly cried when he saw me. Luckily, Jackie Johnson, the physio, managed to patch me up, and I played in the game, which fortunately we won."

Kevin was booked only once in his career, and he's still got the notification letter from the FA in his possession. "It was for dissent in a Durham Challenge Cup tie against Durham City. I was surprised I didn't get more bookings for doing that!"

Not many players turned Nottingham Forest down when Brian Clough and Peter Taylor were the management team there, but Kevin, to the surprise of a great many people, did. Many thought that Kevin could have made the grade at Football League level, but Kevin wasn't interested in joining the Clough revolution at the City Ground.

"Peter Taylor, the Forest assistant manager, came to a game one night, and afterwards threw a load of cash on the table to persuade the club to part with me. Forest asked me to go down there for a week, but I wasn't interested. I was happy to live up here and keep playing for Spennymoor. Ann and I had been married a year, I wasn't bothered about the money, and I was a homely type." Many other clubs who asked Kevin to join them got the same reply.

Fortunately for Spennymoor, the answer was always; "No, I'm happy where I am."

Albert Hickman

Nobody has a definite figure, but Albert possibly holds the club record for the most appearances during fifteen years at the club. Albert could play in defence and midfield and was club captain at 23 years old, and he led the team to many successes in one of the club's heydays in the seventies and early eighties. He picked up seven Northern League winners' medals, four Northern League Cup winners' medals and five Durham Challenge Cup winners' medals, a record that will take some beating.

He started his Northern League career at Ferryhill, scored seven goals in six games, and was quickly snapped up by Moors. "I'd gone from junior football into the Northern League with Ferryhill, and I scored a few goals for them. Mr Spennymoor, Stan Bradley, came to see me while I was working at Thorns one day, and straight away I wanted to join them, because I saw Spennymoor as a big club. I didn't go for the money, it was the prestige.

Albert Hickman

227

Stan had a great eye for a player, but he didn't make a huge number of changes to the team.

"Stan was known as "the poacher" for his ability to persuade players to sign for him. I used to go with him to look at players, and we used to go around their houses. Stan hid around the corner or out of sight, while I knocked on the door to find out if the player was in – we knew he was, of course, because we'd been watching from outside in the car!

"The player would answer the door, I would say; "Would you like to speak to Stan?" and as soon as he said yes, Stan would dash up the garden path and he would be in the house.

"Stan had a charming and pleasant manner which appealed to the player's wife, girlfriend and kids. He would always chat with the wife and play with the kids. Sooner or later, the player would agree to come. If Stan didn't get him the first time, he got him the second time – he was like a Mountie, he always got his man.

"I didn't think I would get in the team straight away, I thought I might get a couple of games in before the end of the season, but I was included after just a few weeks when Billy Lovejoy got injured. To get into that side at such an age was an achievement, but then the pressure was on me to stay in the team, so I had to keep on producing my best week after week.

"Billy, whom I'd replaced, hardly played again, and so I gave him my shirt at the end of that season, after all, he deserved it more than me.

"There were some great players in the team. How Peter Joyce never got an England Amateur cap is beyond me, because he was one of the best centre halves in the country. Graham Defty at right back was an inspiration, Kenny Banks was very good in midfield, and there was Kevin Reilly up front who was a natural goalscorer and had plenty of pace. There were other players such as Butch Simpson, Alan West, Alan Kell, Tommy Holden and Brian Mulligan who were very good players in their own right.

"Billy Robson, our full back, was one of the hardest players I've ever come across on a football field. In the first two minutes in an Amateur Cup tie at Southall, he hit their winger so hard that he went up in the air and landed off the field. I thought he would get sent off, but the referee didn't do anything!

"John Davies was always getting penalties, and some people thought that he was the original diver, but he used to put himself about so much in the opposing penalty area. Centre half Bill Gates demanded respect – when he spoke in the dressing room, you could hear a pin drop. Before a game once, he said; "I demand that you get behind me. When you go in for the ball, show those six studs." Bill played a few games for us before going to the Boro. He came back after he finished playing in the pro game, and never took a penny from the club.

"My dad always encouraged me, and he kept a scrapbook with some press cuttings of what I'd done. He always stuck up for me though – I can remember when I scored twelve successive penalties, and then we were awarded one against Emley at home.

"I completely miskicked, and all their keeper had to do was come out and pick up the ball. My dad shouted from behind the goal; "Did you see that? The ball moved just before he hit it!" Thanks, Dad. We still won the game fortunately.

"I was made skipper of the team at the age of 23 when Kenny Banks was manager. Maybe Kenny thought that that because I gave 100 per cent on the field and that I was studying for my coaching badges, that I could lead by example – and I'd like to think I did during my time at the club."

Moors always fancied themselves in the FA Cup and FA Amateur Cup, and there were some titanic battles against teams from outside the area, particularly Football League teams.

"We knew that we had the ability and the strength in the side to go a long way in competitions. When we played the strong southern teams in the Amateur Cup and the Trophy, and the pro clubs in the FA Cup, we found that there wasn't one that really outclassed us.

"We played Shrewsbury in the 1972-73 season. We drew with them at our place, and played them at Gay Meadow a few days later.

"Our centre forward, John Davies, was up against Jim Holton, who had played for Manchester United, and that must have been the best ever contest of that type I have ever seen between the two. The pair of them gave their all, and had a real battle in the fairest sense of the word. We ran them off the park in the first half hour, and Geoff Parker smashed the ball against the underside of the bar from well outside the box. If that had gone in, it would well have turned the game, but we lost 3-1."

Albert played a key part in the 4-1 FA Cup win over Southport at the Brewery Field in 1975. "We knew that we had a great chance of going through on our ground, and before the game, we were given brand new tracksuits with our initials sewn on to them. We really looked the part. Snow fell that day, there was a big crowd behind us, and we took Southport apart. That was probably one of our most outstanding performances, we outplayed and outclassed them."

Another year, Moors also gave Macclesfield, one of the leading non league clubs at the time, a tough game at Moss Rose before they went down 2-0.

"There was a big crowd in the ground that night. Denis Fidler scored for them with a few minutes left to make the score 2-0. He ran in front of our dugout to celebrate, and stood like a gladiator, so Jack Johnson, our trainer,

chucked a bucket of water over him! I think Jack was as gutted as everybody else."
Despite all the success on the home front, there have been two big disappointments in Albert's career, one in the FA Amateur Cup and the other in the FA Trophy.
"We went to Walton and Hersham in the quarter final of the Amateur Cup, and Dave Bassett, who went on to manage Wimbledon and several other clubs, was in their team. We drew 0-0 down there – John Davies nearly scored late in the game -- and gave them such a good game that Dave Bassett told us that we were the best non league team he'd ever played against.
"In the replay at our place, Bassett was magnificent, and he inspired them to victory. Our place was supposed to be a fortress, but it wasn't that day and they beat us. They eventually got to Wembley.
"I felt worse after we were beaten by Leatherhead in the Trophy semi final in 1978. I couldn't play, because the week before I broke my leg in a league game at Evenwood. It wasn't even one of Evenwood's players, it was one of ours – Steve Lee. We had a corner, he came to the near post where he shouldn't have been, and came down on top of me!
"I would have put my house on us winning the Leatherhead game when we came back to 2-2 on aggregate before half time, but we conceded a soft goal in the second half that cost us the game."
While Bishop Auckland always provided the spice of a local derby, the big battles of the seventies were between Moors and Blyth.
"We were the two dominant sides, and we were so good, that the two clubs were offered places in the Alliance Premier League – today's Conference – because we were so good.
"I wanted to play in the Alliance, because I wanted to test myself and I'm sure virtually all of the other players did as well – but I could well understand the club's financial arguments."
As well as the medals from the local campaign, Albert was also an integral part of several representative sides.
"I was honoured to play for Middlesex Wanderers, who had several England amateur internationals in their side. We played in the England strip in places like Korea and Japan. I had to get my hair cut though when I went to Korea – they weren't going to let me in with long hair!
"We played the Japan national eleven in front of 24,000 in Tokyo and beat them 4-1. Their fans were so disappointed with their team's performance that they threw cushions on the pitch, because the team had been in an intensive training camp for a week preparing for our game. The press went to town on them the following day."

Albert's Spennymoor career came to an end after around 700 appearances in 1981 when he decided to leave for Durham City. "The club offered me the job after Kenny Banks left the club, but I turned it down, because I thought the time was right to bring somebody new in. " When Billy Bell came to the club for his second spell as manager, Albert left the club soon after for the manager's job at Durham, where had some success. "But I missed Spennymoor, it was like a family where we all socialised together."

David "Kid" Curry

"Kid" literally lived a hop, skip and a jump from the Brewery Field.

"We lived just down the road from the ground, and all I had to do was just jump over three fences to get in! Since I was five years old, I used to go and watch Spennymoor in matches, and in training at the Brewery Field. When I was at Spennymoor Juniors, there were three of us invited to go training – me, goalkeeper John Hopper and forward Paul Main - -and I must have made some sort of good impression, because I went straight into the team at right back to play North Shields in a Northern League game. I had a choice to make at that point, either to play for Spennymoor Juniors or Spennymoor United, and Bob Farms, the secretary of Spennymoor Juniors, said without hesitation; "Go to United."

David "Kid" Curry

"I played another Northern League game against Crook, and then the next time I played was at Bury in the second round of the FA Cup, the round after we'd beaten Southport. I came on as sub for Butch Simpson, who broke his arm, so in the space of a few weeks, I was playing on a Football League ground. I was pleased that the junior team never forgot me though. When they reached a cup final against Leeholme Juniors, they had a vote over whether I should be allowed back to play for them, and they voted yes. I came back and scored!"

The young Curry, nicknamed Kid after a television western character at the time, attracted the attention of the Football League clubs. "Spennymoor chairman Jack Smith had played for Plymouth, and so he arranged for me to go down there for a trial. Well, I didn't have a clue where Plymouth was, except that it was at the other end of the country and a twelve hour train ride away. It was a nightmare going, because I'd never been on a train in my life. I think I was homesick before I got there, but at least there was somebody to meet me at that end.

"There were some good players there at the time, like Gary Megson and Paul Mariner, who both had long careers in the Football League, and Paul went on to play for England. But it was too far away from home for me."

"Kid" says that there was some real leg pulling in the Spennymoor changing room before matches. "The banter was great. We used to say to Brian Mulligan; "If you're going to be sick, Brian, go to the toilet now." Albert Hickman used to bring sweets in before every game, and one day he brought in some jelly babies, to which we said; "Are you getting soft, Albert?" Butch Simpson used to thump me in his friendly sort of way, and I ended up with all sorts of bruises. It was all part of the camaraderie, but some lads who came to the club maybe didn't understand."

"Kid" learned the game quickly amongst all the experienced heads around him, but he was once outwitted by Whitby's players. "In the early part of my career, Butch Simpson didn't play at Whitby in a cup tie, and it was my job to face their winger Derek Hampton, who was a real flying machine. I thought I did all right against him, he went where I wanted him to go by angling my body, and he ran the ball out of play several times. Their lads told me afterwards how well I'd done against him – I was chuffed to bits that they praised me.

"In the replay, I changed my game. I chased shadows and couldn't get near him. He tore me to bits. Whitby had done me. I learned from the experience and never let opponents do that to me again.

"Butch got his place back after that, and Kenny Banks put me in midfield, presumably because of all my energy. I used to put myself all over the place, in matches and in training. In fact, when we had training games, I'm sure Brian Mulligan used to check which colour bib I had on, so then he could be on my side. I only ever missed one training session, because of flu. That particular night, there was a knock on our front door, and it was one of the club's committee, wondering if I was all right because I'd missed training. He was that concerned because I hadn't turned up!

"The harder players like Butch Simpson and Billy Robson used to look after me but there was nothing they could do when we played Mossley away in the FA Trophy. Mossley had a big lad playing for them, and I said to him; "You've got big lips," just to wind him up.

"A few minutes later, he elbowed me in the face, and said: "You've got big lips now!" It turned out I'd picked the wrong one to argue with – he was one of the top bouncers at a Manchester nightclub!"

"Kid" didn't pick up many injuries, but one in particular gave him problems. "I suffered a deadleg, and I was given heat treatment, instead of ice. By the time I got home, the leg was really swollen and inflamed. The club arranged for me to see Johnny Watters, the Sunderland physio, and he gave me an X ray, which showed the extent of the injury. He told me that I would be out for six months, just like the Leeds winger Eddie Gray had been. I needed complete rest and an operation, and I couldn't keep myself fit. I was that used to running around.

"I sat on the bus going to Rotherham for the FA Cup tie, and Kenny Banks took one look at my face and said that he could tell I wasn't playing. My weight had gone up from ten and a half stone to fourteen and a half stone! I was eating and drinking too much – I'd always prided myself on being one of the team's top trainers. Not playing was a real shock to my system.

"So when I got the go-ahead to restart training, I gave it everything. I also went for a break to the south of France with Michael Todd, the groundsman. We went to Cannes and St Tropez, and I spent a lot of time running around the Alps. I suppose it was a form of high altitude training, but it did me the power of good, because when I started playing again, I was on fire. When I went for a training run back in Spennymoor, I was the first to touch the castle at the top of the hill near the by pass, and I was first back to the ground. At the end of the season, I won the league's player of the year award -- I felt that was a reward for all my hard work."

Kid's continuing all action performances didn't go unnoticed, and Fourth Division Darlington took an interest. "There was a rumour going around that Billy Elliott, the Darlington manager, was going to offer £20,000 for me, and his assistant, Kenny Ellis, came to see me. But the transfer never happened, maybe the club was wanting more for me, I don't know.

"But I also used to ask myself, "Why leave, when the club is on my doorstep?" We won trophies by playing good football, and we had an excellent team spirit. I accepted the money the club offered me, and I agreed a contract. I could have held out for more money because wages suddenly jumped up right across the board, even at our level, when Trevor Francis was transferred for £1million, but I didn't. I enjoyed being in the centre of the action."

When Kid signed the contract, he had to stop playing Sunday football. "I injured my ankle playing on a Sunday, and we had a big match the following night. I worked at Thorns, the same place as secretary Stan Bradley and my team mate Kevin Reilly. I tried to run off the injury, but I couldn't. I pulled Kevin to one side when Stan wasn't around, and he said "Do you want a word with Stan?" I shook my head – I didn't dare. I hoped that the injury would go away, but it wouldn't.

"In the end, I had to face Stan before the big match. His face was like

thunder, he took me outside, and shouted; "If I'd been younger, I'd have knocked you over the fence!" It wasn't like Stan to lose his temper like that. "I just wanted to play football. Before I signed the contract, I played thirteen games in fourteen days near the end of the season, because the Sunday clubs were catching up with their fixtures in midweek as well.
"I didn't think the games were affecting me, but Stan noticed one night. I went for an easy ball on the halfway line, but the other player beat me to it, and nearly scored at the other end. In the dressing room at half time, Stan told me to stand up. So I did, expecting praise for my first half performance, but Stan pointed his finger at me, and said; "You're knackered! You are playing too much football.""
Moors fans will remember Kid as a whole-hearted, committed player. "I used to relive games in my sleep. If we'd lost, I'd be shouting and swearing in my sleep, and it would be Monday before we could talk the game over again. Fortunately, there weren't many defeats!
"I did have quite a restless night after we lost against Leatherhead, in fact I had two or three! Poor Alan Porter got some criticism for his mistake, but to be fair to Alan, he kept us in the quarter final against Dagenham by pulling off some cracking saves. He kept us in the competition."
But that was one of the few negatives in a Brewery Field career that yielded three Northern League winners' medals, with Durham Challenge Cup and Northern League Cup winners' medals on top. "We worked very hard on our setpieces, and we had several routines. I remember that I headed the winner in one final. Kevin (Reilly) used to whip the corners in, and we arranged between ourselves who would go for it. Geoff Hart whispered to me that he would, but the ball was put out for another corner. This time I could see a gap when Kevin put the ball in the middle, and Albert flicked the ball on for me to run into the net. It was a great feeling to score a goal in an important game like that."
Kid earned recognition for his displays for Spennymoor, and on one occasion went on a tour, organised by the league sponsors Rothmans, to Tenerife and Las Palmas.
"The four leagues sponsored by Rothmans had to send four players each, all of whom had to have gone without a booking throughout the previous season. The four of us from the Northern League were me, Alan Shoulder, Tommy Holden and Fred Hissett. Kevin Reilly should have gone, but he got booked. We played a couple of games, and one of the players who toured with us was Geoff Hurst, the World Cup winner. I really wish that somebody had taken a camera with them, because not many people believe me when I say that I played with the man who scored a hat trick in the 1966 World Cup final."

Kid played for several managers after Kenny Banks left, one of whom was Billy Bell. "Billy was very, very keen, and had picked up several ideas when he'd spent a week at Liverpool. He wanted Kenny Heslop to run fifty, sixty yards to get on the end of crossfield passes from Jackie Sheekey, and he just couldn't manage it. After one game in which Kenny was very red faced, he turned round to Billy said: "How the hell can I do that?"

"Another time, I was out injured, and he asked me to sit in the stand, and count how many yards certain players had run in the game. I forgot to do to it, because I was so involved in watching the game, but that shows how much Billy thought about the game – he thought about statistics like that long before the Premier League did them!"

Kid decided to leave Spennymoor in 1985, when Tony Monkhouse was manager. "I can't remember which game it was, but there was a young lad called Gary Lowes playing for us then. He was making runs all over the pitch, getting into the right positions. I thought to myself; "I used to do that, but I can't now. It's time to pack in.""

Colin Richardson

Colin was a member of the Bob Bell revolution in 1966, but he was brought to the club by Bob's predecessor, Jackie Newton.

"I'd been to West Brom as a kid, and when I left there, I went to Willington and Ferryhill, where Jackie was manager. When Jackie got the Spennymoor job, he came with Jackie Smith to my mother's house at Fencehouses to persuade me to sign. Old Jackie Smith was a lovely man, he was a little bloke who smoked a pipe and was very professional. He looked after me and Graham Defty really well.

"Jackie Newton was an old pro, who was very good at what he did. He told us things, but never showed us very much. When Bob Bell came along, he changed all that. He brought a new level of professionalism to the club, and was very meticulous. Instead of telling us to run around the pitch, Bob had us doing shuttles. He introduced 4-4-2 with two wide men and two out and out front players. We used to train at Chester-le-Street Grammar School, and everybody turned up every week because we really respected Bob.

"He liked to play the game the right way, and when he talked, we listened, and he didn't like dissent on the field of play. He brought some very good young players to the club, like Billy Lovejoy, Michael Maley and Albert Hickman. He wasn't scared to put them in, because in those days, Northern League teams had an average age of between 26 and 32, and youngsters usually had to start in the Wearside League and work their way up.

"Bob was very good in his preparations, he always had a good idea of what the opposition was going to do. His desire and organisation were superb, he was very supportive of his players - -especially when they were going through a bad time -- and he was very good at getting people on his side. He didn't make many changes in his squad at all, he maybe only brought in two or three players a season. He even brought in a fitness coach. Bob was a lovely fella, and that was why people respected him so much. I learned a lot from him which I used when I became a manager.

"There was only once in five years when Bob slipped up, and that was before we played Wrexham in the FA Cup in 1969. Bob said that he'd seen Wrexham play, and in their team was a full back whom he reckoned could bomb on a bit, but made his own mistakes and couldn't shoot, so he told us to back off him and the full back would end up giving the ball away.

"For twenty minutes we held our own against Wrexham, I think I'd put one of their lads in the stand with a tackle! The score was 0-0 when this particular full back picked the ball up, so just as Bob had told us, we backed off. But the full back kept going, and hit a belter of a goal from 30 yards to put them in the lead! We all stood and looked at each other, and I turned and looked at the bench, where Bob had his head in his hands. Peter Joyce, who was a man of few words, said in the dressing room at half time; "What the hell was all that about?"

"Bob, with Stan Bradley and Jackie Smith, built a real platform for what was to come. The team that won the treble in 1968 had everything. There were some excellent passers of the ball, some battlers, players who could look after themselves and players from all over the park who could score. We could mix it if we wanted, we could play if we wanted.

"If there was one disappointment, we didn't win the Amateur Cup. We had a couple of good runs, but the biggest blot on my career was when we lost to Prestwich Heys, how we never got past them, I'll never know. We lost Billy Lovejoy through injury in the first half, and for the last fifteen minutes, everybody except me played at centre forward. We just couldn't score. I've never seen a set of players so despondent after a game, even Peter Joyce, the hard man of the team, was in tears.

"We played another Amateur Cup tie away at Skelmersdale, and the home fans weren't too happy because we won. We were all sat in the bus, when Micky Maley ran to the back of the bus and shouted; "Someone's just thrown a brick through the window!" There seemed to be hundreds of people all trying to rock the bus and turn it over, and we couldn't get off." Colin rates Kenny Banks as the best player he ever played with. "Kenny had a very upright style, and seemed to glide over the ground. There were times when you couldn't get the ball off him, and he had a wonderful ability to score goals, with no backlift whatsoever.

"We played Stockton, who were then in the Northern Regional League, in an FA Cup tie. Stockton always had a good side during the days when they played on their ground in the High Street. It was a great end to end game against them, and their keeper took a goal kick. He cleared the ball straight to Kenny on the halfway line, who hit it on the volley, straight back over the keeper's head!

"Peter Joyce was also a magnificent player. He had the ability to slide in for the ball and drag it away, almost as if he had a hook. He was a wonderful attacker of the ball, and he had qualities which you very rarely see nowadays. John Tobin was an unsung hero, because he knew how to make great runs and take chances. Dave Crampton was a very good keeper, not many attackers roughed him up – and when they tried to, they had Peter Joyce to worry about!

"Peter wouldn't stand any nonsense on the field against any of his team mates. We played at Crook one day, and after a corner, Graham Defty was down in a heap, with blood all over him because of a cut across his eyes and nose. He told Peter who'd elbowed him, and play restarted. But while the ball was at one end, Peter was going the opposite way, chasing the lad who had elbowed Graham! Their lad ran off the pitch, and into the stand! The word got around after that, and players at other clubs said that they would get revenge for Graham."

Colin remembers some really big crowds packing into the Brewery Field as they chased the treble in 1968 and glory in the FA Cup and FA Amateur Cup. "There were some games when the club had to shut the gates after kick off because there wasn't room for everybody to get in. Some mates of mine came down from Dunston for the Goole game – the first time the club used floodlights -- and it took them ninety minutes to get into the ground. Some people were still coming in at quarter past eight – and the official attendance was nothing like the number that was in the ground! The club must have made some money that night.

"The supporters were brilliant, and whenever I went back to the Brewery Field, they always made me welcome. It was a wonderful club, and couldn't get better support. We had a game in Nottingham on a Wednesday afternoon, and thirty busloads of supporters turned up! When we came out on to the pitch, all we could see were black and white scarves, hardly any home supporters. We won the game 3-1. We used to get around 2,000 watching us every week, probably enough to pay for the floodlights thirty times over!

"The club provided us with club blazers, and ten bob (50 pence) a week was deducted from our wages to pay for them. We seemed to be paying the club back for ages. We played Whitley Bay in the final of the League Cup on a Saturday, and drew 0-0. Jackie Meggeson was the treasurer at the time, and when we got our money, we got the usual pay for a draw, with another deduction for the blazers. Peter Joyce went to see Jack, and said: "How much are these blooming suits going to be?"

"The replay against Whitley Bay was on a Monday at North Shields. Now, when we played on a Saturday we got full wages, in a midweek we used to get half. We won the game against Whitley by 3-2, and we were all naturally happy after being presented with the cup.

"Jack Meggeson came in with the pay packets, and when Peter opened his packet, the mood suddenly changed. "There's something wrong here," said Peter. "We should get three quid because we've won, and there's only thirty bob in." There was hell on, Stan Bradley was shaking like a leaf. Jack said; "It's a Monday, you get half the money for a midweek game!"

So we ended up with less money for winning the league cup than we did for drawing! But to be fair, everybody knew that Spennymoor was never a big paying club. When I left, I went to Whitby for £9 a week, a bit more than what I was on at Spennymoor

"I always seemed to play well at Whitby, and scored regularly there. Whitby used to push up against us, and Bob Bell told me to run from the back and beat the offside trap. It always worked."

After his playing career finished, Colin was very successful in management, and he was appointed manager of Moors in 2000, but didn't stay very long. "It didn't work out, because of the club's finances, and the goalposts moved so many times."

Billy Blenkiron

Billy played for the club in its Midland League days, after Moors quit the North Eastern League in 1960.

The team had some long trips to places like Peterborough, Grantham and Skegness, and Billy said: "I was first on the bus and last off for away games. Occasionally we stayed overnight, but there were some long journeys and we didn't get back until really late from some trips, there were no motorways.

"I was only 17 at the time, and had never heard of some of these places, but the travelling didn't really bother me. In a way it helped me when I went to play cricket for Warwickshire. To me, sport is a way of meeting people and making friends

"We had some big crowds at home in the Midland League, but then the gates began to fall, and the club decided it was too expensive to play in that league, and turned amateur. There were some very good players at the club in those days, like Norman Field who had been a pro at Portsmouth.

"I once scored a hat trick in the Midland League against Scarborough, but

I had to come off with about ten minutes left with concussion. The old pros of Scarborough didn't like being shown up by a youngster. Somebody crunched me in a tackle -- I wasn't ready for it.

"When we went back to the Northern League, I was badly injured in a game and the club said that they would look after me until I recovered, which they did. They had a bloke on the committee, Laurie Lightfoot who worked for the Provident."

Brian Healy

Brian was signed by manager Mattie Pearson at the start of the 1992-93 season when the club started its third season in the Northern Counties East League.

"Mattie was starting his first full season, and he was very determined to win promotion to the UniBond League. I'd been playing for Gateshead, but wanted to leave because all my mates had left. I could have gone somewhere else, but Trevor Beaumont, who was one of the club sponsors, and Mattie persuaded me to drop down three steps from the Conference. I told him that I would help take the club up to the UniBond League Premier, which would mean two promotions in two years.

Brian Healy

"I could see what Mattie and his assistant Dave Barton were trying to do at Spennymoor, and we all built up a fantastic team spirit. Some outsiders thought we were a bit cliquish, but we weren't, we were a close knit little club. There were no bad apples at all. Yes, I had my arguments with Mattie, but we totally respected each other. Mattie and Dave worked really well together, they kept everybody very relaxed.

"I didn't start all that well. I think it was my second or third game when I was sent off, I lost my rag with somebody. I got suspended for that, and I was suspended again for the end of the season, I missed the last six games including the game that mattered, when we won promotion against Winterton on the last day of the season. Dean Gibb came in and replaced me as captain, and I wasn't allowed to collect the championship trophy.

"The second year was just as good. We had the momentum going, and we won promotion again. It sounds daft, but I liked playing away better than I did at home. The atmosphere going there and back on the bus was amazing, it was a sense of all being in it together. We were very determined to win games.

"Mattie persuaded me to stay on to try and get promotion to the Conference, but unfortunately, it didn't work out. We were probably two or three players short of being a promotion winning side, and midway through my fourth season I left for Morecambe."

Brian scored one of Moors' most memorable goals, a hook shot over his right shoulder, in the Durham Challenge Cup final over Bishop Auckland in 1994.

"I remember not playing well at all throughout the game, and then the ball came into the box, and I hooked it in over my shoulder.

"A few days later, I went on holiday, and by sheer coincidence, Tony Lee, who was manager of Bishop Auckland at the time, was at the same resort. We were both in the bar one night, at separate ends, and we just ignored each other. So I cheekily sent him a drink via the waiter with a message; "I can't give you the Durham Challenge Cup, so you can have this instead!" I didn't keep my Durham Challenge Cup medal, I gave it to one of the lads who wasn't playing. Winning was enough for me, but I wish I'd kept it now!

"I scored a better goal against Accrington Stanley in the FA Cup, a 25 yarder that flew into the top corner. But I was really disappointed with a penalty that I missed against Colwyn Bay in the FA Cup. I hit the bar with it, and they went down the other end and scored."

Ralph Wright

Ralph had two spells at the club sandwiched in between clubs in the Football League and the USA.

Ralph was part of Bob Bell's team that won the treble in 1968, and after playing for five Football League clubs plus New York Cosmos and Dallas Tornados in the States at the same time as Pele, George Best and Eusebio, he returned to the Brewery Field just before the start of Moors' FA Cup run in 1977.

"I was offered a couple of full time contracts at pro clubs, but I was getting married at the time, and I decided to play part time football and get myself a proper job. So I decided to return to Spennymoor.

"I hadn't played for six weeks, but after two weeks' training, I was close to full fitness. I couldn't get a game for Spennymoor at first because it was the Northern League, but the professional game was completely different, and I was the only one with experience as we prepared to play Rotherham in the FA Cup second round in 1977.

"I picked up the Northern Echo on the way to Rotherham, and read the

team – and I wasn't in it. I told Kenny Banks that it couldn't be right, because Rotherham would destroy us. I was furious because I'd read the team in the paper, I wouldn't have been if I'd been told properly.
"We stopped to get something to eat at the Danum Hotel just outside Doncaster, and I decided that I wasn't going all that way to watch the team get hammered, so I went into Doncaster, and caught a train home. I joined Whitley Bay the following night."

Craig Veart

Craig is credited with scoring one of the fastest goals in the club's history.

It happened at Whitby in the UniBond League Premier Division. "I scored direct from the kick off. I told the lads on the ball to split apart, and I hit it over David Campbell in the Whitby goal and into the net. Somebody once mentioned it on Century Radio. I phoned in and I don't think they quite believed me, so David phoned in to confirm it."

Craig was one of the players who arrived at the club at the start of the Mattie Pearson revolution in 1991. He was playing as a left back at Gateshead, and he jumped at the chance to play for Mattie at the Brewery Field. "I wasn't happy playing in the position Gateshead were using me in. Mattie, though, said he wanted me to play on the left side of a three man midfield, which suited me fine, and eventually I played alongside Brian Healy and Jason Ainsley, both very good players. We had a really good mix of players, with Keith Gorman, Andy Shaw, Ralph Petitjean, John Cooke and Wes Saunders. Several of them had Football League experience, for example, Wes had played for Newcastle, and Brian would go on and play in the Football League for Torquay.

"Not all of them were hard players. I remember Jason once got stretchered off and taken to hospital during one away game, and when the game finished, he'd come back from hospital and was limping around the dressing room with his shin all swollen and strapped up. He was still in his strip, but then, when he started to get changed, we noticed that he'd just stuffed lots of toilet paper down his sock!

Craig Veart

"Our best season was 1993-94, when we became the first team from the First Division to win the UniBond League Cup. We played Hyde United at Harrogate, and we won with ten men, because I managed to get myself sent off. I went flying in for a tackle, which was deemed to be a straight red. Looking back now, the ref was probably right, although I didn't think so at the time. We won nearly everything we entered for a couple of seasons and with the players we had at the time, we always felt very confident.

"After the two promotions, we got to the top of the UniBond Premier Division, but the club couldn't afford to keep the momentum going, and one or two of the players decided to leave.

"I left for Bishop Auckland at the end of the season, but I came back to Spennymoor when Peter Mulcaster was manager. When Peter quit, Rob Jones, who later played for Hibs in the Scottish Premier League, and I were made caretaker managers. We didn't do badly at all – we played four, won two and drew two. We decided to do as much as we could to relax the players, so we had them sunbathing in the corner of the pitch before one game!"

Craig was involved in some big cup ties with the Moors. "One of the best pre match warm ups I ever had before any cup tie was at Wigan, who were in the Fourth Division then, in the FA Cup.

"Wes Saunders had been to this stage of the competition several times before, and knew how important it was to get the players settled before the game. He liked a tipple, and so he produced a bottle of whisky and a pack of cards, sat everybody down in the dressing room and started a game of cards away. We played "Chase the Ace" and the loser had to drink a shot of whisky. I think Wes managed to lose a couple of times.

"The Wigan manager came into the dressing room, and his eyes nearly popped out of his head when he saw what was going on. But the cards and the whisky really relaxed the lads, and we went very close a couple of times early on when the score was 0-0.

"We lost quite a bit of money when we played Colwyn Bay in the first round a year later. We were so confident of going through having beaten them twice already in the league, and were strong favourites, that we put £500 on ourselves – and lost!

"A few of us liked a bet, we used to put £10 per week away to bet on horses. We had an accumulator once, and our first three horses all came first, so we had quite a bit of money going on the last one – we were in line to win thousands. Keith Gorman chose the last horse, which was running after we'd finished a game somewhere, so he phoned somebody on a mobile during the race to hear how it was doing – it finished last! Poor Keith took some stick and had some beer poured over him!"

Craig's displays in his first spell led to interest from several clubs higher up the ladder, in particular Halifax Town, then managed by former Hartlepool defender John Bird.

"John phoned me up and said that he wanted to sign me, but the deal fell through because the club asked too much for me. I thought that I could go back into pro football – I'd been on Middlesbrough's books when I was sixteen -- because I was only 24 at the time. I was really disappointed that it didn't work out. But the great times at Spennymoor made up for it."

Robin Gill

Robin was the first choice full back between 1982 and 1988.

"I could have signed for Bishop Auckland, but I decided to join Spennymoor – and I was really pleased that I did, because my debut was against Bishops and we won 4-0!

"John Heaviside was manager for my first two seasons, and then Billy Bell took over from him. Billy was a disciplinarian, and had a lot of rules which you had to follow. He was a bit of an eccentric as well, and would never talk to the press. But you couldn't doubt his enthusiasm for a game of football. Even when he went on holiday, he would go and watch Leeds or Liverpool in training and try and pick up some coaching tips.

"Tony Monkhouse took over from Billy, and during his first full season we played Football League club Tranmere in the FA Cup. It was tremendous playing against full time professionals, it's something you aim for as a non league player. We could have won that game, they just had more experience than us.

"We had a good team around about then, and we had a long unbeaten run in which we beat Blyth, Bishop Auckland and Chester-le-Street away from home. There was a fantastic atmosphere in the dressing room at this time, and that definitely helped us to win matches.

"One of our best performances was against North Shields. We had a bad first half, in which went 3-0 down, but I scored a rare goal, when I ran from the halfway line and fired past the keeper. Whether that inspired the rest of the lads I don't know, but we went on to win 4-3!

"It all turned sour for me one night when my wife was involved in a car accident, and I was fined £8 by the club for not turning up for training.

"I complained about the deduction and I got my money back from the club, but everything seemed to go sour after that, which was a bit of a shame, because I thoroughly enjoyed myself until then."

Spennymoor Ladies Football Club

The ladies' team began playing at the Brewery Field in 2006-07, and finished fifth in the NERWF League, and at the time of writing, are top of the league in season 2007-08.

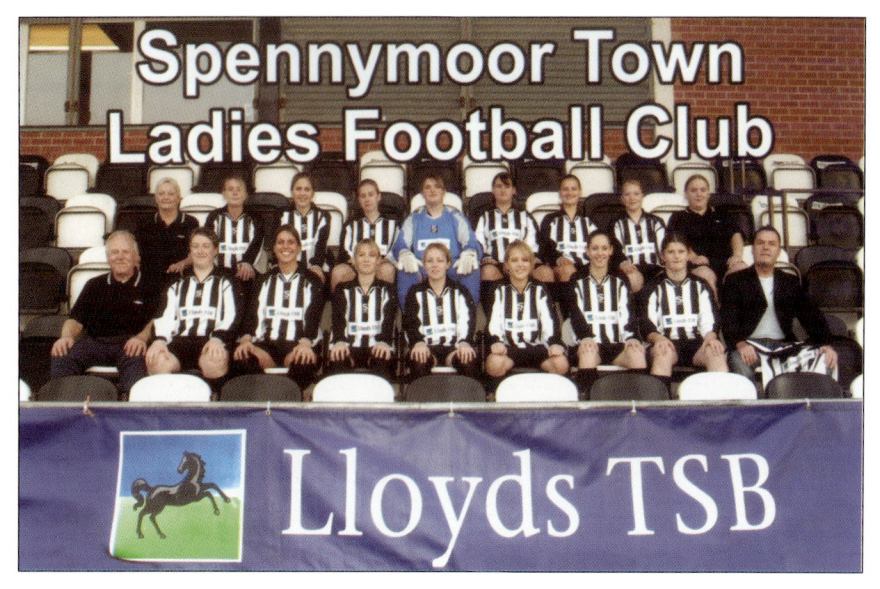

Back row: Olive Dodds (Secretary), Katie Huntington, Lindsay Robinson, Fay Burn, Stephanie Hartley, Kirsty Finlayson, Elaine Behan, Leigh Williams, Amanda Dodds (Coach). Front row: Alan Dodds (Manager), Victoria Ireland, Kelly Rushworth, Kirsty Williams, Sam Clay, Kari Rostron, Nadine Dyer, Sarah B. Jackson, Graham Thompson (Lloyds TSB).

Postscript

Spennymoor Town is thriving as this book goes to press. The club has had an excellent run in the FA Cup beating teams from above it in the national league system, and the supporters, players and officials are very proud to be part of its everyday life.

The club's renaissance shows how much can be achieved when everybody pulls together, and that's been shown many times in its history. Thomas Grant first proved that with organisation, help and encouragement, great things can be achieved. When he arranged for the football club to move into the Brewery Field, surely he would never have envisaged the glittering road to glory the club was about to embark upon? Did he manage to learn of the club's rapid progress after he emigrated to Canada?

Local football is more than just what happens on the field, it's also about being an integral part of the community. Maybe the crowds in 2007 are only a fraction of what they were in the days when admission to the Brewery Field was only tuppence and over 6,000 turned up for games in the post war years; but the Brewery Field, like many other football grounds at all levels around the country, is a place where people who have similar interests can gather every week. Not for them the highly paid stars of the Premiership and the expensive admission prices; more the sheer love and passion they have for their local football team.

Spennymoor United/ Town is fiercely proud of its history, and few other clubs can lay claim to a better tradition. It briefly crossed the author's mind to compile a list of Spennymoor players who had progressed into the Football League, but it was too big a task, because there have been so many. Many people were heartbroken when United folded in 2005, but just as many people were delighted when it rose from the ashes. The heart of the club still beats strongly - -and hopefully it will for a long time yet.

Acknowledgements

This book wouldn't have been possible without the help of so many people. There are contributions from fans, players, officials and managers in the book for which I am very grateful, but there are two very knowledgeable individuals who are particularly worthy of mention and should be recognised.

Ted Mellanby has been a Spennymoor fan for many years, and he has been a goldmine of information going all the way back to when Spennymoor United was formed in 1904, and for the formative years before that. Whenever I've had a query, Ted has invariably provided the answer from his treasure trove of cuttings, photos and documents. Without him, this book would never have been as detailed as it is.

Barrie Hindmarch for many years lived, breathed and ate Spennymoor United. I met him several times to pick his brains about events over the years, and on learning more about the exploits of Spennymoor United in his fifty year association with it as man and boy I can say without fear of contradiction that Barrie, helped by his late wife Joyce, was one of the biggest, if not the biggest, driving forces in the club's history.

Club chairman Alan Murray, whose idea this book was, persuaded me to do it with his huge encouragement and enthusiasm. I must also thank him for giving me half the film rights if the book is adapted as a Hollywood movie.

Thanks are also due to Phil Gallagher for his sponsorship of this book. Phil was no mean footballer himself in his younger days, and played on the Brewery Field for Hartlepool Boys.

Thanks also (in no particular order) for their invaluable cuttings, answers and help to Jon Le Poidevin, Gordon Nicholson, Brian Hunt (Northern Goalfields), Mike Amos (Northern League chairman) Albert Hickman, Kevin Reilly, Vince Williams (Over 40s league), Tottenham Hotspur FC, Charlton Athletic FC, Liverpool FC, Bolton Wanderers FC, Gordon Sharrock of the Bolton Evening News, Frank Tweddle (Darlington FC historian), Des Beamson, the staff at Darlington Library, Alan Alcock and Alan Platt from the UniBond League, Andrew Wilkinson from the Middlesbrough Evening Gazette, Kevin Luff from Darlington FC, Graham Smith, Garry Nunn, Frank Smith, Mel Whitehouse, Alan Ryder, the Northern Echo, the Sunday Sun, the Journal, and the late lamented Evening

Despatch and Auckland Chronicle. I must also thank Ian and Lee at Lintons Printers in Crook for their valuable help and expertise in putting the book together. If I've inadvertently missed you out, then my apologies and thanks for your help. Some innocent little snippets have turned out to be absolute gems.

Thanks also to my wife Audrey, my daughter Hayley and my son Andrew for putting up with my fourth book. Told you I was busy!

About the Author

Ray has followed non league and professional football for many years. In his goalkeeping days at King James School, Bishop Auckland, he was watched by the local Manchester United scout, who was waiting for a bus outside the ground, and promptly let one through his legs. He was also once on the books of Northern League club Shildon.

Ray has written about non league football for the Northern Echo for 21 years, as well as being Darlington correspondent for BBC Tees for the last 17. He has commented on two Wembley play off finals with Darlington, and the 1997, 1998, 1999 and 2001 FA Vase finals with Whitby Town, Tow Law, Bedlington and Whitley Bay respectively. He is in full time employment in the finance department of a plastics company in Newton Aycliffe, and is married with a wife and two grown up children.

Also co-written by the author with Andrew Wilkinson:

Farewell to Feethams 2002

Three Times a Quaker (David Hodgson) 2004

The B****** in the Black (Jeff Winter) 2005